MINERVA PARKER NICHOLS

MINERVA PARKER NICHOLS

THE SEARCH FOR A FORGOTTEN ARCHITECT

Architectural Archives, University of Pennsylvania
Distributed by Yale University Press, New Haven and London

If I fail, I should then know where to strengthen my armor.

— Minerva Parker [Nichols],
The Churchman, March 21, 1891

FOREWORD
THE ELUSIVE ARCHIVE 11
Despina Stratigakos

PROLOGUE
REQUIEM FOR A BUILDING 15
Heather Isbell Schumacher

BIOGRAPHY
FINDING MINERVA 21
Molly Lester

PORTFOLIO
A SUBMISSION TO THE HISTORIC AMERICAN BUILDINGS SURVEY 81
Elizabeth Felicella

CATALOGUE RAISONNÉ
THE ARCHITECTURE OF MINERVA PARKER NICHOLS 177
William Whitaker

WRITINGS

MINERVA PARKER NICHOLS: THE AGENCY OF WOMEN IN BUILDINGS AND TEXTS
Franca Trubiano

301

ACKNOWLEDGMENTS 327
INDEX 331
COLOPHON 336

NOTE TO THE READER

Contributors to this book have treated the name of our subject, Minerva Parker Nichols, as well as her contemporaries, in various ways. Some authors refer to her as "Minerva," to avoid confusion and to avoid using her married name alone. When directly citing historical documents, in which she is referred to as "Parker," "Nichols," or "the architect," we have not modified those naming conventions.

The following abbreviations are used in the captions and endnotes:

AAUP	Architectural Archives, University of Pennsylvania
AABN	American Architect and Building News
HABS	Historic American Buildings Survey
PRERBG	Philadelphia Real Estate Record and Builders' Guide

MINERVA PARKER'S WORK-SHOP.

Minerva Parker in her 14 South Broad Street office, ca. 1891. It was in this room in early 1889 that Parker became the first woman to establish an independent practice in architecture.

FOREWORD

THE ELUSIVE ARCHIVE

Despina Stratigakos

THE ELUSIVE ARCHIVE

How I wish this book had existed when I was a student pursuing the fugitive histories of women architects! In the 1990s publications on women in architecture were rare, and few libraries had them on their bookshelves. When I traveled to Europe to begin dissertation research on Germany's first women architects, I planned to visit archives and then write about what I had found. I never expected that their shelves would be bare as well.

For months, I traveled from archive to archive, only to hear the same response: we have no collections on women architects. With my funding running out, I worried that I would have to change my dissertation topic. How could I write about women architects if their traces were nowhere to be found in the archives?

Determined not to give up, I hunted for alternative sources. I pieced together personal and professional histories through flea market finds, family heirlooms and stories, women's magazines, association newsletters, school records, and more. Whenever possible, I turned to the buildings themselves and their occupants, who sometimes possessed knowledge passed down from one owner to the next. I even bothered the neighbors, hoping they might remember long-gone builders and residents.

Archives themselves provided important contextual information: property records, directories, building codes, and so forth. In Berlin, where

FOREWORD

entire neighborhoods were destroyed by bombers during the Second World War, plans of nonextant buildings were transferred from municipal building offices to the regional archive. This made access to plans easier but did not change the fact that many of the buildings I sought were gone, erased from the landscape like the women who had designed them.

As I met the children and grandchildren of women architects, another archival hurdle arose: Families sometimes entrusted me with valuable historical materials, including family photographs and, in one case, an entire student portfolio. Where could these documents go? Finding archives to take them became an unforeseen extension of my work.

Today, in the United States, the number of local, university and regional archives that actively seek to collect materials on early women architects remains small. As a result, their histories are still largely unknown in the very places and contexts where they worked. Curious students continue the cycle of searching for answers, visiting archives, and leaving empty-handed.

Minerva Parker Nichols: The Search for a Forgotten Architect aims to address many of these challenges by reimagining the role of the archive as an active agent in the production of women's architectural histories. Alongside its more traditionally understood function as a repository for found historical collections, the archive becomes a dynamic generator of new knowledge as well as a space to reflect critically on its own practices.

The project emerged from the decade-long research on Minerva Parker Nichols undertaken by architectural historian and preservation planner Molly Lester. For the exhibition, Lester collaborated with co-curators Elizabeth Felicella, an architectural photographer; Heather Isbell Schumacher, archivist at the Architectural Archives at the Weitzman School of Design at the University of Pennsylvania; and William Whitaker, curator of the Architectural Archives. This interdisciplinary team consulted with local and visiting experts; investigated and mapped buildings; commissioned new archival objects, including Felicella's photographs; and

THE ELUSIVE ARCHIVE

organized public programming to accompany the exhibition. The Pew Center for Arts and Heritage generously supported their efforts.

I hope that this innovative and exciting project becomes a model for other cities and archives. *Minerva Parker Nichols: The Search for a Forgotten Architect* reveals how histories of women architects can be recovered through creative and dedicated teamwork. Across our national landscape, many more such histories await the sleuths and storytellers to give them form.

Despina Stratigakos
Professor of Architecture
University at Buffalo

PROLOGUE

FIG 1: This view is one of eight photographed by George A. Eisenman for HABS in May 1973, just days before the buiding was demolished. [HABS-PA-1522-1].

PROLOGUE

REQUIEM FOR A BUILDING

Heather Isbell Schumacher

REQUIEM FOR A BUILDING

In March 1977 journalist Anna Quindlen was assigned to cover the Philadelphia New Century Club's centenary. She arrived at the Barclay Hotel in Philadelphia and spoke with longtime members, including Ada Kearney, who lamented, "This is a nice place. It is not like our club, however. I wish you could have seen our clubhouse ... I was sick when it had to go."[1] The New Century Club of Philadelphia was founded in 1877 as part of the burgeoning women's club movement, inspired by the women's pavilion at the Centennial Exposition in Philadelphia a year earlier. A women's social club for upper-middle-class White Protestants, the New Century Club also operated as a space for civic and charitable work, particularly around issues that affected women of all classes.

In March 1891 the club announced that it had purchased the property at 124–126 South Twelfth Street with the intention of building a clubhouse, and that it had hired Minerva Parker (later, Minerva Parker Nichols), a twenty-eight-year-old architect from Philadelphia, to prepare plans and supervise construction. Despite her youth, she had already amassed an impressive portfolio—nearly forty designs and completed buildings, including, perhaps most notably, the Queen Isabella Association

---

1. Anna Quindlen, "With Traditional Gentility, A Club Bows to Modernity," *New York Times*, March 10, 1977.

PROLOGUE

Pavilion for the Chicago World's Columbian Exposition. In August 1889 she had made history when she opened her own practice, becoming the first woman in the country to practice architecture independently.

For the next eight decades, the clubhouse served as a center of activity for the New Century Club. Minerva was regularly invited back to participate in important anniversaries, including the club's seventieth anniversary in 1947, where it was reported that the architect, then aged eighty-five, was still working. In 1965, with the full support and endorsement of the club's membership, the Philadelphia Historical Commission designated the building as a local historic landmark. But as membership dwindled in the 1970s, the club suffered financially. Young women now had other opportunities for socializing and the club's political power and relevance diminished. As Quindlen observed, "After 100 years of lobbying for women's rights and providing a place for its members to study and congregate, the club has lost all but its air of gentility to agencies and organizations more modern than itself, to younger leaders, to more specialized groups. All it has left now is lunch."[2]

On January 26, 1973, New Century Club members submitted an application to the Philadelphia Historical Commission to have their building demolished. After learning of the proposed plan, Adelaide Baker, Minerva's eldest child, asked the commission to reconsider the situation, highlighting the historic significance of the building and its designer. Commission member John M. Dickey thanked Adelaide but informed her that the demolition would be approved. He stated that the building's poor structural condition and its exterior character, which he described as "obsolete," made the possibility of its restoration remote.[3] In another letter, the commission noted that the New Century Club was the only remaining structure on the block and was surrounded by parking lots.[4]

---

2   Quindlen, "With Traditional Gentility."
3   John M. Dickey to Adelaide Baker, March 23, 1973, Philadelphia Historical Commission Archives.
4   Margaret B. Tinkcom to James C. Massey, April 10, 1973, Philadelphia Historical Commission Archives.

REQUIEM FOR A BUILDING

The commission recommended photographing the building inside and out for documentation in the Historic American Buildings Survey, and placing all relevant archival material with the Historical Society of Pennsylvania [FIG 1]. By June, the building had been demolished and the site cleared. The club disbanded in 1978.

Minerva Parker Nichols: The Search for a Forgotten Architect, the exhibition that this book accompanies, takes the demolition of the New Century Club in Philadelphia as a point of departure for a critical examination of Minerva's life and work. For the curatorial team, the moment of cultural change and vulnerability present in the built environment during the 1970s provides an interesting and complex lens through which we can reflect upon gaps in the archival record, the often inadequate tools used by architectural historians, historic preservationists, and archivists to document and reconstruct the past, as well as the social, cultural, and economic structures that perpetuate inequities across these disciplines. This book represents the exhaustive research necessary to piece together Minerva's biography, to compile her catalogue raisonné, and to photographically document her extant buildings.

Though heralded in her time, Minerva is absent from today's architectural histories. She was not named in Quindlen's 1977 article, nor did Minerva leave a substantial archival collection of her work. A handful of her drawings for a single design are in the Architectural Archives at the University of Pennsylvania; a dozen or so others are housed in the collection of her daughter, Adelaide, at Harvard's Schlesinger Library; New Century Club collections reside at state historical societies; and some materials remain with Minerva's descendants. Separated, they are fragments that tell us extraordinarily little about their creator.

These glaring absences provoked discussion amongst our curatorial team and our colleagues about the professional practices that perpetuate them, helping to shape our approach. In the archives, this was often the archival practice of provenance—that "records created, accumulated

PROLOGUE

and/or maintained by an individual or organization must be represented together, distinguishable from the records of any other creator"—and how it can further obscure attribution for an unexamined story such as Minerva's and make the process of discovery more difficult. On the historic preservation side, conversations centered around the Historic American Buildings Survey national database, to which the New Century Club photographs were added at the time of the building's demolition. While the database serves as a rich historical record of our nation's built environment, it has also been utilized as a convenient vehicle for "preservation" when the wrecking ball looms.

But the story of Minerva's life and work, as well as our project, is not just one of loss, but also of hope. Dozens of Minerva's buildings *do* survive, as you will see in the portfolio section of the book, continuing to serve as useful and much-loved homes or, in the case of some of her public buildings, as successfully repurposed spaces. In the absence of an archive, we set out to create one, stepping behind the camera with architectural photographer Elizabeth Felicella to document Minerva's remaining projects. The choice to embed an artist in this project opened new opportunities, engaging us not just as historians, but as active agents in the creation of material as we experienced these spaces today.

Like all ambitious projects, this one is built upon the many decades of work by others to collect and interpret Minerva's story, beginning with *The Baddest Day, and Other Favorite Stories*, an oral history recounted by Minerva to her grandchildren in 1944. In 1973, perhaps struggling with the loss of the New Century Club in Philadelphia and concerned with her mother's legacy, Adelaide Baker began writing *Minerva Invicta*, a book about Minerva's pioneering career as an architect. Unfortunately, Adelaide died the following year, but she left behind a rich (though fragmentary) manuscript and related family correspondence. Twenty years later, Kathleen Sinclair Wood picked up the story's threads for her thesis, *Minerva Parker Nichols: Pioneer American Woman Architect*. Our own project, built on a decade of research by Molly Lester, takes on the question of what Minerva built and works toward an interdisciplinary approach to recovering lost or forgotten architectural history. With each of these projects, more archival materials were knitted back together, deepening our understanding of this history. It is also worth noting that each attempt at writing Minerva's story reflects the cultural moment in which it was written, further demonstrating how remarkably the "making" of history has shifted over the last century and how it continues to evolve.

We are once again living through a time of social change and upheaval, and the process of reexamining our past in order to build our future is challenging and often painful. And yet, there is much to be hopeful about: this project aligns itself with similar efforts that aim to address gaps in the record or to reinterpret stories that have been historically misconstrued. Our process-centered approach has also revealed the limitations of diversification alone. We are inspired by archivists such as Jarrett Drake, Michelle Caswell, and Marika Cifor, who challenge all of us involved in memory work to push past these initial diversifying efforts to envision new theories and practices outside the dominant Western framework.

Archives are a natural place of origin and culmination for this critical cultural work. In her book *Crafting History: Archiving and the Quest for Architectural Legacy*, architectural historian Albena Yaneva observes that "the collection operates as a contextual machine providing a broader relational space where new dialogues and transversal reading of works become possible."[5] She characterizes the archive as a "multiverse," where value depends on "the mingling of people and works" rather than deriving from any single collection. We set out to create an archive for Minerva in the absence of one. Ultimately, the real value of our work is not to create a new silo of materials under her name, but rather to contribute to the collective mingling of the archive. Heard together, any and all archived

---

5.   Albena Yaneva, Crafting History: Archiving and the Quest for Architectural Legacy (Ithaca, NY: Cornell University Press, 2020), 182.

PROLOGUE

stories—Minerva's among them—become richer, reflecting the complicated and compelling worlds in which they were created. The contributors to this book are hopeful that they will provoke engaging conversations for generations to come.

BIOGRAPHY

FINDING MINERVA

Margaret (Molly) Lester

FIG. 1: A portrait of Minerva published in 1893 in *Woman's Progress*, a magazine founded and edited by one of her clients.

BIOGRAPHY

The career of Minerva Parker Nichols (1862–1949) spanned seven decades. When she entered the field of architecture in the early 1880s, only seventeen women were active in the profession in the United States. At the time of her death, over one thousand women identified themselves as practicing architects.[1] She began her career in the dynamic decades following the Civil War, as America, on the threshold of modernity, confronted profound questions of class, race, and gender. In her earliest years of practice, she designed several houses for suffragists; in her final years, she focused her attention on the question of homes for World War II veterans. Her longevity is staggering, and yet, because her public career shifted after an intense seventeen-year period, her legacy has either been overlooked or misunderstood. The very fact that she successfully entered the field of architecture in the early 1880s and was the first woman to establish and maintain an independent practice demands examination.[2] She may be the most famous architect you've never heard of [FIG. 1].

Yet, even as she was a perceptive architect, Minerva was also a daughter and sister in a nuclear family that needed her, a writer for publications that celebrated her, a teacher for students who learned from her, a wife and eventually a mother in a new family circle that leaned on her, and a reformer for causes that concerned her (in every sense of the word). She moved among other women as a colleague and counterpart, a client and a supervisor, and even possibly as a rival. She worked with artists, developers, industrialists, suffragists, tradespeople, congregations, schools, social clubs—and even a pair of macaroni manufacturers.

To understand what Minerva built—both tangibly and intangibly—one must examine the many roles that she maintained throughout her life and how these complex identities informed her work, contributed to it, perhaps distracted her from it, and ultimately deepened it. Some of the most revealing clues to her work have emerged from the overlaps between her identities, as they blend within the traces of her life.

Beginnings, 1862–1875

Born on May 14, 1862, in rural Timber Township, Illinois, Minerva Parker was the younger daughter of John Wesley Parker (ca. 1834–1863) and Amanda Doane (1836–1921) and the younger sister of Adelaide Parker. While John Parker worked as a schoolteacher, his wife maintained the family farm and raised their two daughters. The family lived in the small town of Lancaster, not far from its steamboat landing on the Illinois River; their homestead was some fifteen miles southwest of Peoria and one hundred fifty miles from Chicago (by then the eighth largest city in the United States, with a population just over one hundred ten thousand). The area had a fine and diverse timber reserve by the late 1820s, attracting eastern settlers, who lobbied the federal government to displace Native Americans in order to claim and develop land. Minerva's grandfathers, Samuel Parker (1798–1886) and Seth Brown Doane (1798–1876)—both carpenters—sought land grants here precisely because of the region's abundant timber resources.

Just three months after Minerva's birth, as the Civil War made its way into nearby states, John Parker enlisted in the Illinois infantry of the Union Army on August 7, 1862, serving as a sergeant under the command of his wife's brother-in-law, Colonel Allen Fahnestock. On July 23, 1863, when Minerva was just fourteen months old, her father died of dysentery in a makeshift field hospital near Murfreesboro, Tennessee.[3] His body had to be exhumed from a temporary grave for the journey home, where he was buried next to his infant sons, Arthur and Herbert.

Minerva never knew her father, but his death was a seismic event, reverberating through her entire life and propelling her toward a future that demanded she work. Her mother, widowed just three weeks after her twenty-seventh birthday, with two children under the age of four, became one of hundreds of thousands of women stripped of their husbands by the Civil War. For several years after John's death, Amanda leaned heavily on her parents, Seth and Lucretia Doane, and her sister Sarah (known to Minerva as Aunt Sudie) and her family. Amanda's extended family helped raise her daughters, and these circumstances drew Minerva into close contact with her maternal grandfather.

Born in Dana, Massachusetts, in 1798, Seth Doane is remembered in family histories as a "builder, architect, and master mechanic."[4] The son of a sea captain, he joined three of his brothers in work as a "housewright" (or house carpenter) in the Boston area. He proved himself a skilled mechanic and worked in Boston for a time as a builder, before migrating to Florida and then to New Orleans. When he finally returned to New England, he met and married Lucretia Melvina Johnson in 1823 in Waltham, Massachusetts.[5] The couple was living in Boston by 1825, a pivotal year in the history of labor relations in the United States. The city's journeymen carpenters went on strike for a ten-hour workday, and while their action was unsuccessful in the short term, the notion of labor contesting terms of employment was unprecedented. Seth is recorded in city directories for that year as a housewright, and it is likely that he worked as a journeyman and participated in the strike. By 1827 the family was living in Lowell and Seth was presumably active in the great building campaign associated with the construction of the textile mills at Lowell and the associated worker housing.

Lucretia bore eleven children; Amanda, Minerva's mother, was the seventh child and the fourth daughter. With their growing family, Seth and Lucretia migrated to Albany, New York, and later to Buffalo, traveling via the Erie Canal.

All the while, Seth accumulated experience as a builder. In 1834, he felt the pull westward, as the United States seized and settled Indigenous lands west of the Mississippi River. He moved his family to Fort Dearborn, Illinois, an encampment that would become the city of Chicago, chartered by the State of Illinois in 1837. Seth probably built some of the earliest houses in the not-yet-city, which had a population of around three thousand at the time. The family lived there for five years before Seth moved them on, this time to Canton, Utica, and finally Orion Township in central Illinois.[6]

In the course of these moves from New England to the Midwest, Seth traded housebuilding for prairie schooners, establishing a measure of local renown as a craftsman of the wagons that carried settlers further west. After decades of itinerant living, their family growing even as they moved hundreds of miles at a time, Seth and Lucretia finally planted themselves in Orion Township, lingering for over three decades as they welcomed more children and eventually grandchildren—including Minerva. In the years between 1862 and 1870, and particularly after her father's death in 1863, Minerva spent considerable time there with her grandparents, fascinated in particular by her grandfather's stories and Swear words.[7]

Understanding of Minerva's early childhood in Illinois is based on a series of stories she told her grandchildren late in life. Most strikingly, in considering the roots and formation of America's first woman to practice as an independent architect, it is clear from these stories that Minerva's memories were filtered through the buildings in which she grew up; she articulated each phase of life in her childhood and early teens according to vivid descriptions of each successive home—at least two of which were designed by members of her own family.

First, there was the stately house built by Seth and Lucretia in Orion Township. Located about ten miles from the Parkers' farm at Timber Township, Illinois, the Doanes' large white Colonial house looked more like the buildings in the small New England towns where Seth and Lucretia were born than those of the Illinois prairies where the couple eventually settled. Seth constructed a house that "looked like any good Georgian house," Minerva later recalled. "[It was] a white Colonial house that would have been at home on the streets of Salem or Plymouth, Massachusetts," despite the fact that "there was no need for fine houses in Illinois then." The house became a formative schoolroom for Minerva, inculcating a love of design and a respect for the practices of construction. On days when Amanda struggled with her workload, her older daughter's arthritis-like disability, and her younger daughter's rambunctiousness, she sent Minerva to the farm to spend time with her grandparents, Aunt Sudie, and Minerva's favorite play companion, her cousin John.[8]

For several years, Minerva took note of the big Doane house and all the work—by the women in particular—that sustained it. In the big room just inside the front door, Minerva would read on the stone floor, ingrained in shades of green and yellow and flecked with red, illuminated by light from the many windows that she described as having "deep gilt cornices" and "long Nottingham lace curtains looped back over French gilt rosettes." In the loom room, she would watch her grandmother weave textiles on a massive sewing loom. The kitchen had a modern cookstove, "a marvel of modernity and a concession to the daughters of the household" who kept the home running. A basket next to the kitchen fireplace was filled with a tumble of rags ready to be woven into carpets, "one of the few outlets for the artistic skill of the women," according to Minerva. A second basket in the corner was heaped with corn cobs, which young Minerva fashioned into houses when she was fidgety, to keep out of trouble. "I think I can even remember when I hardly walked, sitting on a quilt building houses."[9]

In the barn, Seth Doane channeled his granddaughter's outsize energy, teaching her drawing and building skills [FIG. 2]. He had done the same with her mother, taking Amanda for walks and later asking her to sketch her observations from memory. A farmer and carpenter, he repurposed his own building materials as drawing surfaces. As he made seats for prairie schooners from wide planks of white pine, he would periodically plane boards into thin surfaces for Minerva to draw on, as he had for Amanda. While Minerva used these drawing scraps, she watched her grandfather craft the wood into more substantial creations.[10] When she was done, he would plane them to use again for drawing.

Despite her grandfather's loving influence, Minerva reserved her greatest respect for her mother and Aunt Sudie. She was aware of their burdens, noting, as her mother sewed for neighbors to bring in extra money, the stresses and difficulties of living on a war widow's pension. "The marvel was that these women, overworked, unhappy, without modern methods to chart their way in child care, succeeded in providing long happy days for their [children]."[11]

By about 1868, five years after her husband's death, Amanda felt confident enough to move her daughters to a series of small towns, eventually settling in Normal, Illinois [FIG. 3]. The move from her Timber Township home was destabilizing at first for Minerva, as she watched her childhood possessions and memories being packed onto a wagon: "Perhaps nothing in the world is harder on a child than the dismantling and dismembering of a home that has grown to be the very warp and [weft] of...life," she said over seven decades later, once again reflecting on her childhood by way of the physical spaces that defined it.[12]

Nevertheless, the move had positive effects on Minerva's future. Encouraged by friends and trained by her father, Amanda designed a house in Normal for her small family, using funds from the sale of a farm in Iowa that she and her late husband

FINDING MINERVA

FIG. 2

FIG. 3

FIG. 4

FIG. 2: Minerva spent significant time on her grandparents' farm, where her grandfather, Seth Doane, taught her to draw.

FIG. 3: Minerva (*right*) with her sister, Adelaide, and mother, Amanda.

FIG. 4: Minerva likely during her teenage years.

had purchased as newlyweds. Her friends oversaw its construction, ensuring that it was finished by the time Amanda ushered her family across the porch and inserted her key in the front door.[13]

As with her grandfather's house in Orion Township, Minerva could vividly describe her mother's house in Normal. She could recall its layout, with its enclosed stair leading to the bedrooms above, the long, narrow dining room, and the kitchen "so stream-lined that it was a forerunner of the modern kitchen."[14] Her mother—who "feared nothing," in Minerva's telling—busied herself with building a new life. She took in boarders—at least nine at a time. In 1870 alone, she was managing a bustling household that included her two daughters (aged ten and eight), a twenty-two-year-old student, a music teacher, two "nurserymen," a blacksmith, and a grain merchant, his wife, and their four-month-old daughter. In Normal, Minerva attended school for the first time.[15]

By 1873, Amanda moved the family to Chicago. Although she was there for a relatively short period, Minerva witnessed, consciously or not, the aftermath of the fire of 1871: a modern construction site of extraordinary size and intensity. With over two thousand acres and eighteen thousand buildings lost to the blaze, and over ninety thousand people left homeless, Chicago confronted rebuilding on a daunting scale.[16] On October 10, 1871—the day the fire finally died out—the Chamber of Commerce issued a call to rebuild; by November 18, over five thousand cottages were complete or underway. One year later, the city had already put up over $40 million worth of new construction.[17] Even as temporary structures were erected to meet the immediate need after the fire, the city's conscious re-urbanization set the stage for its long-term reimagining—and for what would become the Chicago school of architecture in the 1880s and beyond. This renaissance was made possible by the city's extensive rail and river connections—both of which had hubs within blocks of the Parkers' home on West Madison Street (and later, West Randolph Street).[18]

Although they could not have anticipated the fallout from the fire, this frenzy of rebuilding and apparent economic progress ultimately benefitted Amanda and her daughters. Why they moved from Normal to Chicago is unknown. Perhaps Amanda hoped to find better employment than the smaller town could offer, or perhaps (as some of her grandchildren speculated in the family papers), she was simply a restless person like her father, in which case the city's rebuilding efforts were no doubt stimulating. Whatever the motivation, she and her daughters were quite close by this time, having spent nearly all of Minerva's life as a threesome. It was disruptive, then, when Amanda met Samuel Maxwell around 1875, and married him that year on September 23.[19]

Samuel, born around 1828, had first married Aurelia Swain, who gave birth to three children—daughters Emma and Ellen, and a son, Arthur. Samuel's occupation changed over time: in the early 1860s, he was a daguerreotypist and photographer; as of 1870, he was a manufacturer of cutlery.[20] Around the time of his first wife's death in 1872, he appears to have moved to Chicago, reinventing himself as Dr. Samuel Maxwell, a physician and Quaker medium who could convene spirits.[21]

Samuel and Amanda likely met through their Unitarian connections, and possibly at one of the spiritualist gatherings that he led. Once they were married, the forty-seven-year-old widower was apparently uninterested in living with two young stepdaughters underfoot.[22] It may have been more than a lack of enthusiasm. Writing after Minerva's death, her daughter implied as much: "There are some gaps [in Mother's life story] I may never be able to fill. They must be the [darker] bits she didn't talk so much about—especially her mother's remarriage."[23] After a decade of stressful widowhood, Amanda was doubtless eager to build a life with her new husband and grateful for the support of his income. Around

FINDING MINERVA

the time of her remarriage, she sent Adelaide and Minerva to a private convent school in Dubuque, Iowa, effectively breaking up her little family for the first time since John Parker's death in 1863.[24]

The distance between mother and daughters grew greater the next year, when the Maxwells moved to Philadelphia. With the Centennial International Exposition set to open in the city in May of that year, Philadelphia was the center of the country's attention, and the newly wed Maxwells found themselves drawn to the festivities—and perhaps financial opportunities. At the time, Philadelphia, the "workshop of the world," was at the height of its industrial output and racing to keep up with its own productivity and constructing housing and infrastructure in order to sustain its growth. The city's grid pattern belied the urbanizing disorder of its core, as railroads competed with rowhouses for space, and William Penn's original open squares were increasingly hemmed in by dense construction. The Maxwells were not the only people attracted to the city in the years leading up to the Centennial Exposition: Philadelphia's foreign-born population reached its peak in 1870 (immigrants accounted for 27 percent of the city's six hundred seventy-four thousand residents that year), and the fair itself would draw over 10 million people.[25]

Settled with Samuel in Philadelphia, Amanda sent for her daughters. Their close-knit dynamic was permanently altered and life with a stepfather was not the only circumstance to which the girls had to adjust: by the time the Centennial Exposition closed in November 1876, Amanda was pregnant.[26] Her husband died of consumption on April 11, 1877. His namesake, Samuel Raymond Maxwell, was born three months later, on July 14.[27] Alone in a new city, with three children to feed and widowed again, Amanda could not turn for help to her parents or sister this time. Instead, it fell primarily to fifteen-year-old Minerva to help support the family [FIG. 4].

Student and Servant, 1876–1888

By 1880 Minerva was so occupied with supporting her family that the Federal Census counted her twice. When census officials made their way through the Society Hill neighborhood of Philadelphia, they noted that she lived in the 600 block of Spruce Street with her mother, older sister, younger brother, and five other housemates. By the time census takers reached Cheltenham Township, north of Philadelphia, they recorded Minerva again, this time working in the household of wholesale grocer Horace G. Lippincott and his wife, Caroline. The second entry lists Minerva as a "servant" for the household: she was probably governess to the Lippincott children—governess is the occupation listed in her Spruce Street census entry. It was a job for which she was well qualified, as her brother, Samuel, was three years old by this time, and she had no doubt spent time looking after him while their mother worked.[28]

Art School

Minerva's job would have entailed long days, including train rides between Philadelphia and Cheltenham to tend to the Lippincott children. Remarkably, during this period, she was also enrolled in a two-year program at the Philadelphia Normal Art School at 1523 Chestnut Street. Normal schools were nineteenth-century teacher training colleges; the Philadelphia Normal Art School was established to train art teachers. It was led by principals Caroline and Elizabeth West, while "artists and instructors of acknowledged ability were engaged to assist."[29]

This suggests that before she thought of becoming an architect—or knew that she could pursue that course—seventeen-year-old Minerva may have intended to become an art teacher. Teaching would have been a more conventional

BIOGRAPHY

career, a safer choice. Whatever Minerva's career thinking may have been at that stage, the Normal Art School turned out to offer practical, broadly applicable skills that served her once she set her sights on a career in architecture. The school's curriculum formalized many of the lessons her grandfather had instilled in her, including drawing from memory. Other subjects in the Normal Art School's coursework included: drawing from dictation, drawing from objects, geometrical drawing, freehand drawing, botanical analysis, perspective, and—the two topics most relevant for a future architect—design and historic ornament.

Minerva attended the Normal Art School from 1879, until her graduation in January 1882. How she spent the next two years is unclear: she may have maintained her position as a governess, although later records suggest she began working for unnamed architectural firms around 1883.[30] By the winter of 1884, she had enrolled in the Drawing School at the Franklin Institute, an unmistakable step toward a career in architecture.

Architectural Training in the United States

University-based architecture programs were not yet the norm for would-be architects in the late nineteenth century. Nor was licensure required, and professional affiliations such as the American Institute of Architects were not yet essential (or, in the case of women, even available before the 1880s). In fact, architecture as a profession—rather than a craft or leisure pursuit—was a relatively new concept in the mid- to late nineteenth century. For centuries in the United States and Europe, buildings were designed either by master builders, who learned their craft through apprenticeship and closely guarded it in male-dominated guilds, or by upper-class gentlemen who had the leisure, wealth, and, all too often in the United States, the enslaved laborers to erect buildings based on their studies of classical orders and other precedents.

Collegiate architecture schools, the primary gateway to the profession today, did not exist in the United States until after the Civil War and they did not earn their clout until the end of the nineteenth century. In the decades before those programs rose in prominence, design education was primarily available through technical programs and schools of design. In Philadelphia, the former were represented by the Franklin Institute and the Carpenter Company, among others, and the latter primarily by the Philadelphia School of Design for Women.

Organized in 1824 "to promote the useful arts by diffusing a knowledge of mechanical science," from an early stage, the Franklin Institute emphasized architecture and building.[31] The success of the school rose and fell throughout the century, but by the time Minerva enrolled in classes in the mid-1880s, it was in the capable hands of director William H. Thorne, who led the Drawing School from 1881 to 1916.[32] Under him, the school was reorganized to include classes in mechanical drawing, architectural drawing, and freehand drawing. By 1883–84, the academic year before Minerva enrolled—and the period in which she would have considered the school's reputation and decided to apply—the architectural class had celebrated its largest enrollment to date, approximately fifty students.[33]

The Franklin Institute had much in common with the Philadelphia School of Design for Women, across town; for a few years in the 1850s, they even shared a direct affiliation based on the alignment in their missions.[34] Like the Franklin Institute, the School of Design for Women was established to prepare women for careers in the mechanical and industrial arts. As its enrollment and reputation grew in the nineteenth century, the school made it clear that its intentions with respect to securing employment for its graduates were practical: it wanted to secure employment for its graduates that could be "exercised at their own homes," and with "no exertion of bodily strength." In other words, if the School of Design for Women could equip its pupils with marketable skills as art teachers, textile designers, engravers, and similar occupations, it could help them avoid the degradation—individual and societal—of physical labor on the factory floor. (Training in marketable skills was not available to many low- and middle-class White women or to women of color in general.) In this way, the curriculum provided a path into trade, offering many single White women a route to earning sufficient income to support themselves and any dependents.

Minerva did not study at the Philadelphia School of Design for Women, nor is there any evidence to date to suggest that she applied.[35] The decision cannot be explained by mere logistics: in 1884, the year she started classes at the Franklin Institute, her family lived at 1614 Green Street. The Institute, located at that time at 15 South Seventh Street, was over a mile and a half away. The School of Design for Women, meanwhile, had recently heralded its new home at Broad and Master Streets—a mile from Minerva's own home. The Franklin Institute, then, would have required an extra mile of walking a day—time in which she was not earning money at the Lippincotts' house, or helping her mother to keep house and raise young Samuel, or assisting newly married Adelaide, who was rearing her first child, Nye, in the Green Street house.

Beyond the question of schedules and distances, another more meaningful explanation for Minerva's choice is related to curriculum and ambition. (Clearly, these speculations are not mutually exclusive.) With over a half-century of investment in lectures and hands-on lessons on the subject, the Franklin Institute's Drawing School had a defined course of architectural studies. Two miles north, the School of Design for Women offered lectures in "historic decorative art and architecture," but its "theoretical and technical design" track was only partially concerned with architectural drafting and related applications. This difference in approach was reflected by the typical careers of graduates from each institution. In his 1882 report on the Drawing School, William Thorne alluded to the professional outcomes for his students: "The main feature of the school has been the teaching of drawing, such as would be useful in the workshop and applicable to construction . . . [The] demonstration and application of these principles has always been made to conform with the practice of our best engineers and architects."[36] Graduates of the Drawing School were trained to work alongside engineers and architects—on and off the construction site—and establish their own professional identity in doing so. Meanwhile, by the late 1870s, most graduates of the Philadelphia School of Design for Women went on to become teachers; fewer went on to become working designers and illustrators.[37] Even the women who forged successful careers in the applied arts could not lay claim to their own work; as one historian notes, "an industrial designer did not sign her projects." Instead, her engravings, lithographs, and by extension her professional identity, were credited to the institution that hired her.[38] Perhaps Minerva opted for the Franklin Institute because she already knew what she wanted to do—and wanted to be known for doing it.

Even as the Franklin Institute, the School of Design for Women, and their counterparts were growing in popularity in the mid- and late nineteenth century, most people interested in earning a living in architecture still sought out apprenticeships. Apprenticeships provided hands-on experience and gave immediate access to the spate of construction that accompanied American industrialization and urbanization around this time. As historian Jeffrey Cohen points out: "While the better-known members of the lineage of architects trained by architects are remembered for most of the more ambitious and monumental buildings of the early nineteenth century, it was the men training with builders who were responsible for the great quantity of the structures of the time, including middle-sized houses, both urban and rural, and the preponderance of civic and institutional structures outside the big cities."[39] The Franklin Institute's Drawing School and other technical programs (in Philadelphia and elsewhere) could deepen students' knowledge of the history and principles of design, but such courses cost money and took time (a year at minimum, although many offered evening classes, recognizing that most pupils had jobs during the day). Most importantly, these formal programs did not yet have proven value in the context of professional practice. As a writer for the contemporary trade publication *American Architect* observed, if no state or professional society mandated an architectural degree in order to practice, then "a great many students [were] not willing to give up so much time to the study of architecture."[40]

Why, then, was Minerva so willing to delay her entrance to the profession by seeking out substantial time in the classroom? The primary reason was likely one of access: unlike most fledgling university programs, the Franklin Institute Drawing School and programs that she subsequently attended accepted women as students.[41] Similarly, there was no guarantee that a practicing architect would take on female apprentices. The first university architecture programs to admit women were, not coincidentally, at public land-grant institutions.[42] By 1891 an estimated twelve women had earned degrees from collegiate architecture programs in the United States, but few of these early graduates went on to practice architecture in any professional capacity.[43] Instead, like the graduates of the School of Design for Women, many went on to teach a related subject or left the field altogether.

The Franklin Institute Drawing School admitted its first female students in 1870.[44] Minerva enrolled in the school for the winter 1884 term [FIG. 5]. She spent the next two years, or four terms, taking classes from two practicing architects: Edward S. Paxson and Clement Remington, one of the founders of the T-Square Club (for Philadelphia architects) in 1883. When she graduated in spring 1886, she earned an honorable mention (under the name "Minnie M. Parker") for her "commendable Zeal and ability." Shortly after graduating, Minerva found work with several architectural firms, culminating in an apprenticeship in the office of Edwin W. Thorne (1850–1926), who had recently moved his office from Wilmington, Delaware, to Philadelphia.[45]

Edwin W. Thorne

Twelve years older than Minerva, Edwin W. Thorne began his career as a carpenter, learning the trade in Chester, Pennsylvania, around 1870. In the 1870s, he moved to Philadelphia, where "he learned stair building and the sash and door business, and also became an architect."[46] From this sentence in an account of Edwin's practice, it is clear that the building trades and the profession of architecture remained inextricably linked at this time; Edwin and his eventual mentee Minerva were emblematic of this overlap, alternately identifying themselves as both an architect and a builder (and, in Edwin's case, a carpenter as well). He also occupied a middle ground with respect to pattern books: without formal training in architectural precedents, he leaned on pattern books as sources for his own work. By 1878 Edwin had settled in Wilmington, Delaware, and within a year he began placing notices in Wilmington newspapers advertising his services as a builder, architect, and "a practice mechanic, of varied experience." He announced himself as a jack-of-all-trades who could offer heavy framework, open stairwork, and "all kinds of building and repairing done by day or contract" (consistent with the

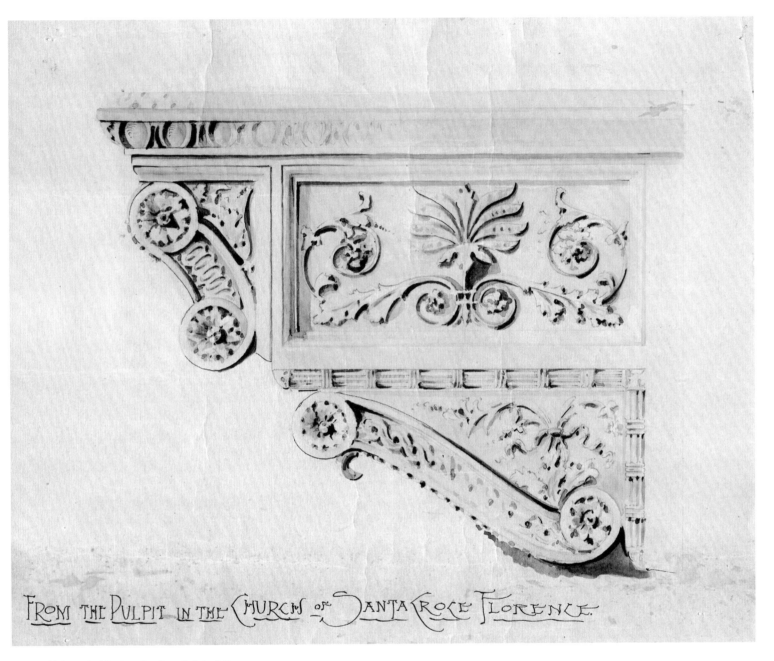

FROM THE PULPIT IN THE CHURCH OF SANTA CROCE FLORENCE.

FIG. 5: Although this drawing is not dated, it seems likely that Minerva created it during her studies at the Franklin Institute Drawing School.

BIOGRAPHY

identity of a builder), combined with "architectural designs, details, specifications, and correct estimates" (in keeping with his presentation as an architect).[47]

Edwin was evidently quite productive in Wilmington, with enough work to bring his brother on as a second carpenter in the firm of E. W. Thorne and Bro. By 1880 the two Thorne brothers had reportedly erected more than forty buildings—acting at times not only as architects and builders but also as developers. Based on the quantity of newspaper notices he placed and the number of buildings he designed and then sold, Edwin seems to have had a knack for drumming up business in Wilmington. He marketed himself to other architects as a useful second for designs, specifications, agreements, and construction supervision; addressing the ladies and gentlemen of the city who were "contemplating building," he made sure they knew that "ALL DRAWINGS ARE PRACTICAL."[48] Between 1878 and 1885, he designed dozens of residences, but also landed jobs working on higher-profile public buildings such as the Wilmington Institute Library (where he was a carpenter for renovations) and Shiloh Baptist Church (where he was the builder, working under architect D. S. Gendell).[49]

A dispute over the bid process for a new public high school, however, alienated Edwin from key Wilmington power brokers and may have driven him to Philadelphia.[50] In the months following the dispute, his business advertisements took on an increasingly despondent tone. By December 6, 1884, his notices in local newspapers mentioned that he had reduced his fees.[51] By the end of April 1886, he gave notice in the Wilmington newspapers that he would henceforth be based on South Broad Street in Philadelphia, "in which city business prospects are said to be good."[52]

Apprenticeship

Before Edwin W. Thorne hired Minerva Parker as his apprentice in 1886, he appears to have had only one other employee than his brother, an English architect whose identity is unknown and whom Edwin took on in 1882. At the time, he celebrated the fact that the Englishman brought over twenty years' experience to his projects.[53] It's unclear how long the English architect worked for Edwin, as there are no subsequent references to him.

If Edwin could command such skilled assistance, why did he hire Minerva just a few years later? Perhaps he was considered difficult to work with, and the only person willing to take that chance was a young woman with few other prospects. Another possibility is that she brought to Edwin's practice some real advantages: with two years of normal art school and two years of drawing school, she had considerably more formal education than he did. Although he had taught himself an admirable number of trades—carpentry, contracting, and design—he had only a fraction of the classroom experience that she had. She could therefore speak to architectural style with more fluency than he could. Moreover, she clearly brought the talent and passion that the Franklin Institute's instructors saw in her to Edwin's office, and was determined to learn from him what she could not glean in drawing school—namely, the business of architecture. Regardless of the Wilmington school competition debacle, Edwin clearly took his work seriously when it came to marketing and management, and Minerva would benefit from his expertise in both.

Edwin and Minerva worked together for approximately two years, operating out of a three-story rowhouse at Broad and Market Streets—across the street from City Hall and just a block from the Pennsylvania Railroad's Broad Street Station. It was an undeniably productive arrangement. Together, they worked on projects in the town of Rutledge (just outside Philadelphia) and in the emerging towns along the Main Line of the Pennsylvania Railroad.

They shared an understanding of the importance of a professional identity in the evolving field of architecture; being known for one's work was critical in securing the sort of bread-and-butter, middle-class residential projects that they pursued. As historian Kathleen Sinclair Wood has pointed out, Edwin and Minerva wrote nearly identical letters to the editors of the *Philadelphia Real Estate Record and Builders' Guide* (hereafter cited as *Builders' Guide* in the text and as *PRERBG* in the notes) in December 1887, appealing to the publication to include the names of designers whenever their project plans were published.[54] Minerva signed her letter M. Parker, one of only two known instances in her career in which she used her initials, obscuring her gender.[55] Unlike industrial designers who never signed their projects, architects recognized that their signatures on a project's drawings could earn them their next commission.

Even as she worked with Edwin, Minerva was eager to hone her own professional identity. In May 1886 she entered a competition administered by *Carpentry and Building*; entrants selected noms de plume for their submissions; hers was "Chicago," a nod to her family roots. Although she did not place among the winners, she earned sufficient plaudits from the editors to merit mention in later issues of the magazine.[56] Her design was published in full in the October 1887 issue, alongside her own descriptions and the editors' commentary [FIG. 6]. Although the magazine misspelled her name—crediting the design to a "Miss Minnie M. Packer, Philadelphia"—these are the earliest known plans published by Minerva.[57]

In its initial commentary on her work, the magazine wrote condescendingly: "A study which gallantry perhaps should cause us to pass by in silence or to say nothing concerning that which is not pleasant to read [because] this design enjoys the distinction of being the only one in the contest coming from a woman."[58] Despite this inauspicious preface, the editors went on to praise her floor plans as "carefully studied," and noted that "the house has more than the usual conveniences." However, they took issue with the artistry of her penwork—"This we would hardly expect from such a source" (women were expected to be inherently and aesthetically skilled)—and the impracticality of some of her construction details. The latter criticism in particular is important to note, given that Edwin prized himself on the practicality of his drawings, and Minerva later marketed herself as similarly pragmatic; perhaps the competition experience in her apprenticeship period inspired her to redouble her efforts to learn about the realities of construction. Despite these shortcomings, the magazine made sure to conclude its analysis with a word of encouragement: "We would not by any means discourage 'Chicago' from her efforts in her chosen field, for we believe that with proper training and careful practice, she can make a name and position for herself."[59]

Early Work

Indeed, evidence suggests that under Edwin's tutelage Minerva served as the lead architect on several projects. No sooner had she submitted the design for the *Carpentry and Building* competition than she parlayed it into an actual commission. On May 27, 1886, the *Morton Chronicle* (published in a suburb of Philadelphia) noted that J. Rugan Neff of Philadelphia and his wife, Emma, were "having a large and convenient frame house built on President Avenue" in Rutledge. The house—which has clear parallels to the *Carpentry and Building* entry submitted by "Chicago" around this

BIOGRAPHY

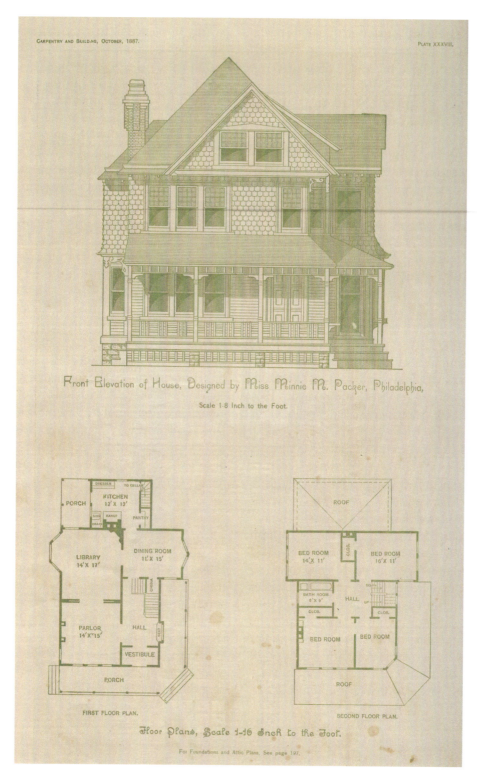

FIG. 6

FINDING MINERVA

FIG. 7

FIG. 8

FIG. 6: Design submitted by Minerva in May 1886 to a competition organized by *Carpentry and Building* magazine, under the pseudonym "Chicago." Although she did not win, her entry was published in a subsequent issue of the magazine. A version of this design appears to have been built in 1886 in Rutledge, Pennsylvania, on behalf of J. Rugan Neff.

FIG. 7: The house at 10 President Avenue in Rutledge, Pennsylvania, modeled after Minerva's *Carpentry and Building* entry and constructed in 1886.

FIG. 8: The design for Isaac Ashmead's house in Wyncote, Pennsylvania, was credited to E. W. Thorne (centered at the bottom of the drawing), but Minerva's signature appears on the upturned lower-right corner of the sketch, indicating that she was responsible for the rendering and suggesting that she may have played a role in the actual design.

time and published a year later—is still standing at 10 President Avenue in Rutledge. It is likely the earliest extant building designed by Minerva [FIG. 7].

Her early commissions took shape in the context of a city where industrial growth and the development of new suburbs were powered by the railroads, their lines radiating in all directions from the city's stations to the outlying counties, transforming colonial-era villages into flourishing nineteenth-century suburbs. Other small towns—particularly along the Main Line of the Pennsylvania Railroad—emerged from former farms and quickly became population centers. As if to demonstrate the power the railroad had in fostering this growth, several of these new towns named themselves for their closest station; today's Narberth, for example, developed in the 1880s as Elm Station.

Edwin and Minerva capitalized on these circumstances, cultivating projects not just downtown—where wealth and development were already concentrated—but in the emerging suburbs, where they could make a mark on the changing landscape. With each new project—and by 1888, Edwin W. Thorne's office was apparently responsible for at least twenty-four—Minerva and Edwin negotiated their working relationship. In February 1888, Isaac Ashmead commissioned a cottage from Edwin, to be built in Wyncote.[60] In May of that year, the trade publication *Builder and Decorator: An Illustrated Monthly* (later *Builder, Decorator and Woodworker*) included a rendering of the resulting design [FIG. 8].[61] Drawn in pen and ink, the rendered cottage was presented at an angle to the viewer, situated in what looked like a fully realized landscape, with a sloping walk at the front and a natural setting behind. In the top right corner of the drawing, a small floor plan translated the evocative perspective view into the pragmatic details of structure and space. Centered at the bottom of the drawing, within the pen strokes of the lawn, was the inscription "E. W. Thorne, Architect." But at the bottom-right corner of the drawing, the sketch was rendered as if the corner of the drawing itself was upturned, and on the winking "underside" of the page, Minerva's name appeared. In some ways, this drawing bears out the hierarchical arrangement we would expect from Edwin's office: his name and title in the center of the drawing, hers relegated to the corner. But, whereas many renderers folded their names into the background (at times, these signatures are practically indistinguishable from the rendered foliage), Minerva carved out space in the layout of the drawing to include her full name. Perhaps this was simply her clever way of representing the project; but if her role in designing this building was more substantial than that of a draftswoman—and based on the overlap between Edwin's confirmed works and her own, this is plausible—then her corner inscription may have been her way of "signing her work" in a deeper sense.

Two other projects in Lansdowne, Pennsylvania, further complicate an understanding of Minerva's working relationship with Edwin. The "fine stone residence" for F. L. Archambault was commissioned in January 1889 and was under construction by April of that year. The project was associated with Edwin specifically, but as built, its turreted design strongly resembles other works in Minerva's portfolio; just a few years later, she called out a comparable design as "so satisfactory" that it was worth sharing with a national audience. [SEE CAT. NOS. 05 AND 38.] Given the standard architect-apprentice hierarchy, one might assume that the turreted buildings should be understood as a design that he created and she borrowed. It seems far more likely, however, that the design shows up in both portfolios because they both had a role in crafting it—Minerva contributing her acumen as a designer to the creation of the form, and Edwin ensuring its structural soundness. In this reading, their commissions hint at a working relationship between Edwin and Minerva that was less stratified and more strategic and took advantage of their complementary skillsets. While these designs were built under Edwin's name, Minerva had already published notice, in April 1888, of her own project for the engineer and industrialist Max Suppes of Johnstown, Pennsylvania, a manufacturer of steel extrusions, who did business with the Pennsylvania Railroad. It is unclear how he learned of Minerva, or what prompted him to hire her. Dispensing with "Minnie," the nickname she had used in childhood and adolescence, Minerva published her name in full—the first time it appeared in the *Builders' Guide*.

Building a Life and Practice, 1888–1896

By the summer of 1889, Minerva had already been producing work under her own name for over a year and was ready to take her chances and go out on her own. When Edwin decided to relocate to "more commodious offices" a few blocks away at 1305–1307 Arch Street, Minerva decided to remain on South Broad Street and hang out her own shingle, becoming the first woman in the country to maintain her own independent practice [SEE ILLUSTRATION ON PAGE 10].[62]

Had she stayed under Edwin's mantle, Minerva would have spent her career executing his designs, adhering to his directives for his clients. In exchange, she would have benefited from his privileges of gender and age in securing work. Instead, she ventured away from that relative security, with no model to build on, no wealthy patrons to launch her, and no presumption of steady work or future clients, choosing boldly, even rashly, to distinguish herself from her female contemporaries who remained in larger practices or partnered with men. Alone, on the upper floors of 14 South Broad Street, Minerva began building her own network to propel her work and influence onto a broader stage.

Minerva as an Architect

From the moment she launched her independent practice, Minerva's accelerating productivity was remarkable. In 1888 she published two notices in the *Builders' Guide*, the next year, she published ten; in 1890, her busiest year in the *Builders' Guide*, she filed thirty announcements, not counting the front-page profile devoted to her by the publication in March of that year, in which several more projects were mentioned.[63] These announcements—which often revisited the same projects at various stages of completion—tracked the progress of projects as she secured them ("Minerva Parker, 14 South Broad Street, is engaged on plans . . . "),[64] consulted with the client and prepared plans ("Minerva Parker, architect, has on boards [the] plans for . . . "),[65] put projects out to bid for contractors ("Minerva Parker, architect, is engaged in securing bids . . . "),[66] selected builders ("Same architect has just awarded the contract to . . . "),[67] and oversaw their construction ("Minerva Parker, who drew the plans, will supervise . . . ").[68] By the end of 1890, when Minerva was twenty-eight years old, more than forty of her projects were underway or already complete.

At this pace, it was not long before people beyond Philadelphia knew about her; by April 1889, she had earned mentions in newspapers as far away as Birmingham, Alabama, Cincinnati, Ohio, and Portland, Maine. Trumpeting the opportunities of "new work for women," as one newspaper headlined her story, the press introduced her to readers around the country, not as a mere novelty, but as a worthy addition to the profession, one who brought indisputable skills to the process of designing and constructing buildings. Reporters and editors celebrated her career, and implicitly commended her adopted hometown of Philadelphia for nurturing it. Minerva's next eight years in Philadelphia were indeed transformational for her life and work, as

BIOGRAPHY

her practice in Philadelphia generated dozens of commissions.

Only one other woman had launched her own practice in the United States. Louise Blanchard opened an office in Buffalo a few years before Minerva went solo in Philadelphia. Unlike Minerva, Louise took on a male partner within a few months, hiring Robert Bethune, whom she eventually married. Minerva took on no partners, laboring alone on her designs. She had no colleague with whom to divide the work or discuss ideas. A young, single woman, she also had to represent herself in a man's world. The stakes were high, as her income was necessary to sustain her family. Success was the only possible outcome: "Should I fail, I would then know where to strengthen my armor," she said in 1891.[69]

Unassisted, how did Minerva get so much work done in these early years? (The question is all the more intriguing if we consider that in 1888–89, she managed to log another year of technical education, this time at the Pennsylvania Museum and School of Industrial Art. Although there is no record of her chosen course of study, she likely received additional training in drawing and/or architectural ornament, or style.)[70] There is no documentation of apprentices or drafting assistants in her firm until later; it was no doubt too financially risky at first, despite the work that must have piled up in 1890, when she juggled an estimated thirty projects in one year alone.

Minerva's productivity can be explained in part by the nature of design work at that time. Whereas architects today are responsible for several sets of designs—conceptual designs, construction details, and as-built drawings, with several iterations in between—in Minerva's time, architects who, like her, specialized in residential work, were responsible for only a handful of sheets, including scaled plans, elevations, and (in some instances) sections. The number of meetings with clients expected of such architects would have been fewer than are expected today. Construction supervision was probably the most time-intensive part of the process, as the architect would prepare detailed specifications for the builders and travel to the site every few weeks to ensure that all was going according to plan.[71] Despite those time demands, an architect like Minerva could toggle between several projects at a time—balancing drawings on the boards for some projects, with site visits for others—in order to maintain a steady pace of work.

Minerva's ability to handle a large volume of projects can thus be explained by her deliberate focus on residential architecture; "specialists in architecture, as in medicine, are most assured of success," she declared.[72] By focusing on homes—in particular, middle- and upper-class houses, rather than the grand estates of the ultra-wealthy—she could complete projects on her own, whereas most commercial or institutional projects would demand collaboration of effort and expertise. (In fact, she lined up several projects that departed from her stated specialty; they will be discussed in further detail below.) Of course, the streamlined pace of her specialization also necessitated more projects—meaning, more paying clients—in order to keep occupied.

By specializing in residential architecture, Minerva both created and solved this problem. Although many of her male counterparts took on similar projects, they did so as an interim source of income for their firms between bigger projects. Minerva did not see these projects as interludes between larger commissions, but as the primary focus of her career—and for good reason. For a woman breaking into architectural practice in nineteenth-century America, domestic architecture was a logical choice of specialty: the same conventions by which White women were deemed the arbiters of taste made it acceptable for women to become designers of homes. As promoted by Catherine Beecher and others beginning in the mid-nineteenth century, an ideal of feminine behavior known today as the "cult of domesticity" linked women's equality (to a point) with domestic efficiency, arguing that if the home was efficiently arranged, women could devote more time to other concerns.[73] This prescription simultaneously freed women from the home and tied them to it.[74] In this context, one could read Minerva's career as merely a small leap from organizing the home to designing it, generating clients by dealing in the very building type they would expect from her as a woman.

However, Minerva brought more than her gender to this specialty. She had clear views on how a house should be designed, taking into account the household's members and the building's physical context. Her designs subtly accounted for public gathering spaces and private family living quarters, articulating the differences between them with graceful archways leading to communal rooms and flat lintels that segued into more intimate spaces. Partitions between private and public spaces often featured massive pocket doors with retractable hardware, so that a wall could be opened—allowing guests to stroll between rooms or seated gatherings to overflow from one space into the next—or the door could be closed, to ensure the most privacy.

Minerva nearly always inserted transitional spaces between food preparation and dining areas, neatly buffering cooking smells with butler's pantries and double-acting hinges. She diverted the back stair away from the kitchen to discourage servants from dawdling (prioritizing domestic efficiency over rest), but also simplified household cleaning by paring down the intricacy of any designed woodwork (prioritizing domestic efficiency *and* rest).[75] One wonders how early these design principles took root in her mind: watching her mother clean their home or run a boardinghouse? Watching a fellow servant in need of a break in the Lippincott household? However young she was when she first took notice of these functional issues, their design solutions became a throughline in her work during her Philadelphia period.

In homes with children, actual or expected, she often reduced the height of stair risers for the benefit of little legs, and designed bookshelves to be accessible, without locks or glass doors, as these were barriers to learning.[76] Bedrooms for young children communicated with their parents' rooms, making it easy to comfort a crying child in the middle of the night.[77] As with the considerations she made for the service functions of home, these accommodations for children's physical and developmental needs likely took root in the Lippincotts' home and her mother's boardinghouse.

Many of Minerva's residential projects were in the Philadelphia suburbs, as they had been when she worked under Edwin Thorne; as in the days of her apprenticeship, she sought out residential projects in the towns developing along the Main Line of the Pennsylvania Railroad, west of the city. In Overbrook, Bala, Elm Station (now Narberth), Berwyn, and elsewhere, she was responsible for work that helped set the tone for the burgeoning suburban towns. She wrote extensively about the importance of designing for context—a house should not thumb its metaphorical nose at its neighbors—but in many cases, she was designing homes that did not yet have neighbors. [SEE, FOR INSTANCE, AN EARLY PHOTOGRAPH OF THE HOUSE SHE DESIGNED FOR MISS MARY POTTS IN 1890—FIG. 9] In these cases, her designs created the context for subsequent homes, presenting four formal elevations (rather than the one presentable elevation on the front and the three shoddier side elevations that cheaper builders typically proposed) that gestured to their future neighbors in every direction.

Although most of her work was in the suburbs, Minerva also designed several residential projects in downtown Philadelphia. Confined to tighter lots and often hemmed in by adjacent buildings that eliminated the need for side elevations, her

BIOGRAPHY

FIG. 9

FIG. 10

FIG. 9: Minerva's design for Miss Mary Potts in Germantown demonstrates how her buildings were often among the earliest developments in Philadelphia's outlying neighborhoods and suburbs.

FIG. 10: The house for Margaret M. Barber (at left, with the corner turret) was constructed on a constrained urban parcel in Philadelphia.

urban commissions found other ways to greet their neighbors—often, by way of complementary architectural styles. Eclectic and revivalist forms were popular in late nineteenth-century America, and Minerva was well versed in many of them from her formal education. In her suburban projects, she particularly favored a transitional style with elements of both the slightly earlier Shingle and slightly later Colonial Revival styles, praising the latter in particular for its "simple dignity, honest construction, and beauty of design." However, those qualities often went hand-in-hand with the more expansive, suburban sites in her portfolio, and were typically expressed using rough-hewn local stone (Wissahickon schist) that would be challenging to incorporate into a downtown site; for these reasons, Minerva's typical transitional style did not lend itself to the constraints of her urban projects. For those commissions such as the Barber house at Broad and Dauphin Streets [FIG. 10], she leaned on more eclectic details, complementing the many layers of a city's construction by using the dominant material in this context (brick), adopting the rhythm of the block's many bays, and contributing a new element such as a jaunty turret to the neighborhood's fabric.

Residential architecture dominated Minerva's portfolio, but her work was not limited to private homes. She also produced plans for a railroad bridge, three churches, including the Unitarian church that she attended, a mixed-use building incorporating a store and dwelling, a hotel, a macaroni factory, an iron foundry, and four women's clubs (two of which were ultimately built).

On the boards, Minerva's drawings were savvy and sophisticated, anticipating the complexities of use, setting, and style for each project. But there are many steps between preparing drawings and completing construction, and for those later phases of each commission Minerva leaned more on her training as an apprentice than on her academics. The process began with writing the specifications for each project; based on a few surviving examples, we can see how these foundational documents set the terms of her relationship with the builders on-site and breathed life into her buildings as they took shape. The specifications amounted to another kind of blueprint: written instructions that addressed all facets and phases of construction, including working conditions and chains of command, appropriate excavation practices, foundation preparation, ironwork, pointing of stonework, millwork, and so on. They needed to be airtight. Internal contradictions or insufficient detail could result in wasted money, squandered time, or a blow to the architect's reputation. But if they anticipated most on-site questions, a good set of specifications could ensure an uneventful build—one in which the architect's influence was felt, and her authority respected, even when she was not present.

Trading on her two years of hands-on work with Edwin, as well as an eye for detail honed by several years of artistic training, Minerva brought determination and knowledge to her site visits. We do not know how hard-won her experience was—how much hostility she encountered before proving herself—but Minerva quickly earned the respect, however grudging, of many of the builders with whom she worked. "She's the most particular and knowing person to work for that I ever struck," one tradesman remarked. "She knows every brick and just where it ought to go. There's no cheating her by smuggling in knotty lumber and leaving the joists sticking out into the chimneys."[78] (With how many other architects did that builder get away with such shortcuts?) One contractor told a newspaper that he "had never worked for an architect who better understood the business," while another went a step further: "She knows not only her business, but mine, too."[79]

These—and many other—quotes about (and by) her, showed up frequently in daily newspapers, weekly magazines, and monthly trade publications. The novelty of a woman working in an

BIOGRAPHY

overwhelmingly male field may have prompted the initial press response to Minerva and her work, but coverage very quickly became substantive, and publications generally took her professional credentials seriously. Which is not to say that it was not regularly colored by a patronizing tone: several articles commented on her looks and one expressed surprise that "Nothing in dress or demeanor would indicate that she ... knew so much more about Doric arches and Corinthian columns than about fancy [sewing] work and cake recipes."[80] But, helped along by builders who vouched for her, including those quoted above, Minerva was received into the profession in generally welcoming terms. She regularly made time for conversations with journalists (even in her later years), and benefited from coverage such as the front-page profile that the *Builders' Guide* gave her on March 26, 1890, at that date, the first profile of an architect ever to appear over the 220 issues of the *Builders' Guide*; Minerva was both the first woman and the first architect to receive such coverage.[81]

Minerva clearly had a knack for marketing, parlaying the natural curiosity about her work into leads for future work. And it paid off in a far-flung constellation of newspaper mentions and commissions. In the eight years she maintained her independent practice in Philadelphia (1888–96), her name appeared in at least 606 newspaper articles in forty-four American states (as well as the District of Columbia) and eight countries, including New Zealand, Jamaica, and France. (This count does not include magazines and trade publications that cannot be assigned to any particular place, as they reached such broad audiences.) In 1890 alone, readers worldwide saw her name at least two hundred forty times, including eleven mentions in separate newspapers on a single day (April 10). That year, her name was published somewhere every three days on average.

Minerva's portfolio increasingly reflected the extent of her publicity. Although most of her work remained concentrated in and around Philadelphia, a handful of commissions show up in places as far away as Canton, Ohio, and Beaumont, Texas. No links to Philadelphia have been discovered for these clients (Esther R. Gaskell and C. F. Johnson, respectively); the pitch of newspaper coverage around this time seems to have translated to work for Minerva, as people likely solicited designs from her via mail. By the end of 1891, approximately three years into her independent practice, she was making around $6,000 a year—somewhere around $200,000 in today's dollars.

There was a circularity to Minerva's chosen specialization and the clientele that sought her out for residential projects: women, in particular, hired her and propelled her to success. There were of course men among her patrons (George W. Christy, Lewis T. Brooke, Frank Wallace Munn, and Henry Bennett, among others), some of whom entrusted her with ambitious projects for large-scale developments. More striking, however, are the many commissions from women—single, widowed, and married—among Minerva's notices in the *Builders' Guide*. Names such as Mrs. Sarah E. Bewley, Miss Elizabeth E. Gallagher, Mrs. Rachel Foster Avery, and more than a dozen others bolstered Minerva's workload year after year, commissioning her to design homes for them (and sometimes husbands or children) or houses that they could rent out for additional income. This speaks to a pattern of increasing legal status and financial independence for women in the late nineteenth century—or at least White women, pointing to the racial limitations of that status and capital.

Minerva's success derived not just from her residential commissions for women; her four projects for women's clubs fueled her reputation locally, nationally, and even internationally. Designed for the New Century Club of Philadelphia, the New Century Club of Wilmingtown, Delaware, the New Century Guild of Philadelphia, and the Queen Isabella

Association at the World's Columbian Exposition in Chicago, these projects relied on women to raise funds, secure the property, determine the building program, hire Minerva as architect, and ultimately manage a substantial square footage once the buildings opened.

Although Minerva's commissions were rare in that they represented a women's club hiring a woman as architect, they were part of a growing movement in the late nineteenth century. Women's clubs and their intellectual cousins, benevolent associations, multiplied in cities and towns in tandem with the suffrage movement, urbanization, industrialization, and the world's fairs that showcased those modern forces. As women gained new measures of social independence, and as the domestic efficiency promoted by Catherine Beecher and others freed up more of their time, they increasingly organized around civic causes—although most women's clubs were segregated (explicitly or in coded terms), with separate clubs for White women and Black women.

Indeed, Minerva appears to have worked entirely and exclusively with White clients, both as individuals and as members of these segregated organizations.[82] Given that her career coincided with the Jim Crow era's constraints on space, education, capital, and property, this is unsurprising. There is no evidence that this absence in Minerva's portfolio was driven by explicit animus, nor is there any record of her acknowledging it or trying to correct for it. But the groundbreaking opportunities that she seized for herself and extended to many other women were not available to all women—and were entirely forbidden to some.

As a building type, a club headquarters was in many ways a scaled-up version of Minerva's specialty. Although clubs were not strictly residential, their building programs had much in common with those for private residences, blending public gathering spaces with private sleeping quarters—in the case of the women's clubs, temporary accommodations where women could stay unchaperoned overnight when visiting. (Hotels, by contrast, often expected women guests to be chaperoned.) Unlike her other domestic projects, Minerva's clubhouses included income-producing amenities to help support club operations such as a large auditorium for big events and smaller public rooms for paid lectures, small concerts, and the like.

Minerva's designs for the Philadelphia and Wilmington chapters of the New Century Club [FIG. 11 AND 12]. were successfully constructed; a third clubhouse, for the New Century Guild of Working Women, may not have progressed past the preliminary drawing stage. Her fourth project for a women's club—the commission for the Queen Isabella Association—was simultaneously her highest-profile one and the biggest one she lost. The association, whose members were known as "the Isabellas," formed in the lead-up to the World's Columbian Exposition in Chicago. As planning for the fair (originally scheduled for 1892, but ultimately held in 1893) anticipated the fourth centenary of Christopher Columbus's landing in the Americas, a Mrs. C. W. Waite stood up at one gathering of women to protest: "Why should Columbus only be honored when Queen Isabella was the one that made the discovery of the New World possible?"[83] (Even at the time, some critics questioned whether Queen Isabella deserved such tributes, given her role in the Spanish Inquisition.)[84] Mobilizing to create a place for professional women that would honor the Spanish queen at the fair, the Isabellas swiftly formed a membership organization to raise funds for a statue of her and a clubhouse to host women who were lawyers, doctors, and the like.

Hearing of their effort, Minerva volunteered her services gratis, probably calculating that the free publicity was worth the lost fees. The amount of coverage the ensuing saga received suggests that

BIOGRAPHY

FIG. 11

FIG. 12

FIG. 11: One of Minerva's most significant commissions was for the New Century Club of Philadelphia, 1891–92.

FIG. 12: The New Century Club of Wilmington, constructed in 1892–3, remains standing. It is Minerva's only surviving public commission.

BIOGRAPHY

she probably got her money's worth. This was no suburban Philadelphia residence; this clubhouse required an entirely different form, and Minerva wrote to Spain (it is unclear to whom) requesting plans of the famous Alhambra palace. By December 17, 1890, she had completed the preliminary plans for the building. Designed around Moorish motifs, it included: a large auditorium; multiple reception rooms; offices for "medical, press, and legal departments"; apartments for women and their children; a nursery; and an emergency room (to be staffed, no doubt, by Isabellas who were doctors).[85] Once built, it would be a testament not only to the organizing power of the women around the country who funded it, but also to the agency of the women who would travel to it, and the prowess of the women who would staff the professional departments within it.

These aspirations were lost, however, in the politicking that soured relations between the Isabellas and the Board of Lady Managers, which was overseeing the commission and construction of a separate fair pavilion, the Woman's Building [FIG. 13]. The design for that project was awarded competitively to a young architect named Sophia Hayden. (Louise Blanchard Bethune was invited to participate in the competition, but rejected the call since the prize purse was a mere tenth of the money that men earned for building designs at the fair.)[86] Once the fair's supervisors delegated authority for any buildings associated with women to the Board of Lady Managers, that board quashed the Isabellas' effort, forcing them to scramble for a site outside the fairgrounds and to downsize their pavilion as a result. Minerva's grand, airy design was scuttled, and a smaller masonry building was erected instead.[87]

Meanwhile, twenty-two-year-old Sophia had struggled through the commission for the Woman's Building, contending with the micromanaging personalities of the Board of Lady Managers (particularly, board chairwoman Bertha Palmer) and her own relative inexperience.

Although she had earned an architecture degree from the Massachusetts Institute of Technology (MIT) a year before—one of the few women among the early graduates of that collegiate program—she had little to no practical training in construction and client management. When she won the design competition, she was plucked from a job as an art teacher and thrust into the high-profile, high-pressure project, responsible for the design and construction of a massive building for what would be a seminal event in American history. After several months, the stress proved too much: in the summer of 1892, Sophia suffered a health crisis.[88]

The press pounced. Quick to point to Sophia's "melancholia" as a reason why women should not practice architecture, the *American Architect and Building News* questioned "how successfully woman with her physical limitation can enter and engage in the work of a profession which is a very wearing one." The magazine jeered at the irony of her collapsing while working on the Woman's Building, positing that "if the building of which the women seem so proud is to mean the physical ruin of its architect, it will be a much more telling argument against the wisdom of women entering this especial profession than anything else could be."[89]

Despite the blow that the Woman's Building—and Sophia, however indirectly—had dealt to her own work, Minerva could not tolerate this insult to her profession and to women practicing it. Within a matter of days after reading the editors' jibes in the issue of November 26, 1892, she penned a rebuke; it was published in the December 10 issue.

> Comment on the success or "lack of success" of the Woman's Building designed by Miss Hayden is unfair to her and to the general architectural profession. The conditions of the competition and the selection of a design made it impossible to secure satisfactory results. What other building, whether given by

FINDING MINERVA

FIG. 13: Minerva (*inset*) designed a pavilion for the Queen Isabella Association (*bottom*), which was to be accompanied by a statue by Harriet Hosmer (*center*). Minerva's design appeared in an issue of Harper's Weekly with Sophia Hayden's design for the Woman's Building (*top*). The Woman's Building was ultimately constructed; Minerva's pavilion was not.

appointment or by competition, could have fallen into the hands of an architectural student without experience or practice?[90]

For Minerva, Sophia's inexperience was to blame for her collapse; her gender had nothing to do with it. Although this could be read as a critique of sorts—faulting her for not landing sufficient apprenticeship training as Minerva herself had—Minerva reserved most of her anger for the *American Architect and Building News* and assigned most of the blame to the Board of Lady Managers that hired Sophia and ran her into the ground, with no allowance for her inexperience.

Minerva's critique was widely circulated and remarkably well received, even in the pages of that same issue of *American Architect and Building News*. Introducing her essay, the editors remarked that they were "pleased to publish elsewhere the protest of Mrs. Nichols [She was married by this time.] who has proved her own ability to work side by side with masculine architects without asking favor on the score of sex."[91] On the one hand, the periodical's prefatory comments are simply more of the same paternalism as their initial piece about Sophia Hayden: eager to pit the exposition's women against each other, they praise Minerva at the expense of Sophia. On the other hand, leaving aside the patent misogyny, we see evidence of the same pattern that played out throughout Minerva's years as an architect in Philadelphia: she earned her place, she earned respect, and she earned an impressive number of commissions—all while contending with other pressures of her own at home.

Minerva as a Daughter and Sister

For the first few years of her independent practice, Minerva lived at home with her family. By this time, they lived at 1614 Green Street, a mile-long walk away from Minerva's office on South Broad Street. While Minerva was designing houses for other people, she and her family lived in a rented house that they shared with several subtenants.

It wasn't that Minerva did not want or seek to design a home for her own family: in May 1889, shortly after forming her own practice, she announced in the *Builders' Guide* that she had completed the drawings for a $4,000 home in the Oak Lane section of Philadelphia for a "Mrs. Maxwell," her mother's second married name; in September 1890, she was engaged in plans for herself, also in Oak Lane, for "a fine little suburban house ... of which she will be the owner."[92] It is unclear if the two announcements refer to the same design, but they were intended for two lots of land in Cheltenham Township, close to the Oak Lane railroad station. Adelaide and Minerva chipped in, and Amanda purchased the property in 1889 from the Oak Lane Land Company, a speculative enterprise founded that same year; the women must have been some of the first investors in it.[93] The same Isaac Ashmead who commissioned a residential design from Edwin and Minerva was one of the charter members of the company; this almost certainly explains how Minerva and her family became aware of the investment opportunity.[94]

Building a new house in Cheltenham would have offered the Parker-Maxwells a fresh start in the city's expansive but developing suburbs; it would also have brought Minerva full circle to design a house for herself in the place where she once worked as a servant and governess. The house did not materialize, however. Instead, the family continued to rent, choosing to expand their boardinghouse on Green Street, and Amanda took out a $1,000 mortgage on the Cheltenham property without executing any of Minerva's plans.[95]

Did they stay put so that thirteen-year-old Samuel could remain in school? Did Minerva decide that the commute would be too long as her workload increased? Or—as seems most likely—were there financial reasons for remaining on Green Street, a need for additional income rather than expenditures? To the last question, we have some record of their financial footing in the years leading up to Minerva's decision to form her own practice, which may help explain why she was willing to take big professional risks.

As a Civil War widow, Amanda was entitled to a pension after John Parker's death; she first filed for it in October 1863.[96] She received $8 per month (retroactive to John's death in July 1863), and an additional $2 per month for each of his two children until they reached the age of 16.[97] She may have paid for the house in Normal, Illinois, with this money. She also owned property at some point on Chicago's South Side that may have been purchased with the help of the pension, in addition to any income she was earning from sewing, and, perhaps, some inheritance from her parents.

However, in June 1873, Amanda was in arrears on some taxes, suggesting that the family had fallen on hard times. When she married Samuel Maxwell in 1875, she had to surrender her widow's pension (although she continued to receive a token sum for thirteen-year-old Minerva). Her pension, which resumed when Samuel Maxwell died and was paid to her until her death in 1921, was paltry for a mother of three, and Samuel's estate did not help very much. Most of his $1,200 life insurance policy went to his children from his first marriage, although Amanda received some funds from his estate on behalf of her newborn son. The family moved several times in the late 1870s and early 1880s—they lived in at least four places in seven years after Samuel Maxwell's death—further evidence that they lived with some financial stress in the first decade after they settled in Philadelphia.

In July 1882 Amanda sold the house and property in Normal for $1,000. This may have netted some income for the family and relieved immediate financial pressure, but it is notable that just a few months later, Adelaide Parker married a salesman named Henry (Harry) M. Griffiths.[98] Did Amanda sell the Normal property so that she could put some or all of the proceeds toward a dowry for her older daughter? Or—given that Adelaide and her new husband moved into the Green Street home and had a baby the following July—were the Normal house proceeds simply keeping the growing household afloat? In either scenario, Minerva, recently graduated from the Normal Art School, was probably still working as a governess and only just starting to line up work with architectural firms and contribute to the household's bottom line.

By 1884 the family had settled at 1614 Green Street, where they remained for several years, expanding next door into number 1612 after abandoning the Cheltenham plans. They were joined in the three-floor brownstone rowhouses by a revolving roster of working- and middle-class tenants who paid rent based on their jobs as fruit salesmen, music teachers, watchmakers, weavers, and more. Although the house was clearly full, it is probably not a coincidence that Amanda's finances were secure enough around this time for her to contemplate investing in speculative enterprises.

In 1884 the New York, Philadelphia and Norfolk Railroad reached Cape Charles, Virginia, running south from Wilmington, Delaware, down the spine of the Eastern Shore of Maryland and Virginia. Sensing an opportunity to develop the areas that the railroad now reached, several investors founded a town in Virginia that they called Parksley, and formed a corporation called the Parksley Land and Improvement Company for this purpose.[99] Amanda Maxwell was one of the original stockholders. In 1885 she purchased one hundred thirty shares in the company, staking a claim in a new town that was one hundred eighty miles from her home in Philadelphia.[100] Valued at $13,000, these shares suggest a high point in the ever-changing fortunes of the Parker-Maxwell family in the 1880s.

It is unclear how Amanda met the improvement company's investors or bought into it, but it must have been through a personal connection: the town was not mentioned in a Philadelphia newspaper until 1889. She may have crossed paths with several of the company's charter members, since they filed their paperwork in Philadelphia and had ties to the region. They included Henry Bennett, a traveling paint salesman from Dover, Delaware; his brother-in-law, Samuel T. Jones (also from Dover);[101] William C. Wilson, of Philadelphia;[102] and Jacob (alternately listed as James) N. Wilson, of Philadelphia. The leading spirit of the group was a woman, Elizabeth Stanton Chadbourne, of Boston. However Amanda encountered the vision for Parksley, she had bought into it by the time Minerva started her apprenticeship with Edwin W. Thorne. Amanda, like her parents before her and later her daughter, was apparently eager to help shape a town from the ground up.

Within five years, the investment had paid dividends—not just for Amanda, but for her daughter as well. In 1889 Minerva placed the first of two notices in the *Builders' Guide* about projects in Parksley, Virginia, announcing to readers that she had prepared preliminary sketches for a three-floor, fifty-room inn in town, replete with an elevator.[103] That notice was followed by one in July 1890 for a brick and shingle house for Henry Bennett himself, and for "a number of two, four, and six-roomed frame houses" for the same company in which Amanda was an investor. We have no record of how Minerva secured these commissions—perhaps she, too, met the founders even before they formed their company— but Amanda's status as an early investor must have helped her now famous daughter land the projects.

It is unclear, however, whether Minerva's plans were ever deployed in Parksley. There is no way of knowing if she traveled down to Virginia to see the sites, let alone superintend the construction of any buildings, and given her productivity in 1890, it is hard to believe she could have left Philadelphia for any significant amount of time. The town is not mentioned in any of the newspaper profiles about her—even as other projects, for other large-scale developers were—and she does not revisit the progress of the hotel or residential projects after the July 1890 issue of *Builders' Guide*. Even if her buildings were constructed, a fire devastated the town's core commercial area in 1896 and dampened the improvement company's progress until the turn of the twentieth century.[104] Whatever their fate, the Parksley commissions demonstrate how Minerva's fortunes rose and fell with her family's throughout her Philadelphia years, as she and her mother and siblings supported one another.

In another sign of how interconnected Minerva's worlds were and the importance of accounting for all of them in a study of her life and work, the sworn witness to several affidavits in Amanda's pension file was Maria Nye Johnson. Trained in Philadelphia as a doctor at a time when women were still breaking into that profession, Maria was a family friend from their Chicago days, a neighbor who lived just a few blocks away from their house on Green Street in Philadelphia, the namesake (it would seem) of Adelaide's daughter, Nye Winifred Griffiths—and, as of 1892, a client of Minerva's.[105] Maria commissioned a residence that year (although it does not appear to have been built). Once again, Minerva's practice may have been based out of her office on South Broad Street, but it could not be separated from her home life on Green Street.

FINDING MINERVA

Minerva as a Writer

Although Minerva's practice accelerated almost immediately after her launch, she still felt that her buildings weren't speaking enough for her. She had already had a taste of submitting her work to publications—in the 1886–87 competition entry published in *Carpentry and Building*, as well as the letter to the editor published in the *Builders' Guide* in 1887—and she quickly decided to incorporate writing into her firm's repertoire, both to hone her thoughts about architecture and raise her profile. As early as 1889, within months of announcing her Philadelphia office, she began writing essays and commentary about the art, practice, and practicalities of architecture. In 1891 she landed a dedicated column in a monthly magazine (the kickoff was accompanied by yet another feature profiling her), in which she published an essay every quarter for the next year and a half. Even then—during her busiest years in Philadelphia—she managed to pen additional pieces for other publications, interspersed with the rhythm of her regular column. In the eight years she maintained a practice in Philadelphia, she published a total of thirteen essays, all the while executing the dozens of drawings and specifications she produced during this period.

It is clear that Minerva was strategic in identifying and writing for an audience that would ultimately serve her work, channeling her effort for the most benefit. Her work appeared in magazines with names like *Housekeeper's Weekly*, the *Business Woman's Journal*, and the *Home-Maker*, with casual references throughout her writing to the architectural client getting what "she" wants, and the architect's experience in working with "her." Just as Minerva chose to specialize in residential architecture, carving out a productive line of work by aligning herself with women who could afford to hire her (and were too often dismissed in other quarters), Minerva tailored her writing to female audiences.

Occasionally she wrote for more traditional trade publications, with predominantly male readers—most notably, her 1892 essay in *American Architect and Building News* in defense of Sophia Hayden. But in general, she focused her writing efforts elsewhere, and with good reason: women were the most likely future clients for her practice; and if they couldn't be *her* clients, she wanted to make sure they were good clients for *someone*. In each of her essays, she pushed women to expect more of their homes, their architects, and—left unspoken in the conclusion, but implied nevertheless—their lives.

In her writings, Minerva asserted the importance of architects as distinct from pattern books and builders—both could be had for less money but came with more headaches—and instructed her readers on the potentially daunting process of commissioning a home. Minerva was a pragmatic guide for middle- and upper-class women in the late nineteenth century, acknowledging their growing financial independence and shepherding them through the confusion of changing professional norms and architectural styles. "Women often seem so helpless when they come to designing their own houses," she wrote in *Housekeeper's Weekly* in June 1893. "I assure you, French novels will seem dull compared with the delight of threading your way through the translation of plans."[106] Her wry tone—combined with a coaxing familiarity in the expression of her expectations that women should educate themselves on the qualities of good design—hooked her readers; she took them (and their architecture) seriously, but not herself.

Many of Minerva's articles, like those of writers in other trade publications such as *Carpentry and Building*, included drawings and plans. But whereas the sketches in many trade publications were accompanied by narratives full of jargon and opaque technicalities—they were, after all, directed toward a readership of builders, who would understand these details—she walked her readers through her own drawings in more accessible terms, describing their real-world outcomes and the client-driven decisions that shaped them. She acted as translator for her drawings, deploying her designs as clear expressions of her process and architectural principles. Thus, her fully realized architecture gave depth to her writing, and her writing in turn helped clarify her architectural perspective.

Although Minerva readily wrote for female readers, bringing an expert conversation about architecture to outlets that might not previously have included it to such a degree, she did not relegate herself to women's magazines or abstain from more traditional, that is, male-dominated outlets and trade publications. In 1893 she contributed her thoughts on the World's Columbian Exposition to the *Times* (Philadelphia), alongside peers such as Frank Furness, Edgar V. Seeler, and Wilson Eyre [FIG. 14]. That she was certainly considered a peer of these esteemed contemporary architects can be inferred from the layout of their renderings amid the full page of commentary, with her image at the center of the sheet. And lest we dismiss this as simply a choice to favor symmetry, since all her counterparts were men: her essay was featured second, preceded only by that of Frank Furness.[107] The next month, she expanded her thoughts on the fair even further, publishing "An Architectural Object Lesson" in *Architecture and Building*.[108]

A third piece published in 1893 marked how far she had ascended in just five years of independent practice: in the September 1893 issue of *Carpentry and Building,* Minerva wrote a short article for the robust commentary section of the magazine. Appearing just six years after her own plans were published anonymously in this same outlet under the pen name of "Chicago," her words this time were published under her full name, without abbreviation or pseudonym. Where previously the editors had dissected her plans, chided her for technical flaws, and offered areas for improvement, she could now submit her critique of the "houses for workingmen" published in a previous issue. Confidently but not vindictively, she drolly noted flaws in their plans, going so far as to propose a design of her own that reflected her deftness in arranging a building program: "I think even a workingman would object to a house where the kitchen could only be reached through a [bed] chamber, or the bathroom through the kitchen." She did not stop there, perhaps conscious that if she commented only on the interior, she risked relegating herself to the spaces most associated with women. In closing, she could not resist addressing a technical flaw of the original design, as if to highlight how much she had learned about the realities of construction since her 1886–87 competition entry: "I would also suggest roofing the front bay or porch under one ornamental gable, thus avoiding the cuts in the roof, which, I think, add more labor than beauty."[109]

Minerva as a Wife

As an independent architect, Minerva may have been a favored daughter of Philadelphia, but she was out of step with American society for much of her twenties—not just in regard to her professional practice and fame, but also to her personal life. In 1890 the average woman was married by the age of twenty-two; at that age, Minerva was still an apprentice for Edwin Thorne.[110] As she launched her practice and her profile grew, she raised eyebrows for her status as a single woman—often, with an incredulous tone that seemed to ask how such an attractive woman could not only be working, but be single as well. It must be said that such incredulity was often expressed by other women—typically, married ones—as in the column that marveled in 1891:

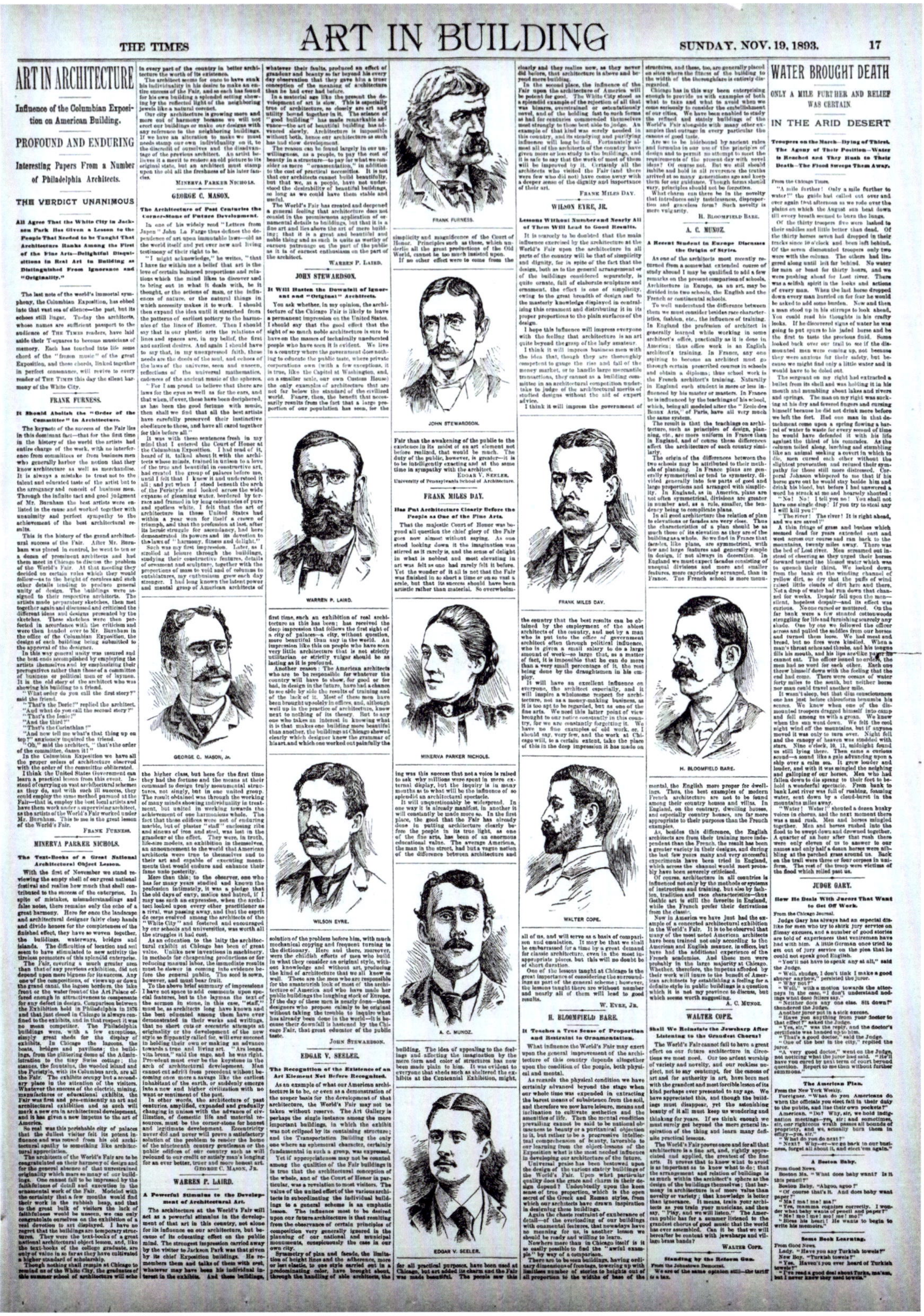
THE TIMES ART IN BUILDING SUNDAY, NOV. 19, 1893. 17

ART IN ARCHITECTURE

Influence of the Columbian Exposition on American Building.

PROFOUND AND ENDURING

Interesting Papers From a Number of Philadelphia Architects.

THE VERDICT UNANIMOUS

WATER BROUGHT DEATH

ONLY A MILE FURTHER AND RELIEF WAS CERTAIN

IN THE ARID DESERT

FIG. 14: Minerva's reflection on the architecture of the World's Columbian Exposition was featured in the *Times* (Philadelphia) in 1893, situating her alongside her male peers from Philadelphia.

BIOGRAPHY

> Any one having talked with Miss Parker and learned of the enormous amount of work done by her could hardly imagine her lacking courage in anything, yet how else account for the state of "single blessedness"? In addition to her demonstrated ability to support a husband, she is a gifted conversationalist and endowed with personal graces much beyond the ordinary, hence the inference that Miss Parker prefers her profession to a husband.[111]

Minerva's unmarried status was a double-edged social expectation: even as they marveled that she could be single, most press outlets clearly allowed for her professional career only because she was single. A married woman could never maintain a practice, they stopped just short of saying.

And yet, Minerva did. On December 22, 1891, she married the Reverend William Ichabod Nichols at the Spring Garden Unitarian Church, a few blocks from her house. Named for his grandfather Ichabod Nichols, a Unitarian minister in New England, William had been the minister at the church since December 1889 [FIG. 15]. By the time they met, twenty-seven-year-old Minerva, a lifelong Unitarian, was already a famous architect and—closer to home—a familiar Sunday school teacher at the church [FIG. 16]. Forty-one-year-old William was apparently quite an eligible, albeit older, bachelor amid the gossiping church members.[112]

When Minerva and William married in December 1891, the *New York Times* published a wedding announcement for the couple—publicity that likely reflects on her professional standing at the time.[113] Nearly 1,500 invitations were sent out for what would become "one of the prettiest weddings of the season."[114] Guests included members of the Munn and Justice families—both of which had commissioned Minerva to design their homes—as well as Paul Sartain, nephew of Emily Sartain, a prominent member of the New Century Club of Philadelphia. Standing in for her deceased father and stepfather, the Reverend Dr. William Henry Furness—father of renowned Philadelphia architect Frank Furness—gave Minerva away.[115]

Given the period in which Minerva practiced, it would be reasonable to assume that her career and her marriage did not overlap—that any discussion of Minerva as architect would be superseded by consideration of Minerva as wife. This was treated as a given in the press in the months before and shortly after her wedding: "Miss Minerva Parker... has married a minister," the *Lincoln Daily Nebraska State Journal* wrote in February 1892. "Her architectural work is in all probability ended."[116]

Apparently, William himself expected as much: in a letter written to his brother Edgar in May 1891, seven months before the wedding, William could not contain his love for Minerva, and his pride in her career:

> You and Julia [Edgar's wife] have set before me so attractive a specimen of a home, that I have concluded to try if I cannot have one of my own, and have succeeded in finding a woman willing to enter with me upon the undertaking. The name of this venturesome lady is Miss Minerva Parker, a member of my [Unitarian] society, and a teacher in the Sunday School ... If we ever [should] get so far as to build a house, we should possess a special advantage, for Miss Parker has been educated as an architect, and in eight years' experience has achieved quite a reputation.[117]

Even so, his admiration was colored by the assumption that she would stop working after their wedding, and by the concern that their marriage would cause her to resent him for ending her career.

FINDING MINERVA

I wonder that she [should] have consented to abandon a work in which she is so much interested and has been so successful, and I almost tremble when I think what I am allowing her to do for me, but it seems to have come about naturally, and I hope I may be able to prevent her from regretting the sacrifice.[118]

William need not have worried; Minerva apparently had no intention of abandoning her work. Her wedding on December 22, 1891, did not prove to be the end of her career, but merely the briefest of interruptions: on December 23, she was back on site at the New Century Club of Philadelphia, supervising its construction in time for it to open early in the new year.[119]

Minerva as a Teacher

Minerva met her future husband when she was volunteering as a Sunday school teacher. Bolstered by her training at the Philadelphia Normal Art School, she took many opportunities during her years of independent practice to teach. Calling on the same confidence and competence that spurred her to promote her work as a writer and to launch her own office in the first place, she lectured widely during her Philadelphia period. Her most significant position began in 1891, when she accepted an offer by principal Emily Sartain to teach at the Philadelphia School of Design for Women. Emily was a founding member of the New Century Club of Philadelphia, whose headquarters Minerva was in the midst of designing when she accepted the offer to teach architecture and historic ornament. It was a subject to which she had given considerable thought by this point, having already spent years studying it, writing about it, and designing dozens of buildings that made use of the real thing. Her course was part of the Technical Design track, alongside various courses in botany (drawing), theoretical design, and more.[120]

For the next four academic years, Minerva was part of a faculty that included luminaries Alice Barber Stephens and Samuel A. Murray; given the press coverage announcing her new class in 1891, Minerva was clearly considered a star in her own right.[121] Yet, according to the school's financial records from those years, she was not treated as one in terms of her pay. It declined annually between 1891 and 1895 from a starting salary of $115 for the 1891–92 school year, to $100 (1892–93), $90 (1893–94), and finally $80 in 1894–95, for her final year of teaching.[122]

The most striking revelation of the archival administrative records of the school, however, is that Minerva was not only paid less than her fellow teachers but her salary was surpassed by none other than the man who occasionally served as her employee. Eight years younger than Minerva, Herbert P. Onyx worked on at least two projects as Minerva's renderer (her 1890–93 design for a house in Bala, Pennsylvania, for Francis Jordan Jr. and Mary Amelia Jordan and her 1890–91 commission for Frank Wallace Munn and his wife Martha; SEE CAT. NOS. 37 AND 38).[123] Herbert was a graduate of the University of Pennsylvania's architecture program, the Pennsylvania Academy of Fine Arts, and the Manual Training School. He was also, as of 1889, Edwin W. Thorne's apprentice—which means that Minerva either shared Herbert with her former mentor, or hired Herbert away from him, in another instance of overlap between Edwin's practice and her own.[124]

Herbert started teaching at the School of Design for Women in the 1892–93 school year, a year after Minerva. He listed his work address as 14 South Broad Street, suggesting that he was working at least part-time for Minerva at this point (which coincided with the Jordan and Munn commissions).[125] During the 1893–94 school year, he was even boarding in her home: his faculty address was 1616 Mount Vernon

BIOGRAPHY

Street, William and Minerva's address after they married.[126] Yet, for each of the three years that their teaching posts overlapped, Herbert earned more than Minerva: when Minerva earned $100 in 1892–93, Herbert was paid $114; the next year, she earned $90 to his $109.50; the third and final year that they overlapped, she received $80, while his pay escalated to $139.[127] They taught in the same study track (Technical Design), and taught the same number of students and subjects each year, so this pay disparity cannot be explained by any difference in class size. Herbert held degrees from the University of Pennsylvania and the Pennsylvania Academy of Fine Arts—prestigious institutions, to be sure, but as already discussed, these credentials were not necessarily superior to Minerva's at this stage in the professionalization of architecture. Instead, there was likely a simpler reason for the differences in their salaries.

There is no indication that Minerva was aware of these pay disparities, but even if she were, she may have decided that the sacrifice was worth it, taking into account the visibility and professional connections that the position offered; after all, she almost certainly owed the teaching post to her New Century Club connection with Emily Sartain. She may also have been driven by a passion for the role, eager to teach a new generation of young women about the possibility of contributing high-grade architecture to the world. For the latter theory, we can adduce evidence from the World's Columbian Exposition: at the fair where her own project for the Queen Isabella Association was scuttled and where she came to Sophia Hayden's defense, Minerva and her School of Design students won an honorable mention.[128] [SEE CAT. NOS. 36 AND 56.]

Whatever her motivation in accepting a relatively low salary, Minerva returned on a weekly basis, for four years. She taught nearly one hundred students in that time. It is unclear whether any of her students followed in her career footsteps, or whether she remained in contact with them after leaving her teaching post in 1895. (According to the class lists and student addresses, she secured housing for some of them at her mother's boarding house, suggesting a longer-term relationship with at least some of the students.)[129]

The School of Design for Women was not the only outlet for Minerva's teaching while practicing as an architect during these years; she also had public speaking engagements. In 1891 she gave a talk about architecture to the council of the General Federation of Women's Clubs.[130] In March 1892 she contributed preliminary drawings to a conference in Philadelphia, exhibiting her work alongside seventy-four other architects; two months later, she spoke in the New Century Club's drawing room on Spanish architecture and the Alhambra—presenting her research for a commission that did not come to fruition in a building of her own design that did.[131]

Minerva as a Mother

In November 1894, three years into her marriage, Minerva gave birth to a daughter, whom she named Adelaide for her older sister. In the years leading up to the birth of Adelaide, Minerva's design work tapered off; possible explanations include both economic and personal ones. On the economic front, in the volatile climate of the late nineteenth-century American economy, the Panic of 1893 was one of the more significant depressions to affect the country while she lived in Philadelphia. In the personal realm, Minerva may have reconsidered her priorities, deciding that her commitments to writing, teaching, supporting her family, and embracing her new marriage outranked commissions. But a more compelling reason why Minerva's productivity trailed off after 1891 may have been related to her health: in mid-1892, she miscarried twins while traveling through New England (presumably, visiting William's family).[132]

The psychological and physical toll of this event could easily have disrupted her practice and led her to reprioritize her commitments.

On June 29, 1892, Minerva announced a project for a house for Dr. Maria Nye Johnson, whose medical career and complicated family situation made her something of a nomad. The house appears not to have been built. That may have been because the client's itinerant lifestyle ultimately shelved the project. Alternatively, the commission may have been a casualty of Minerva's miscarriage, which occurred on July 8.

In 1893 Minerva and William moved from the Green Street house to 1616 Mount Vernon Street, a few blocks away. At this time Minerva also surrendered the office on South Broad Street and announced that she would be working from home. In giving up the office two years into her marriage and a year after her miscarriage, Minerva seemed to concede some of her working independence. At the same time, women had always conducted substantial work at home and for many of them having a separate office was not a legal, financial, or socially acceptable option until the late nineteenth or early twentieth centuries. Minerva's announcement asserted that the move would change nothing, indeed it would allow her to take on more—not less—work: "Mrs. Minerva Parker Nichols, so well known as architect ... has recently removed her office to her residence, 1616 Mount Vernon Street. Mrs. Nichols will now be able to devote more time to her practice."[133]

After the birth of Adelaide, Minerva started a baby book, marking the child's milestones and pasting in photographs of her, William, and herself. She continued the practice in the same book for each of her three subsequent children. The baby book is notable for the photographs of Minerva herself, and for the record it provides of her life in her own words. It is also useful for what it tells of Minerva's professional life: in physical terms, her home life and her career had never overlapped more. Like the list of guests at her wedding, the baby book sheds light on Minerva's network of Philadelphia connections that both grew from and contributed to her architectural practice. The names of people who sent gifts when Adelaide was born includes "Miss Grew," who gave the baby a pair of socks.[134] This notation almost certainly refers to Mary Grew, a Philadelphia abolitionist and suffragist. A Unitarian like Minerva and William, she gave a talk at a major suffrage meeting in 1882 at Spring Garden Unitarian Church; twenty-year-old Minerva may have been in attendance.[135] A co-founder of the New Century Club, Mary may have helped Minerva secure the commission for the Philadelphia chapter.[136] Alternatively, the commission may have been what brought them together and served as the starting place for their friendship. The baby book also provides reminders of the ties binding Minerva to the father of one of Philadelphia's most famous architects: on December 29, 1894, the Reverend William Henry Furness, who gave Minerva away at her wedding, baptized Adelaide at the Spring Garden Unitarian Church.[137]

Minerva as a Reformer

In launching her own practice, Minerva showed herself a reformer. Throughout her career, she took vocal positions on several issues affecting women, finding outlets for her views in her writing, speaking engagements, and interviews, but she was careful about the movements to which she lent her time and name, committing herself only to causes that intersected directly with her working life.

She was unquestionably a suffragist, stating in one of her *Home-Maker* essays, "I am politically in favor of 'woman's rights.'"[138] She appreciated the ways in which suffrage would benefit her personally and women generally, but she was more interested in setting the stage for activists than speaking herself. Unlike her clients who were central to various nineteenth-century suffrage organizations—Rachel Foster Avery and Jane Campbell were the most prominent, but several other clients appear on the rosters of suffrage organizations—Minerva's support for suffrage was firm, but understated.

On other fronts, however, she did not keep silent. Her public and unequivocal support for Sophia Hayden in the pages of the *American Architect and Building News* stood out not only as a defense of a particular woman, but as a wider call for women to join the architectural profession. This was a theme in her working life—and in particular, during her years with her own formal practice and fame to draw on—as she was concerned, first and foremost, with reforming the field of architecture to make space for women within it.

Minerva was vocal about the barriers that kept women out of the profession in the first place, as well as the day-to-day conditions that kept them from succeeding once they were working. One of the only known instances of Minerva publicly advocating for reform—as opposed to giving an address at a routine speaking engagement—was in connection with dress reform. Far from being incidental to her working life, the topic was critical: the corsets of the late nineteenth century reduced by half the lung capacity of their wearers.[139] On the construction site, Minerva's corset made her job twice as hard; small wonder that she mentioned in an interview that she "[didn't] mind walking over scaffolding a bit, but [she drew] the line on ladders."[140] It comes as little surprise, then, to find her name among the list of speakers at an 1893 dress reform rally in Chicago.[141] She may have preferred to be known for her designs than for any "notoriety,"[142] but to the extent that dress norms affected her work, she was an outspoken proponent of reform.

Dress reform was only one focus of Minerva's advocacy efforts in 1893. She was also involved in the early stages of a progressive housing effort in Philadelphia. Inspired by similar efforts in New York City to address poor living conditions in tenements, the Model Dwellings Association was established in 1893 with the stated purpose of "the erection of dwellings with sanitary improvements at moderate rentals for the working class."[143] At the intersection of social reform and the built environment, the organization was one that Minerva might be expected to align herself with. She and William were early subscribers to it, purchasing stock and investing in the group's efforts to develop affordable housing and to lobby for policy changes. The association was ultimately short-lived, disbanding after two years, in 1895.[144] But this particular reform movement seems to have planted seeds that bore fruit throughout Minerva's later career.

Minerva as a Colleague

Throughout her years practicing in Philadelphia, Minerva took pains to give credit to and collaborate with other women, as colleagues as well as patrons. A speech she gave in 1896 celebrated all the women she knew to be practicing architecture, praising their distinct skill sets and contributions to the field. Louise Blanchard Bethune, regarded by Minerva as a seminal figure in the field and pointed to frequently in her public remarks, was among the eight architects she named in the speech: "Perhaps no woman has won a more deserved success in architecture than Louise Bethune, of Buffalo."[145]

For at least one project, Minerva hired Elizabeth Abel, a stained glass artist, and similarities in decorative glass in several buildings designed by Minerva suggest that she and Elizabeth worked together regularly. Both were members of the New Century Guild, a New Century Club offshoot that focused on supporting workingwomen—Minerva's membership dating from November 1892.[146] Given her collaboration with Elizabeth, it would be interesting to know whether Minerva hired other fellow Guild members to design details for her projects, or indeed any of her own students from the Philadelphia School of Design for Women, or former classmates from the Philadelphia Normal Art School, the Franklin Institute Drawing School, or the Pennsylvania School and Museum of Industrial Art. The record is sparse, but it is entirely plausible that her buildings were in fact full of the work of women.

Yet, there were limits to her network of professional women. Although she may have hired her former or current students to contribute decorative details to her designs, there is no evidence that she ever trained a woman as an apprentice. Herbert P. Onyx is the only person known to have worked under her as a draftsman. Where Edwin W. Thorne gave Minerva her big break by hiring her as his apprentice and opening the door to the profession, she does not appear to have done the same for any other women. Perhaps in hiring Elizabeth Abel (and any other artists who were women) to contribute to her work, she was finding other ways to hire women where she could.

Leaving Philadelphia

One year after stepping down from the faculty of the Philadelphia School of Design for Women, Minerva left Philadelphia with her family. In 1896 William resigned his position at the Spring Garden Unitarian Church and accepted a post as the general secretary of the Brooklyn Bureau of Charities. Minerva quietly packed up her drawings and papers; there was no major announcement in the local press, or even the *Builders' Guide* that had covered her practice so diligently since publishing her first letter in 1887. With their daughter Adelaide, William and Minerva moved to Brooklyn in early 1896. For the first time since her boarding school exile two decades earlier, Minerva would be living more than a few blocks away from her mother and siblings.

But the move to Brooklyn did not sever Minerva's ties to Philadelphia. According to the baby book, she made several trips back to Philadelphia, as she continued to introduce baby Adelaide to her friends. After living there for twenty years and maintaining a business as one of its most famous residents for eight, she had many friends and connections there.

As it had many times previously, the nature of Minerva's work changed when she moved to Brooklyn, shifting the dense layers of design, writing, teaching, and activism. Her later career should not be viewed as a postscript to her productive life and significance, as it has been in too many architectural histories—if they acknowledge her at all. Rather, her post-Philadelphia years are best understood as an evolution: Minerva remained a designer for the rest of her life; the only thing that changed was what she designed.

Minerva in the New Century, 1896–1949

In March 1896 Minerva and her family moved to 53 Pineapple Street in Brooklyn, before moving a few months later to their long-term rental at 280 Prospect Place. A month after arriving in Brooklyn, Minerva received a letter from Lois Lilley Howe. Born two years after Minerva, Lois had attended the School of the Museum of Fine Arts in Boston before enrolling in a two-year architectural program at MIT. Graduating in 1890 (when Minerva's practice was at its busiest), Lois pieced together work from various architects before taking on her own commissions around 1894.[147] As Minerva observed in a note she wrote on the letter, Lois had won second prize in the competition for the Woman's Building at the World's Columbian Exposition

BIOGRAPHY

FIG. 15: William Ichabod Nichols, ca. 1891.

FIG. 16: Minerva, likely around the time the family moved to Brooklyn.

FIG. 17: In Brooklyn, Minerva and William rented a house at 280 Prospect Place, where they would raise their four children.

FIG. 15

FIG. 16

FIG. 17

FIG. 18

FIG. 18: Minerva created a baby book to document the growth of her four children. Alongside descriptions of one child learning to sit up, she or William pasted photographs of her latest architectural project at the Browne and Nichols School.

in Chicago, placing behind fellow MIT graduate Sophia Hayden.[148]

Lois wrote in response to a letter from Minerva; Minerva's side of the correspondence does not survive among Lois's papers in the MIT archives, but we can infer from her reply that Minerva was looking for work.

> My dear Mrs. Nichols,
>
> ...I am sorry I can not give you at present much of an account of the work of the women architects in Boston or those graduating from the Boston Institute of Technology. Miss Hayden, who built the [Women's] Building at the World's Fair, is now I believe in a decorator's office.
>
> I myself, as you see by the above heading, have established my own office, but as [for] having been in business for a short time have not done much. Scarcely [*illegible*] to write about.
>
> I will, however, try to make some inquiries which may lead to more information, at least.
>
> Meanwhile, I remain,
> Yours very sincerely,
>
> Lois Lilley Howe [149]

As fruitless as her letter to Howe turned out to be, it demonstrates that Minerva had a network of professional relationships to tap and that her ambitions remained alive after she left Philadelphia. The more we learn about Minerva's chapters in Brooklyn and elsewhere from 1896 until her death in 1949, the more we understand that these decades should be regarded as her later career, not as post-career years. In reexamining her life and career, we see not a brief flurry of work extinguished by the demands of marriage and motherhood, but rather the sustained, enduring presence of architectural practice in her life.

Nevertheless, Minerva's move to Brooklyn undeniably altered her career trajectory. In Brooklyn, she gave birth in 1897 to her second daughter, Caroline, and in 1899 and 1905 to sons John and William. With four young children, she worked from home, balancing motherhood with her work as an architect, reformer, teacher, and writer [FIG. 17]. Her drafting board was in steady demand—architectural commissions included the dollhouse she designed for her children. They now used her board, much as she had once used the boards her grandfather prepared for her to draw on.[150]

In 1897 Minerva completed plans for a new building for the Browne & Nichols School in Cambridge, Massachusetts.[151] Her brother-in-law, Edgar Nichols, was a co-founder of the school, and helped enlist her to design the three-story brick building. Photographs of the completed school building appear in the same baby book that tracked her children's growth, between a description of baby William learning to pull up into a sitting position, and an explanation of John's namesake [FIG. 17].[152] The photographs—and the project itself—reinforce the link between motherhood, education, and architecture in her later career.

The school's catalogue of 1898 celebrated its new home in a description that was almost certainly written (in part or in full) by Minerva, given its emphasis on the building's materials and technical specifications:

> The rooms are large and high, finished in natural ash throughout, and the walls are tinted a soft buff. The windows were constructed on the principle that it is easier to keep light out when it is excessive, than to get it in when it is deficient.

The heating and ventilating is of the most approved kind, a gravity system, with indirect radiation. An upward current is established by steam coils in large ventilating ducts leading to the roof from the level of the floor of each room; and fresh air from out of doors is drawn over single or double steam coils in the basement up through iron ducts opening into each room through large apertures eight feet from the floor. A constant supply of over fifty cubic feet per minute of warm fresh air for each pupil is thus kept in gentle circulation without [draft]. The heating of the ample halls and the conservatory is reinforced by direct radiation. The plumbing, baths, and sanitaries, which are ventilated into an independent system, are of the best design.

In all, the building presented "a perfectly ventilated hall [that] offers superior facilities for lectures, parties, exhibitions, and other entertainments."[153]

Farther afield, Minerva was also responsible around this time for a project in Saco, Maine, where her husband was born and where his family retained ties. In 1884 William's father, John, had built a small cottage for his family near Old Orchard Beach, three miles outside Saco. For many years, the cottage was part of a compound loved by multiple generations of the Nichols family. Around the turn of the twentieth century, John gave the cottage to William and his family. Minerva "tactfully enlarged [the house] with skill," apparently adding a rear shed and barn as part of the project.[154]

In 1900 Minerva took on two commissions, one for the Hackley School in Tarrytown, New York, the other for her husband's Bureau.[155] For the school, Minerva designed an addition for the growing student body. Frances Hackley, the school's founder, and Sarah Goodhue, an early trustee, were Unitarians, possibly key to how Minerva secured this commission—her business network included numerous Unitarian connections.[156] For the Brooklyn Bureau of Charities, she designed a rooftop addition for one of its buildings on Marcy Avenue. The organization ran workrooms, laundries, and a woodyard at this address, and by 1904, a day nursery (or nursery school, in today's terminology); Minerva's third-story addition likely made this newest social program possible. These were the only commissions that she advertised in the New York edition of the *Builders' Guide*; none of her other projects completed after 1896 were announced or featured in the local trade publication.[157] The Hackley School project was also mentioned in an extended profile of Minerva published in the *San Francisco Chronicle* in 1901—a spread that included a photograph of Minerva with her young children [FIG. 19].[158]

William's job at the Brooklyn Bureau of Charities was physically and emotionally demanding. While Minerva maintained a light stream of paid work, the Bureau became a focal point for the family throughout his tenure. Minerva became the chairwoman of the subcommittee overseeing one of the Bureau's three day nurseries. The Central Day Nursery was based at the Bureau's headquarters, 69 Schermerhorn Street in Brooklyn, a little less than two miles from the Nichols' house at 280 Prospect Place. Day nurseries played a critical role in alleviating the burdens of working-class women, tending to poorer children while their parents worked and educating mothers about healthiest child-rearing practices.[159] At one meeting of a federation of day nurseries, a speaker cast their mission in gruesome but vital terms: "Every mother knows she can't drop her baby out of a three story window, but she doesn't know that she must not feed it on stale milk or put it in the same bed with two adults."[160] Minerva was a corresponding secretary at that gathering, speaking up for the importance

FIG. 19: Minerva continued to garner press even after her move to Brooklyn. This full-page profile in the *San Francisco Chronicle* in 1901 includes photographs of several projects and a portrait of Minerva with three of her four children.

of building trusted relationships with tenement residents in order to best support them.

Minerva's synopses on the day nurseries, contributed annually to the Bureau's organizational reports, were an outgrowth of her writing, shaped by the reformist tendencies she had shown in Philadelphia. With parallels to her essays in the *Home-Maker*, her annual reports expressed a social mission particularly in speaking of women as caregivers: "Our aim has been as far as possible to supply for the children the happiest and healthiest conditions, that they may be benefited, and the mothers encouraged and instructed in the wise care of their little ones," she wrote in the 1898 report.[161]

In her *Home-Maker* essays, Minerva had noted how her buildings offered beautiful and functional living conditions to their residents: "Don't be afraid of light and air, they are the things that do most to beautify our homes," she wrote in the April 1891 issue.[162] In her reports to the Brooklyn Bureau of Charities, her response to living conditions was more urgent, as the children in the day nursery's care lived in housing far below the standards than those enjoyed by her clients. The stakes were higher than beauty: "Two of the babies, who for months were daily members of the nursery flock, died during the year."[163] As her subcommittee devoted its time to activities like clothes drives and Christmas festivals, Minerva remained concerned with the significant contributions that well-designed buildings could make to the health, safety, education, and happiness of young children.

As she and the other volunteers worked to improve the lives of poor children, Minerva harbored no illusions about whose labor was the most honorable in these situations. Speaking to a convention of charities in 1904, she punctured the self-congratulatory tone among the attendees:

> I want to speak of one form of social co-operation that seems to me so far has been overlooked. We have spoken of what we do for these people, but we have said nothing about what they do for themselves and we have entirely ignored all that they do for each other. No [volunteer] ever does for her "case" what a woman in a tenement house does for her next door neighbor.[164]

Although she did not allude to her architectural career in this speech, it nevertheless encapsulates the same attention to women's labor and social care that was threaded throughout her life as a design professional.

Minerva's experience with the working mothers of the day nurseries may explain why, in 1904, she was quoted in a newspaper lobbying *against* women working outside the home:

> A regular meeting of the [New York League of Unitarian Women] was held on Friday…The topic of the day was "The Effect of Business Life on the Character of Women." . . . Mrs. William I. Nichols made an urgent plea for the home life, expressing the opinion that every woman who doesn't actually need the money should keep in her own home.[165]

This position is quite surprising in the overall trajectory of Minerva's life and work. In the years before and after this gathering, Minerva promoted the opportunities for women to enter the field of architecture and pursue successful, professional careers in it. Even after leaving Philadelphia, she continued working, though somewhat less, throughout the years her children were growing up. Did she come to reconsider her views in light of what she learned in the day nurseries and from watching the travails of the workingwomen? Perhaps. Her comments may also represent an effort to recast her own choices—the decision to reduce her practice and devote most of her time to her family—as the right and moral ones.

FINDING MINERVA

These motivations may underpin her comments to the New York League of Unitarian Women, but they sidestep the key phrase: "every woman *who doesn't actually need the money*." From the time she was a teenager, Minerva had always needed the money. When she lived with her mother and siblings in the boardinghouse, her work offset the household's financial burdens. Even after she married, her income bolstered her husband's salary as a clergyman. When William took the job in Brooklyn, he apparently took a substantial pay cut.[166] Just three years before the meeting at which she spoke about women who didn't need to work for money, she made it clear to a journalist that she could not count herself among them: in a profile of Minerva in the *San Francisco Chronicle*, reporter Ida Husted Harper wrote: "Some important piece of work is constantly on hand, developing under the busy brain and fingers, *partly because of the financial returns it will bring* [emphasis added] and partly because of the architect's love of her art."[167] Minerva's comments to the Unitarian women of the New York League may point to some ambivalence that Minerva felt in her later career about her overlapping responsibilities as architect, wife, and mother. They may also be the honest words of a woman who was, by this point in her life and career, simply tired.

As the years went on, William's work took a toll on him (and, more than likely, on Minerva). For more than a decade, he had seen at close range the deprivation in Brooklyn's poorest neighborhoods, brought on by the crushing impacts of industrialization and urbanization that had far outpaced improvements to infrastructure and sanitation. While Minerva was tending to the basic needs of young children in the nurseries, William's job required him to manage work programs, testify in sensitive social services cases, and generally work around the holes in the late nineteenth-century social safety net [FIG. 20].

By the time their son William (later known as Bill and referred to that way here, to avoid confusion with his father) was born in 1905, William and Minerva were eager for a getaway closer to Brooklyn than the Maine house. They spent one last summer at the Old Orchard Beach house in 1906, then looked for a summer cottage closer to home. Around 1907 William found a rundown farmhouse on Sharp Hill Road in Wilton, Connecticut—a short train ride from Brooklyn and a rural respite on weekends. The house was dilapidated when he first drove Minerva and the children up to it in a horse-drawn wagon [FIG. 21]. Their oldest child, Adelaide, wrote about the experience in her book *Return to Arcady*:

> Beneath [the maples'] checkered shade, we saw, for the first time, our house. Its wide eaves, its watching windows with small humorous panes, made a face of friendly welcome. It was for us! Mother looked at Father and he smiled back triumphantly. The magic that was to work wonders took over.[168]

For the children, the house became part of a childhood idyll. But for Minerva, once convinced that it was worth the trouble, the rundown cottage represented her next project. From the family's first walk-through, she crafted a vision for improvements (as recounted by Adelaide):

> "I thought as much," said Father... "But if we open up the old fireplace again..."
>
> "And of course we must," broke in Mother firmly...
>
> Mother's eagle eye was already measuring up the windowless oak-beamed storeroom with the stone chimney-breast making one wall.

BIOGRAPHY

FIG. 20

FIG. 21

FIG. 20: The Brooklyn Bureau of Charities ran several day nurseries for working-class children. Minerva chaired a committee overseeing one of the nurseries.

FIG. 21: Around 1907 William and Minerva purchased an eighteenth-century cottage in Wilton, Connecticut, to serve as a country retreat. Minerva oversaw renovations to the house, which remained in the family for over two decades.

FINDING MINERVA

"This will be a wonderful room when we put in a couple of dormers," she said. "We'll leave the hand-hewn beams and the chimney-breast and finish it right up to the ridge of the roof."[169]

Even over their picnic lunch on the first day at the house, "Mother was already talking of tearing out partitions and paper walls."[170] Her work, undertaken over an unknown number of months or years, resulted in a home that the family loved and returned to for over twenty years. It remains standing today.

The family traveled back and forth from Brooklyn to Wilton for several years; the second home helped assuage some of William's working stress. But around 1909, the Bureau's board noticed a decline in his health and sent him and his family on a restorative trip to Europe. A surviving scrapbook of photographs from this trip tracks a rich itinerary that included Scotland, England, Italy, and France. A few offer glimpses of the family—particularly, daughters Adelaide and Caroline, and a woman who was likely Minerva's mother, Amanda. But these are rare, as the scrapbook does not capture many people at all. Instead, most of its fifty-five pages feature photographs of buildings, including cathedrals, townscapes, castles, and monuments. The preponderance of these subjects and the absence of photographs of Minerva, suggest that she was the family's photographer; indeed, although the photographs are well-composed, they often present unconventional vantage points (oblique and off-center views of an otherwise symmetrical building, for example), as if to make a study of the massing of the buildings, the volumes of the open spaces before them, and the relationship of the elements in the streetscape.

Back home in New York, Minerva was apparently involved during this period in larger projects than just the little Wilton house. According to biographical fragments written by her grown children years later, she worked on at least two non-residential projects during her Brooklyn years: the Cathedral of St. John the Divine, in Manhattan, and the Riverside Apartments (or Riverside Apartments) in Brooklyn. These accounts, not yet corroborated by other archives, are plausible, given the timing of those projects' construction and the relationships that Minerva is known to have established in New York. Moreover, the fact that Minerva's children mentioned these projects in their partial biographies of her suggests that they heard about them from Minerva herself.

The Cathedral of St. John the Divine was designed and expanded in several stages, beginning in 1892, and continuing until 1941.[171] During the period when Minerva lived across the East River in Brooklyn, the first phase was underway, under architects Heins & LaFarge; it culminated in 1911 with the completion of the crypt, choir, and crossing.[172] Although Minerva was not the primary architect on any stage of this project, and her name does not show up on any of the Heins & LaFarge drawings archived at Princeton University, she may nonetheless have contributed studies and details that informed those drawings—apparently (according to her children) based in part on her observations during the trip to Europe.

The Riverside Apartments commission is also difficult to account for in secondary sources, and here again, Minerva was not the architect of record. Built around 1890 (when Minerva was exceedingly busy in Philadelphia), the complex of 260 apartments was originally designed by William Field & Son. But as in the case of St. John the Divine, it is conceivable that Minerva worked on alterations or studies that were not documented to the same extent they would have been if she had been the primary architect. In the case of the Riverside Apartments, it is established that Minerva knew the man who conceived of and financed the project: Alfred T. White, one of Minerva and William's closest friends in

BIOGRAPHY

Brooklyn, was on the board of the Brooklyn Bureau of Charities, and, like many of her clients, was a Unitarian.

At a time when conditions were squalid in so many tenements, the Riverside Apartments were seen as such a humane alternative that journalist, photographer, and reformer Jacob Riis described them as "the beau ideal of the model tenement" in his influential book, *How the Other Half Lives*.[173] They offered working-class residents the opportunity to live in "pleasant homes" at a moderate rent, and prioritized domestic privacy for their tenants.[174] The scope of any work that Minerva may have undertaken for Alfred T. White is unclear, but if she did indeed design improvements to the Riverside Apartments after their initial construction, this would represent a reprise of her work with the reformist Model Dwellings Association in Philadelphia. In fact, the Model Dwellings Association cited the Riverside Apartments in its prospectus for the organization in 1893, the year that Minerva and William joined.

By 1912 William's health had declined so much that he resigned from the Brooklyn Bureau of Charities, and the family moved to the Wilton house, making full-time use of it for a while. In March 1913 William returned to the pulpit, accepting a position at a church in Deerfield, Massachusetts.[175] It did not take long for Minerva to work the move into her own career, overseeing alterations to the church's historic building, originally constructed in 1824. Appointed chairwoman of the committee coordinating the project, she stewarded a scope of work that included the installation of a hot-air furnace and the electrification of the historic chandelier, as well as more cosmetic restoration projects such as interior painting and refinishing the pulpit and other woodwork.[176] Once finished in October 1913, one local newspaper wrote that, "the meeting house as renovated and restored is one of the most beautiful of New England's rural meeting [houses] and in some of its features is unique."[177] On November 28, 1913, the congregation celebrated the rededication of the meetinghouse and the installation of William as minister—an occasion in both of the Nichols' careers.[178]

In 1916, with William's health worse than ever, Minerva found an eighteenth-century house to buy in Hingham, Massachusetts, where William had been ordained over forty years before.[179] As William faded, Minerva channeled her sorrow into restoring their home. Adelaide later wrote:

> To take Father back to his Arcady, Mother found a home for us to buy in Hingham. She restored a sedate white brick town house with her indomitable energy and skill. With its fine wainscoting and mantels, it was a fit background for the family heirlooms that had come by way of Deerfield and Cambridge…Pouring her energy into this labor of love, she warded off the darkening shadow cast before the inevitable anguish of the final loss.[180]

Much as she had for the Wilton house, she applied her architectural skills to the challenge of blending old and new. Viewed with the alterations to the Deerfield church completed during this period, and the project in Saco, Maine, a pattern in Minerva's decades of practice after Philadelphia becomes clear: her work had expanded to include preservation projects.

In November 1917 William died in Hingham after a long illness.[181] Widowed with four children aged twelve to twenty-three, Minerva was just fifty-five; she would live another thirty-two years, in an echo of her mother's decades of widowhood.[182] Indeed, Amanda herself was still alive at this time, having buried two husbands, two premature babies, and the husbands of both her daughters. In the Hingham and Wilton houses, Minerva mourned William's absence. Adelaide wrote of that time: "Afterward, she was prostrated by the waves of grief, too utterly weary to rise. I had never seen her break before. Those were days too bitter for tears."[183]

FINDING MINERVA

FIG. 22: Minerva in front of 82 Clinton Avenue in Westport, Connecticut, one of the last buildings she designed, August 1949.

BIOGRAPHY

Grieving, Minerva moved several times in the next few years, eager to stay close to her children, siblings, and mother. In 1921 she suffered another blow, when her mother died. At the time of her death, Amanda was living with Minerva and three of Minerva's four children in Milton, Massachusetts (the fourth was at college). Having lost both her husband and her mother, Minerva would not be separated from her children. She put the Hingham house up for sale in 1922 and, after her daughter Adelaide married Jack Baker in 1924, designed a house for them at 82 Clinton Avenue in Westport, Connecticut [CAT. NO. 77]. Minerva described the white two-story house, known as Lower Guard Hill, as "early American and miner camp"—a nod to Jack Baker's job as a mining engineer [FIG. 22].[184] In 1925, a year after designing Lower Guard Hill, Minerva lost her sister, Adelaide. (Their half brother, Samuel, would outlive Minerva, dying in 1962.)

Beginning in 1929, Minerva designed a new house in consultation with Jack. Located just up the hill from Lower Guard Hill, the new house at 78 Clinton Avenue was known simply as Guard Hill. Adelaide and Jack moved into the new house when it was completed, while Minerva lived in the lower house; the growing family traipsed up and down the hill—past a frog pond—to visit each other. At some point, Minerva's niece Nye Winifred, daughter of her sister Adelaide, came to live with her at Lower Guard Hill, and became known to Minerva's grandchildren and great-grandchildren as "Aunt Peedie."[185]

The two Westport houses that Minerva designed for her family—as well as a third house nearby, designed for the neighboring Lubrecht family—represent a significant counterpoint to Minerva's earlier works. Constructed nearly three decades after her time in Philadelphia, these houses demonstrate her evolving approach to design. With details influenced by the Arts and Crafts movement and the American revivalist tendencies of early twentieth-century architecture, they depart from the eclecticism she deployed in many of her earlier works of the 1880s and 1890s and demonstrate that she was still actively attuned to the prevailing architectural movements.

Her design for Lower Guard Hill, for example, created a playful rhythm with the dormers and the roofline, imbuing the house with a cottage-like quality that is much more informal than her late nineteenth-century designs. At Guard Hill she emphasized the craftsmanship and materiality of the woodwork. The entrance hall is intimately scaled, with a heavy wood door, overhead beams, and a rough-hewn post, bracket, and balustrade at the stair. But the arrangement of the foyer beckons the visitor into the adjacent great room; there, the vaulted ceiling beams emphasize soaring openness, the inverse of their effect in the foyer—and a volume not found in any of her earlier known works [FIG. 23].

Both of the houses on Guard Hill were probably influenced by her experience restoring the Wilton cottage. The very fact that Minerva restored that cottage, together with similar projects like the Deerfield church and the Hingham house, can be seen as dovetailing with the contemporaneous Arts and Crafts movement, which valued traditional craftsmanship and what was considered a lost way of life. The traditional eighteenth-century features in the Wilton house seem to find their twentieth-century equivalents in the Westport houses: the timber beams in the ceiling, the substantial fireplaces and hearths, the banks of windows. She even incorporated a small interior casement window at Guard Hill, looking down from the upstairs hallway into the great room; a similar window exists in the Wilton cottage, and almost certainly inspired its counterpart in Westport.

In 1937 septuagenarian Minerva was still busy and newsworthy—and aware of the current movements in architecture. That year, the *Philadelphia Inquirer* ran a long article about her under the

FINDING MINERVA

FIG. 23: The great room at Guard Hill was the center of life in the house, and demonstrated Minerva's evolving approach to design, materials, and craftsmanship.

FIG. 24: Late in life, Minerva designed a house for the Lubrecht family. The residence was situated on a property across the street from Guard Hill the site of two houses Minerva designed for her daughter Adelaide and son-in-law Jack Baker.

FIG. 23

FIG. 24

BIOGRAPHY

headline "Pioneer Woman Architect Still Active at Age of 75." Having traveled to Philadelphia for her granddaughter's birthday, Minerva casually gave an interview while waiting on a train platform, cane in hand. She used the interview as an opportunity to voice her support for "slum clearance"—recalling not just her work with the Brooklyn Bureau of Charities, but also her involvement in the Model Dwellings Association in Philadelphia a half-century earlier. She also mentioned that she had designed a house "as lately as last year," likely a reference to the house for the Lubrecht family at 73 Clinton Avenue, Westport [FIG. 24].[186]

She opined on the "pure functionality" of architecture, aligning her body of work with proto-modernism in the late nineteenth and early twentieth centuries. Yet, reflecting on the state of architecture in the late 1930s, she decried the most extreme expressions of modernism that prized austerity above all: "[Those designs are] as freakish as the over-ornamentation of the hideous architecture of the Gay Nineties."[187] Well aware of the work of modernist architects who rejected any sense of history, Minerva insisted on an expansive approach to architecture that could recognize the "good out of every period"—including the more than fifty years of history that comprised her own working period.

The interview she granted in 1937 was part of a larger effort (however subconscious) to craft her own retrospective narrative in her waning years. Minerva had always demonstrated a knack for marketing and self-promotion in her work; as she reached her eighties, she did the same for her life. In 1944 she sat down with her grandchildren to share the anecdotes recorded in *The Baddest Day, and Other Favorite Stories*; other than her professional essays and speeches, this is one of the only records that survives in Minerva's own voice, and it offers the most detailed account of her formative childhood years. Beyond the stories themselves, *The Baddest Day* is a family archive made by many hands: Minerva's accounts are accompanied by illustrations drawn by her daughter-in-law Francis D. Nichols, and photographs compiled by Minerva's niece Nye Winifred Griffiths. After Minerva's death, her children made various attempts to write her biography and grapple with the throughlines and incongruities of her life. She herself lived at the house at 82 Clinton Avenue, Westport, until her death on November 17, 1949. She was active in architecture almost to the end: just two years earlier, at an anniversary event in Philadelphia at the New Century Club headquarters that she designed, she mentioned, according to a newspaper article, that she was drawing up plans for veterans' housing.[188]

When she died, the *New York Times* ran a headlined obituary for her—a fact even more remarkable given the newspaper's present-day "Overlooked No More" series, which acknowledges how many significant individuals did not receive such treatment in its pages. The obituary highlighted all phases of her career, noting her designs for the New Century Clubs and the Browne & Nichols School, as well as her involvement with the Brooklyn Bureau of Charities and other reformist enterprises. Shaped by the input of her children, the *New York Times* piece was testimony to the fact that Minerva kindled meaningful work—and a sense of self as a designer—for her entire life [FIG. 25].

FIG. 25: Minerva at Guard Hill with John and Carol Baker, circa 1940.

BIOGRAPHY

NOTES

1 "A Thousand Women in Architecture: Part I," *Architectural Record* 103, no. 3 (March 1948): 105.

2 This essay (and indeed, this entire book and its companion exhibit) deliberately avoids referring to Minerva as a "woman architect"—despite the many historical and contemporary instances of such phrasing. To describe her as a "woman architect" would imply that an architect (with no preceding word to modify it) is presumptively a man, and that she is therefore some derivative form of the profession. Minerva herself rejected the framing of herself as a "woman architect" (or "lady architect," as one newspaper called her).

 I confess that some of my own past writing about Minerva did not take this framing into consideration. On this front, I have been strongly influenced by Karen Burns's essay critiquing this phraseology, "The Woman/Architect Distinction" in *Women, Practice, Architecture: "Resigned Accommodation" and "Usurpatory Practice,"* ed. Naomi Stead (London: Routledge, 2014).

3 Private collection, Carrie Baker.

4 Private collection, Carrie Baker.

5 Alfred Alder Doane, *The Doane Family and Their Descendants, with Notes Upon English Families of the Name* (Salem, MA: Salem Press, 1902), 272–73.

6 Decisions to move seem to have been taken by Seth: Lucretia never approved of the decision to leave Chicago, and refused to cede her "dower rights" to properties there. (Doane, *The Doane Family*, 272)

7 Minerva Parker Nichols, Frances D. Nichols, and Doane Fischer, *The Baddest Day, and Other Favorite Stories: As Told in Ga-Ga's Own Words about 1944 and In Short Hand by Frances D. Nichols Who Did The Illustrations* (D. Fischer, 1997), 1–2. Copy at Peoria Public Library.

8 Nichols, Nichols, and Fischer, *The Baddest Day*, 2.

9 Nichols, Nichols, and Fischer, 5.

10 Nichols, Nichols, and Fischer, 5.

11 Nichols, Nichols, and Fischer, 15.

12 Nichols, Nichols, and Fischer, 27.

13 Nichols, Nichols, and Fischer, 28.

14 Nichols, Nichols, and Fischer, 28.

15 Ancestry.com, *1870 United States Federal Census* [database on-line] (Lehi, UT, USA: Ancestry.com Operations, Inc., 2009), images reproduced by FamilySearch.

16 Ross Miller, *The Great Chicago Fire* (Urbana, IL, and Chicago: University of Illinois Press, 2000), 18.

17 Miller, *The Great Chicago Fire*, 22.

18 Private collection, Carrie Baker.

19 According to some accounts, they may have met when she was sick and a patient of his, but this has not been confirmed. They did live in the same building—409 West Randolph Street—according to the 1875 city directory; as they married later that year, it is unclear whether they met as neighbors there or moved there as a couple after their marriage.

20 Ancestry.com, *1860 United States Federal Census*; Ancestry.com, *1870 United States Federal Census*.

21 "Religious News," *Chicago Tribune*, September 21, 1873.

22 Minerva apparently never mentioned to her children that Samuel Maxwell had been married and had other children; in more than one instance as they wrote about her life, they referred to him as a lifelong bachelor. Minerva and Adelaide clearly did not have a relationship with their stepsiblings, who lived elsewhere during the entire time that Samuel and Amanda were married.

23 Private collection, Carrie Baker.

24 Private collection, Carrie Baker.

25 Dorothy Gondos Beers, "The Centennial City, 1865–1876," in *Philadelphia: A 300-Year History*, edited by Russell F. Weigley (New York and London: W. W. Norton, 1982), 421–22, 467.

26 Private collection, Carrie Baker.

27 Private collection, Carrie Baker.

28 Amanda was listed as a "lady's physician" according to the 1880 census; according to her daughter Adelaide, she engaged in some sort of massage-based healing work at various points in the late nineteenth century.

29 "Normal Art School Closed," Philadelphia Inquirer, February 15, 1884.

30 In 1891, a letter from Minerva's husband, William I. Nichols, to his brother stated that Minerva had eight years' experience in architecture. Moreover, in an interview in 1937, Minerva said, "I had an office...which I opened after I had been connected with other architectural firms in the city." Both of these references suggest that she made connections with practicing architects early, even as she continued to pursue additional coursework in the field.

31 Although the institution is known today as a science museum, divorced from architecture and design, its nineteenth-century incarnation promoted the connection between the mechanics (as practiced by Seth Doane), science, and the art of design.

32 "William H. Thorne [obituary]," *Philadelphia Inquirer*, February 24, 1926.

33 Jeffrey A. Cohen, "Building a Discipline: Early Institutional Settings for Architectural Education in Philadelphia, 1804–1890," *Journal of the Society of Architectural Historians* 53, no. 2 (June 1994): 156.

34 Sarah Allaback, "'Better than Silver and Gold': Design Schools for Women in America, 1848–1860," *Journal of Women's History* 10, no. 1 (Spring 1998): 98.

35 The board minutes in the Franklin Institute's archives do not list her as an applicant at any point in the 1880s.

36 Quoted in Cohen, "Building a Discipline," 156.

37 F. Graeme Chalmers, *Women in the Nineteenth-Century Art World: Schools of Art and Design for Women in London and Philadelphia* (Westport, CT: Greenwood Press, 1998), 107.

38 Allaback, "'Better than Silver and Gold,'" 96.

39 Cohen, "Building a Discipline," 139.

40 Quoted in Mary N. Woods, *From Craft to Profession: The Practice of Architecture in Nineteenth-Century America* (Berkeley, CA: University of California Press, 1999), 78.

41 During her two years at the Drawing School, Minerva studied alongside a handful of other women.

42 Cornell University established its architecture program in 1871, accepting women from the start. Although no women sought it out initially, Margaret Hicks was the first to graduate from Cornell with a Bachelor of Architecture degree in 1880. She died prematurely in 1883, at the age of twenty-five, cutting short any career as a peer of Minerva's. The University of Illinois awarded its first architecture degree (to a male student) in 1873; six years later, Mary L. Page graduated from Illinois, the first woman to earn a degree from an American architecture program.

43 Woods, *From Craft to Profession*, 76.

44 Seemingly, admission of women met with little resistance from school leaders, based on the minutes of the Committee on Instruction.

45 Although we cannot rule it out entirely, it does not seem that the Franklin Institute's William H. Thorne and Edwin W. Thorne were related. They definitely were not brothers, or first or second cousins. Any as-yet-undiscovered familial connection might suggest that Minerva gained her apprenticeship along the following lines: an architect relocates to Philadelphia and needs an assistant. He asks his relative for a recommendation, since his relative runs a school for would-be architects, and a standout student is recommended to him, etc.

46 "Thorne Bros., Architects," *Daily Republican* (Wilmington, DE), June 26, 1880.

47 "Edwin W. Thorne, Architect and Builder," *News Journal* (Wilmington, DE), February 10, 1879.

48 "Architects," Morning News (Wilmington, DE), September 27, 1882; "Notice. To Ladies and Gentlemen," *Morning News* (Wilmington, DE), October 30, 1882.

49 "The Wilmington Library," *News Journal* (Wilmington, DE), December 2, 1881; "The Shiloh Baptist Church," *Daily Republican* (Wilmington, DE), July 17, 1882.

50 In May 1884, after having submitted a bid for a new public high school, Edwin took issue with the process, demanding payment for his drawings and publicly criticizing the school board and their procedures. The move was not well received, and at the meeting of the school board on November 10, a member denounced any accusation of impropriety as "a lie out of the whole cloth," and said that "the person who uttered it [Edwin Thorne] was a liar." "City School Board," *Daily Republican* (Wilmington, DE), November 11, 1884. There is no record of how Edwin responded to these comments at the meeting.

51 "Notices," *Daily Republican* (Wilmington, DE), December 6, 1884.

52 "Removal," *Daily Republican* (Wilmington, DE), April 27, 1885.

53 "To Those Intending to Build," *Daily Republican* (Wilmington, DE), September 16, 1882.

54 Kathleen Sinclair Wood, "Minerva Parker Nichols: Pioneer American Woman Architect" (master's thesis, University of Delaware, 1993), 8.

55 M. Parker, letter to the editor, *PRERBG* 2, no. 50 (December 19, 1887), 598.

56 The publication's commentary on a single entry could be split across several issues, which could be both confusing for the reader and an enticement to continue subscribing.

57 *Carpentry and Building* 9, no. 10 (October 1887): 196–97, plates XXXVIII, XXXIX.

58 "Seventeenth Competition," *Carpentry and Building* 8, no. 10 (October 1886): 186.

59 "Seventeenth Competition," 186.

60 According to the *PRERBG*, Isaac Ashmead was associated with the Spring Garden National Bank. Located at Twelfth and Spring Garden Streets, the bank was just a few blocks from Minerva's home. Based on this proximity, perhaps she had a role in landing this client and commission.

61 *Builder and Decorator* 6, no. 3 (May 1888): [supplement].

62 In Buffalo, Louise Blanchard launched a practice a few years earlier than Minerva; within a few months, though, she had partnered with Robert Bethune, who would eventually become her husband. For more on Louise and the rapport between her career and Minerva's, see p. 58.

63 Although the *PRERBG* is not the only source we use to assemble the roster of Minerva's portfolio, it is a primary one; Minerva clearly was meticulous in filing these notices during her Philadelphia years, proving in the process that she could both secure and execute a range of commissions.

64 *PRERBG* 5, no. 36, September 10, 1890, 545.

BIOGRAPHY

65 *PRERBG* 5, no. 44, November 5, 1890, 685.

66 *PRERBG* 7, no. 22, June 1, 1892, i.

67 *PRERBG* 7, no. 26, June 29, 1892, i.

68 *PRERBG* 6, no. 16, April 22, 1891, 241–42.

69 "Minerva Parker," *Daily Inter Ocean* (Chicago), January 17, 1891, 11.

70 The Pennsylvania Museum and School of Industrial Art, *Circular of the Committee on Instruction, 1889–1890* (Philadelphia: Pennsylvania Museum and School of Industrial Art, 1890), 47, https://archive.org/details/schoolcatalog8889penn/page/46/mode/2up.

71 Jeffrey Cohen, email message to author, August 22, 2022.

72 Frances Elizabeth Willard and Mary A. Livermore, eds., *A Woman of the Century: Fourteen Hundred-Seventy Biographical Sketches Accompanied by Portraits of Leading American Women in All Walks of Life* (Buffalo, NY: Moulton, 1893), 536.

73 Steven Conn and Max Page, eds., *Building the Nation: Americans Write About Their Architecture, Their Cities, and Their Landscape* (Philadelphia: University of Pennsylvania Press, 2003), 324.

74 The "cult of domesticity" should not be confused with the idea of separate spheres, which suggests that women occupied the domestic realm while men worked outside it. As Minerva's own career demonstrates, such a categorization—conceived by later historians evaluating women's opportunities in the nineteenth century—creates a dichotomy of two domains whose boundaries were, in fact, much more nebulous. Nineteenth-century literature employed the idea of the "woman's sphere" in reference to the concept of domesticity, but the framing of these associations as discrete and separate domains of public and private, or as male and female spaces, was done by twentieth-century historians. While Minerva as a case study belies the concept of "separate spheres," women of color in general are representative of the faults in that framing, as so many of them had worked outside the home—often in other people's homes—for centuries, out of financial necessity or as enslaved laborers. (See Andrea J. Merrett, "From Separate Spheres to Gendered Spaces: The Historiography of Women and Gender in 19th Century and Early 20th Century America," *The Proceedings of Spaces of History/Histories of Space: Emerging Approaches to the Study of the Built Environment, College of Environmental Design, UC Berkeley* [Berkeley, CA: University of California, Berkeley, 2010], 3–4.)

75 Minerva Parker, "Practical Homes," *Home-Maker* (January 1891): 63–65; Minerva Parker, "Practical Dwellings," *Home-Maker* (December 1891): 445.

76 Parker, "Practical Homes," 64.

77 "Illustrations," *American Architect and Building News*, February 11, 1893: 95.

78 Ida Husted Harper, "A Woman Who Is the Architect of Her Own Fortunes," *San Francisco Chronicle*, April 14, 1901.

79 Joseph Dana Miller, "Women as Architects," *Frank Leslie's Popular Monthly*, June 1900: 200; Harper, "A Woman Who Is the Architect of Her Own Fortunes."

80 "Miss Parker, Architect," *Semi-Weekly Interior Journal* (Stanford, KY), May 29, 1891.

81 In fact, the *PRERBG* rarely featured any people on its front page, choosing instead to profile new buildings. Only seven prior issues included front-page stories about people; all men, they tended to be speculative builders or real estate operators.

82 One of Minerva's clients, Emma Williams Brooke (married to Lewis T. Brooke), appears to have "passed" as White; some of Emma's ancestors were Black, but she was recorded as White in several official documents. Thus, there is no indication that Minerva knowingly worked with any clients of color.

83 "The Isabella Idea," Adelaide Nichols Baker Papers, Schlesinger Library, Harvard Radcliffe Institute.

84 "Isabella of Castile, Reply to Bergenroth, Ewald and Tucker," *Queen Isabella Journal* 1, no. 2 (April 1890): 1. Sophia Smith Collection of Women's History, Smith College.

85 *PRERBG* 5, no. 50, December 17, 1890, 784.

86 Sarah Allaback, *The First American Woman Architects* (Champaign, IL: University of Illinois Press, 2008), 48.

87 "The Isabella Hotel," *Queen Isabella Journal* 3, nos. 2 and 3 (1892): 12. Sophia Smith Collection of Women's History, Smith College.

88 Jeanne Madeline Weimann, *The Fair Women* (Chicago: Academy Chicago, 1981), 145.

89 "Chicago: The Architect of the Woman's Building," *American Architect and Building News* 38, no. 883 (November 26, 1892): 134.

90 Minerva Parker Nichols, "A Woman on the Woman's Building," *American Architect and Building News* 38, no. 885 (December 10, 1892): 170.

91 "To Our Subscribers," *American Architect and Building News* 38, no. 885 (December 10, 1892): 158.

92 *PRERBG* 4, no. 20, May 22, 1889, 243.

93 Writing in 1904 about this purchase, Adelaide Parker indicated that the property was "purchased jointly by myself, my sister, and mother." Only Amanda's name is on the deed and mortgage, but this means that Adelaide and Minerva almost certainly contributed to the purchase funds.

94 "Oak Lane Land Company," Entity Number 0000257375 [Domestic Business Corporation], Pennsylvania Department of State.

95 "Approved Pension Application File for Amanda M Doane Parker."

96 "Approved Pension Application File for Amanda M Doane Parker."

97 "Approved Pension Application File for Amanda M Doane Parker."

98 "Approved Pension Application File for Amanda M Doane Parker."

99 Cara Burton, *Historic Parksley, Virginia: A Self-Guided Walking Tour* (Accomac, VA: Eastern Shore Public Library, 2018), [2].

100 Parksley Land and Improvement Company Records, Eastern Shore of Virginia Heritage Center.

101 Burton, *Historic Parksley, Virginia*, [2].

102. Parksley Land and Improvement Company Records, Eastern Shore of Virginia Heritage Center; Cara Burton, *Historic Parksley, Virginia*, [2]; Arthur King Fisher, *Reminiscences of Parksley, Virginia (1896–1912)* (n.p.: Arthur King Fisher, 1979), 4.

103 *PRERBG* 4, no. 33, August 21, 1889, 391.

104 Fisher, *Reminiscences of Parksley, Virginia*, 7–8.

105 Private collection, Elizabeth Halsted.

106 *Minerva Parker Nichols, "An Uncultivated Field," Housekeeper's Weekly, June 10, 1893.*

107 "Art in Architecture," *Times* (Philadelphia), November 19, 1893.

108 Minerva Parker Nichols, "An Architectural Object Lesson," *Architecture and Building* 19, no. 27 (December 30, 1893): 318.

109 Minerva Parker-Nichols [sic], "Houses for Workingmen," *Carpentry and Building,* September 1893: 238.

110 *United States Census Bureau, "Figure MS-2: Median age at first marriage: 1890 to present" (Washington, D.C.: United States Census Bureau, 2022), https://www.census.gov/content/dam/Census/library/visualizations/time-series/demo/families-and-households/ms-2.pdf.*

111 Mary Temple-Bayard, "The Woman Architect," *Times* (Philadelphia) *Sunday Special*, September 13, 1891, 9.

112 Private collection, Carrie Baker.

113 "Among Philadelphians," *New York Times*, December 27, 1891.

114 "A Unitarian Wedding," *Philadelphia Inquirer*, December 23, 1891; "Nichols-Parker," *Times* (Philadelphia), December 23, 1891.

115 "Nichols-Parker," *Times* (Philadelphia), December 23, 1891.

116 "Of Art and Archaeology," *Lincoln Daily Nebraska State Journal*, February 14, 1892.

117 Private collection, Elizabeth Halsted.

118 Private collection, Elizabeth Halsted.

119 Helen E. Scheeble, "Pioneer Woman Architect Still Active at Age of 75," *Philadelphia Inquirer*, November 28, 1937.

120 Philadelphia School of Design for Women, *School List* 1887–1897, Connelly Library [Archives], Moore College of Art and Design.

121 "The Building Boom," *Philadelphia Inquirer*, September 14, 1891.

122 Philadelphia School of Design for Women, *School List* 1887–1897, Connelly Library [Archives], Moore College of Art and Design.

123 Minerva Parker, "Practical Homes," 757.

124 Board of Public Education, *Seventieth Annual Report of the Board of Public Education, First School District of Pennsylvania comprising the City of Philadelphia* (Philadelphia: Dunlap & Clarke, 1889), 95.

125 Philadelphia School of Design for Women, *School List* 1887–1897.

126 Philadelphia School of Design for Women, *School List* 1887–1897.

127 Philadelphia School of Design for Women, *School List* 1887–1897.

128 Signed by Bertha Palmer, whose politicking drove the Isabellas out of the fairgrounds, the honorable mention certificate for Minerva may have been a consolation prize or peace offering for the events surrounding her pavilion. However, such an assumption in no way diminishes the recognition that Minerva received on behalf of the School of Design. (Private collection, Carrie Baker.)

129 See Mary Hearn (?) in the school's 1893–94 class list, residing at 1614 Green Street. Philadelphia School of Design for Women, *School List* 1887–1897.130.

130 "Cycle Department: Federation Notes," *Home-Maker* (June 1891): 273.

131 "Novel Exhibition: Seventy-Five Architects Display Their Work at the Exchange," Philadelphia Inquirer, March 22, 1892; "Met About Town: At the Unitarian Club," *Philadelphia Inquirer*, May 13, 1892.

132 *Ancestry.com. Massachusetts, U.S., Death Records, 1841–1915 [database on-line] (Provo, UT, USA: Ancestry.com Operations, Inc., 2013).*

133 "What Women are Doing," *Daughters of America* 7, no. 10 (1893), 16.

134 Private collection, Elizabeth Halsted.

135 Ira V. Brown, *Mary Grew: Abolitionist and Feminist* (1813–1896) (Selinsgrove, PA: Susquehanna University Press, 1991), 158–59.

136 Brown, *Mary Grew*, 155.

137 *Private collection*, Elizabeth Halsted.

138 Parker, "Practical Homes," 65.

BIOGRAPHY

139 As a cause, dress reform gained significant steam at the turn of the twentieth century, in tandem with the suffrage movement. (Cynthia Zaitzevsky, *Long Island Landscapes and the Women Who Designed Them* [New York: W. W. Norton, 2009], 258.)

140 "A Lady Architect," *Indianapolis Journal*, February 23, 1890.

141 "Many Leaders Talk on Dress Reform," *Chicago Daily Tribune*, May 24, 1893.

142 "A Lady Architect," *Indianapolis Journal*, February 23, 1890.

143 *Prospectus of the Model Dwellings Association of Philadelphia* (Philadelphia: Model Dwellings Association, 1893), Historical Society of Pennsylvania.

144 "To Abolish the 'Slums,'" *Jewish Exponent* (Philadelphia), April 21, 1893; "Model Dwelling Association to Dissolve," Jewish Exponent (Philadelphia), November 1, 1895.

145 *Minerva Parker Nichols, "Women as Architects," Third Biennial, General Federation of Women's Clubs (Louisville, KY: Flexner Brothers, 1896), 267.*

146 New Century Trust Records (Collection 3097), Historical Society of Pennsylvania.

147 Allaback, *First American Woman Architects*, 104.

148 Lois won $500 for her entry, compared with Sophia's $1,000—paltry prizes compared to the men's winning purses. But Lois fared much better in her career than Sophia, beginning with a trip to Europe with her mother and sisters paid for with her prize money. (See Allaback, *First American Woman Architects*, 104.)

149 Private collection, Carrie Baker.

150 Private collection, Carrie Baker.

151 After a series of twentieth-century mergers, the institution survives as the Buckingham Browne & Nichols School.

152 The baby book is layered, chronologically. Having proceeded through the book tracking Adelaide's growth, Minerva doubled back as each of her three other children was born. Thus, the school photographs are pasted in between pages related to William and John.

153 *The Browne and Nichols School for Boys, No. 20 Garden Street, Cambridge, Mass.* (Cambridge, Massachusetts: Browne and Nichols School for Boys, [1898]), [10], Buckingham Browne and Nichols School Archives.

154 *The Browne and Nichols School for Boys*, [10].

155 James Chester Flagg, "Across the Lawn: Hackley School," *Unitarian*, June 1908, 219.

156 *Annual Report of the American Unitarian Association, for the Fiscal Year May 1, 1906–April 30, 1907* (Boston: American Unitarian Association, 1907), 46–47.

157 *Real Estate Record and Builders' Guide* [New York], July 7, 1900, 7.

158 Harper, "A Woman Who Is the Architect of Her Own Fortunes."

159 Although we know that women of color worked in the day nurseries, it is unclear whether any of the children in the care of the nurseries were non-White; this has implications for which working mothers saw their burdens alleviated by the day nurseries.

160 "Tenement Mothers," *New York Daily Tribune*, April 14, 1905.

161 The Brooklyn Bureau of Charities, *Nineteenth Annual Report* (Brooklyn, NY: Brooklyn Bureau of Charities, 1898), 15 [Brooklyn Bureau of Community Service Records (Arc.129), Series 1, Center for Brooklyn History].

162 Parker, "Practical Homes," 757.

163 Brooklyn Bureau of Charities, *Eighteenth Annual Report*, 24.

164 Isabel C. Barrows, ed., *Proceedings of the National Conference of Charities and Correction at the Thirty-First Annual Session Held in the City of Portland, Maine, June 15–22, 1904* (Boston: George H. Ellis, 1904), 606–7.

165 "Religious Intelligence," *The Christian Register,* December 8, 1904, 1368.

166 Harper, "A Woman Who Is the Architect of Her Own Fortunes."

167 Harper, "A Woman Who Is the Architect of Her Own Fortunes."

168 Adelaide N. Baker, *Return to Arcady* (New York and Westport, CT: Lawrence Hill, 1973), 7.

169 Baker, 15.

170 Baker, 18.

171 Later, alterations took place between 1979 and 1982. Donald G. Presa and Jay Shockley, *Cathedral Church of St. John the Divine and the Cathedral Close: Designation Report*, edited by Kate Lemos McHale (New York: New York Landmarks Preservation Commission, February 21, 2017), 1.

172 Presa and Shockley, *Cathedral Church of St. John the Divine*, 2.

173 Constance Rosenblum, "A Building with a Heart of Gold," *New York Times*, December 9, 2011, https://www.nytimes.com/2011/12/11/realestate/brooklyn-heights-habitats-a-building-with-a-heart-of-gold.html.

174 Marcus T. Reynolds, "The House of the Poor in American Cities, *Publications of the American Economic Association* 8, no. 3 (March–May 1893): 90–91.

175 "Nichols, William Ichabod," Unitarian Universalist Association, Minister Files, 1825–2010, Harvard Divinity School Library.

176 "Deerfield: Meeting House to Be Renovated," *Greenfield* (MA) *Recorder*, September 10, 1913.

FINDING MINERVA

177 "Local Notices," *Holyoke* (MA) *Daily Transcript*, October 27, 1913.

178 Private collection, Elizabeth Halsted.

179 For unknown reasons, William's was the only name on the deed, but their daughter Adelaide gave credit to Minerva for the choice.

180 Baker, *Return to Arcady*, 137–38.

181 It was likely cancer, but he had had recurring bouts of illness—exacerbated by stress—for much of his life.

182 Interestingly, William's obituary in *The Brooklyn Eagle* says that he is survived by his wife, "Minerva Maxwell." This is the only known instance of Minerva using her stepfather's surname, rather than her father's. It is unclear who wrote the obituary or contributed the information to the newspaper. "W. I. Nichols Dies; Leader in Charity," *Brooklyn Daily Eagle*, November 5, 1917.

183 Baker, *Return to Arcady*, 138.

184 Scheeble, "Pioneer Woman Architect Still Active."

185 Aunt Peedie moved into Adelaide and Jack's house, after Minerva's death in 1949.

186 Scheeble, "Pioneer Woman Architect Still Active."

187 Scheeble, "Pioneer Woman Architect Still Active."

188 Mary Padgett, "New Century Club Marks 70th Year with Luncheon," *Philadelphia Inquirer*, March 11, 1947.

PORTFOLIO

A SUBMISSION TO THE HISTORIC AMERICAN BUILDINGS SURVEY

Elizabeth Felicella

A SUBMISSION TO HABS

Between 2019 and 2022, I photographed nearly all of Minerva Parker Nichols's known extant buildings in accordance with the submission guidelines of the Historic American Buildings Survey (HABS). These require that structures be captured on black-and-white negative film using a large-format view camera that can correct for perspective on site. All HABS submissions require both an original negative and contact print of each view for subsequent digitization and archival storage. I worked with an 8 × 10 Deardorff view camera that happened to be as old as Nichols's earliest buildings.

    We began considering HABS as a permanent repository for our planned photographic documentation after one of our earliest outings as a team. HABS is an extensive collection of architectural photographs, measured drawings, plans and field notes, administered by the National Park Service and housed at the Library of Congress. Its stated mission is to "preserve the architectural legacy of America," including vernacular and regional forms, for which it provides ample accommodation. We knew that the only work by Nichols archived in HABS was her New Century Club in Philadelphia (1891–2) submitted in 1973, the year of its demolition, and that although she herself was noted in an original data sheet that accompanied the submission, her name was not an operable search term in the database on the Library of Congress website. That was our starting point.

PORTFOLIO

But what I soon came to appreciate in the context of HABS—my own constant point of reference within the overall project—is that "things" in that collection speak among themselves with as much authority as any individual author speaks through them. Perhaps, given the breadth of the collection and its early focus on the vernacular, a Nichols porch or fireplace or front door, no matter how exquisite, would always be one among many porches, fireplaces and front doors in the archive. A door's having existed—having been crafted, planed, and hung by someone; having been opened and closed as many times and by as many people as it had; having been worn, altered, or lovingly preserved—was as much the point of its inclusion in HABS as a design attributed to a particular author. And this would be just as true for the photographs I would take. The guidelines I followed were meant to ensure correspondence and consistency within the archive over time, and to foster a conversation already well underway.

The photographic process reinforced an important aspect of this: the many intricacies, often unacknowledged—historical, technical, social—that we inevitably step into even before we set to work. Looking through a view camera, there is no mirror to automatically right the world. So, for me, what remains of Nichols's work was always projected upside down and reversed onto the ground glass of my camera. On the one hand, this meant it was up to me to make sense of the inversions; on the other, the apparatus through which I was seeing—another thing with its own history and its own voice—was always exceedingly present. The tension between seeing what was before me, twice inverted through a wooden box of a camera, and the impulse to skip ahead, to "auto correct" so as to fit within the framework of my own present, my own now, was instructive. It was a constant reminder that there is meaning in both the making and archiving of photographs that lies far beyond personal vision and understanding. And that similarly, as an architect, Nichols had worked in and among technologies and conventions that now carry meaning in ways she could never have imagined.

A SUBMISSION TO HABS

In the end I arrived at my own inflection of our starting point. Although Nichols's absence from HABS was something to be addressed, the missing voice was not hers alone; it was also that of the many voices of the things she had propagated. What Nichols had left to the world and what was available to me to photograph was a living archive with its own erasures, mutations, markings of time and change, a collection of things that speak in acquired accents entirely unknown to her.

This portfolio was selected from 247 final views. Another selection was utilized in an exhibition at the Architectural Archives at the University of Pennsylvania that centered on a professional and biographical timeline for Nichols constructed by the research team. The documentary function of the photographs was primary to the project. But for me, that is not their only register. Over time, the things I had photographed had taken on lives of their own, particularly the many corridors, doorways and stairs—freed from the task of illustrating Minerva Parker Nichols's narrative, they could become portals to less orderly histories and reflections on time. An alternate installation that I came to imagine is a projection of the photographs onto the stage of Nichols's New Century Club (1892-93) in Wilmington, now the Delaware Children's Theatre. Each "thing" would be cast as itself: newel post played by newel post, cornice played by cornice, window detail, doorknob, stair riser. Together, what this ensemble would enact for us would be a pivot from the past to the present, a performance in which the most compelling dramatic tension centers on us, here in the present, rather than on a distant and ultimately unknowable past. The act of constructing a history would drive the plot. Performance finished, the cast of things would exit stage left, the curtains would close, ready to draw back at a later date—for yet another staging, another audience, another day.

PORTFOLIO

PLATE 1   John Rugan Neff House, 1886, 10 President Avenue, Rutledge, Pennsylvania   [HABS-PA-6836-2]

PLATE 2 Joshua H. Witham House, 1887, 128 Linden Avenue, Rutledge, Pennsylvania [HABS-PA-6837-1]

PLATE 3 Isaac Ashmead House, 1888, 170 Fernbrook Avenue, Wyncote, Pennsylvania [HABS-PA-6828-5]

PLATE 4 F. Millwood Justice House, 1889–90, 1104 Montgomery Avenue, Narberth, Pennsylvania [HABS-PA-6817-1]

A SUBMISSION TO HABS

PLATE 5   F. Millwood Justice House. Porch detail [HABS-PA-6817-5]

PORTFOLIO

PLATE 6   F. Millwood Justice House. Staircase at entry hall [HABS-PA-6817-8]

A SUBMISSION TO HABS

PLATE 7 F. Millwood Justice House. Fireplaces [HABS-PA-6817-13]

A SUBMISSION TO HABS

PLATE 8 Mary Potts House, 1890, 535 West Hortter Street, Philadelphia, Pennsylvania [HABS-PA-6826-11]

PLATE 9 Mary Potts House. Detail of stair landing [HABS-PA-6826-7]

PORTFOLIO

PLATE 10   Edward Y. Taylor and Harriet Potts Taylor House, 1890, 533 West Hortter Street, Philadelphia, Pennsylvania [HABS-PA-6827-1]

PLATE 11 Edward Y. Taylor and Harriet Potts Taylor House. View of rear elevation [HABS-PA-6827-4]

PLATE 12 Edward Y. Taylor and Harriet Potts Taylor House. Service passage under staircase [HABS-PA-6827-8]

A SUBMISSION TO HABS

PLATE 13 William P. Painter House, 1890, 1016 Main Street, Darby Borough, Pennsylvania [HABS-PA-6821-2]

PORTFOLIO

PLATE 14 Rachel Foster Avery House, Mill-Rae, 1890–91, 13475 Proctor Road, Philadelphia, Pennsylvania [HABS-PA-6818-4]

A SUBMISSION TO HABS

PLATE 15 Rachel Foster Avery House, Mill-Rae. Detail of rear elevation [HABS-PA-6818-8]

PLATE 16   Rachel Foster Avery House, Mill-Rae. Staircase at entry hall   [HABS-PA-6818-16]

PLATE 17   Rachel Foster Avery House, Mill-Rae. Fireplaces [HABS-PA-6818-14]

A SUBMISSION TO HABS

PLATE 18   Rachel Foster Avery House, Mill-Rae. Bedroom [HABS-PA-6818-18]

A SUBMISSION TO HABS

PLATE 19   Francis Jordan Jr. House, 1890–93, 320 Cynwyd Road, Bala Cynwyd, Pennsylvania [HABS-PA-6831-18; PHOTO BY JOHN BARTELSTONE]

A SUBMISSION TO HABS

PLATE 20   Francis Jordan Jr. House. Detail of parlor window   [HABS-PA-6831-7]

PLATE 21 Francis Jordan Jr. House. Staircase at second floor
[HABS-PA-6831-17; PHOTO BY JOHN BARTELSTONE]

A SUBMISSION TO HABS

PLATE 22 Francis Jordan Jr. House. Detail of rear elevation
[HABS-PA-6831-19; PHOTO BY JOHN BARTELSTONE]

PORTFOLIO

PLATE 23 Frank Wallace Munn House, 1890–91, 1014 Oak Lane Avenue,
Philadelphia, Pennsylvania [HABS-PA-6819-3]

PLATE 24 Frank Wallace Munn House. Side elevation [HABS-PA-6819-7]

PLATE 25 Frank Wallace Munn House. Staircase at entry hall [HABS-PA-6819-10]

PORTFOLIO

PLATE 26   Frank Wallace Munn House. Detail of balcony at third floor [HABS-PA-6819-1]

PLATE 27 Frank Wallace Munn House. Detail of third-floor dormer [HABS-PA-6819-11]

PLATE 28 William J. Nicolls House, 1891, 337 East Curtin Street, Bellefonte, Pennsylvania [HABS-PA-6832-3]

PLATE 29 William J. Nicolls House. Detail of main elevation [HABS-PA-6832-2]

PORTFOLIO

PLATE 30   William J. Nicolls House. Entry hall and staircase [HABS-PA-6832-7]

PLATE 31   William J. Nicolls House. Interior detail [HABS-PA-6832-12]

PLATE 32 William J. Nicolls House. Side elevation [HABS-PA-6832-6]

PLATE 33 Twin Houses for Sarah Jane Campbell and Mary A. Campbell, 1891–92, 417–419 West School House Lane, Philadelphia, Pennsylvania [HABS-PA-6820-1]

PLATE 34 Twin Houses for Sarah Jane Campbell and Mary A. Campbell. Side elevation
[HABS-PA-6820-4]

PLATE 35 New Century Club of Wilmington, 1892–93, 1014 Delaware Avenue, Wilmington, Delaware [HABS-DE-352-1]

PORTFOLIO

PLATE 36   New Century Club of Wilmington. South elevation [HABS-DE-352-4]

A SUBMISSION TO HABS

PLATE 37 New Century Club of Wilmington. View of balcony and south wall in auditorium
[HABS-DE-352-15]

PLATE 38 New Century Club of Wilmington. Balcony detail [HABS-DE-352-11]

PLATE 39 New Century Club of Wilmington. View of proscenium and musicians' gallery [HABS-DE-352-17]

PLATE 40   New Century Club of Wilmington. Interior detail of dining room   [HABS-DE-352-26]

PLATE 41 New Century Club of Wilmington. Staircase at second floor [HABS-DE-352-20]

A SUBMISSION TO HABS

PLATE 42   New Century Club of Wilmington. View of third-floor stair hall [HABS-DE-352-25]

A SUBMISSION TO HABS

PLATE 43   House for the Moore Brothers, 1892, 7350 Zimmerman Avenue, Pennsauken, New Jersey [HABS-NJ-1271-1]

PORTFOLIO

PLATE 44 House for the Moore Brothers. Exterior detail [HABS-NJ-1271-4]

PLATE 45   House for the Moore Brothers. Staircase at second floor [HABS-NJ-1271-12]

A SUBMISSION TO HABS

PLATE 46 House for the Moore Brothers. Interior details [HABS-NJ-1271-15]

A SUBMISSION TO HABS

PLATE 47 House for the Moore Brothers. View of dining room [HABS-NJ-1271-9]

PLATE 48 William and Minerva Parker Nichols House, 1907–9, 36 Sharp Hill Road, Wilton, Connecticut [HABS-CT-487-7]

PLATE 49   William and Minerva Parker Nichols House. Closets in second-floor bedroom   [HABS-CT-487-6]

A SUBMISSION TO HABS

PLATE 50 John and Adelaide Baker House, Guard Hill, 1929, 78 Clinton Avenue, Westport, Connecticut [HABS-CT-484-1]

PORTFOLIO

PLATE 51 John and Adelaide Baker House, Guard Hill. Entry hall and staircase [HABS-CT-484-10]

A SUBMISSION TO HABS

PLATE 52   John and Adelaide Baker House, Guard Hill. View of living room [HABS-CT-484-7]

PLATE 53   John and Adelaide Baker House, Guard Hill. View of living room and staircase [HABS-CT-484-6]

PORTFOLIO

PLATE 54   Charles A. and Gertrude R. Lubrecht House, 1936, 73 Clinton Avenue, Westport, Connecticut [HABS-CT-486-1]

PLATE 55   Charles A. and Gertrude R. Lubrecht House. View of entry [HABS-CT-486-4]

PLATE 56   Charles A. and Gertrude R. Lubrecht House. Interior detail [HABS-CT-486-8]

PLATE 57 Charles A. and Gertrude R. Lubrecht House. Stair hall at second floor [HABS-CT-486-6]

CATALOGUE RAISONNÉ

THE ARCHITECTURE OF MINERVA PARKER NICHOLS

William Whitaker

01
Houses for the Rutledge Mutual Land Improvement Association

ca. 1886–1890

William A. Huff Cottage, ca. 1897

Various locations,
Rutledge Borough, Pennsylvania

Still standing, with some structures altered.

Established in 1885, Rutledge is a railroad suburb located ten miles from Philadelphia. It advertised to potential residents a home, "away from the constant din of a city, from its bustle, its distractions, and its evil influences." Businessmen, doctors, journalists, lawyers, mechanics, ministers, and teachers represented the range of professionals who chose to invest in Rutledge—known as the Workingman's Colony—the smallest, self-governing borough in Pennsylvania.

The development of the town was channeled through the Rutledge Mutual Land Improvement Association. Most members of its board resided in the town. Behind the scenes, a circle of backers that included George W. Handcock, a real estate operator, engineer, and surveyor, who was responsible for laying out the town (as he had done at Wayne, Pennsylvania, for investors Drexel & Childs), as well as realtor Lewis T. Brooke (an important supporter of Parker's early career) drew on a stable of architects to attract investment and to spur building. Among the architects working in Rutledge were Albert Ellis Yarnall (later of Yarnall and Goforth) and Edwin W. Thorne—both of whom had their offices at 14 South Broad Street in Philadelphia alongside realtor Brooke. Thorne—Parker's employer—was particularly active in the early development of Rutledge, producing twenty-four plans for the association by February 1888, amounting to half of the total number of structures appearing in J. L. Smith's 1889 survey of the borough.

Parker's involvement in the development of Rutledge is confirmed through her design of 10 President Avenue, built in the summer of 1886 for groceryman John Rugan Neff (1849–1924) and his wife Emma (1854–1920). The house is clearly based on Parker's submission to *Carpentry and Building's* Seventeenth Competition in May 1886 (completed a month before her graduation from the Franklin Institute Drawing School; SEE FIG. 6, P. 34). The fast pace of development in Rutledge provided the young architect with

CATALOGUE RAISONNÉ

John B. Plant Cottage, ca. 1897

an opportunity to demonstrate her abilities in an atmosphere where future supporters (like Brooke) might take notice, providing a strong motivation for her efforts. Thorne's office (which likely consisted of just Thorne and Parker at this time) produced several designs in which Parker probably participated, including: 12 Linden (for James Thompson); 16 Linden (for Robert Witham); 24 Linden (for Daniel Watson); 108 Linden (for Harry Smedley); 128 Linden (for Joshua Witham); 227 President (for Rudolph Pabst); 129 Sylvan (for Charles Roberts); 205 Sylvan (for William Huff); and 4 Rutledge (for John Plant). The house at 21 President (for George Close), while not confirmed as a design by the Thorne office, shares a close resemblance to the 10 President design, and suggests Parker's direct involvement.

REFERENCES

Philadelphia Inquirer, August 13, 1885.
Morton Chronicle (Delaware County, PA), May 27, 1886.
PRERBG 2, no. 13 (April 4, 1887): 148.
PRERBG 2, no. 26 (July 4, 1887): 304.
PRERBG 2, no. 30 (Aug. 1, 1887): 353.
Carpentry & Building (October 1887): plates 37–39.
PRERBG 2, no. 40 (October 10, 1887): 472.
PRERBG 3, no. 3 (January 23, 1888): i.
PRERBG 3, no. 5 (February 6, 1888): 53–54.
[Rutledge Mutual Land Improvement Association], *Rutledge*. ca. 1897. Promotional brochure.
Rutledge Borough research files
HABS No. PA-6833, PA-6834, PA-6835, PA-6836, PA-6837, PA-6838

02 Isaac Ashmead House

1888

Ashmead House, north facade, 2022

Manager of the Old City branch of the Spring Garden National Bank, Isaac Ashmead (1841–1902) served as a cavalry soldier in the Civil War and speculated in real estate ventures, including the Oak Lane Land Company (through which Parker's mother had acquired real estate—SEE CAT. NO. 6). In February 1888 Ashmead commissioned Edwin W. Thorne to design a "stone and shingled house with slate roof." The house was built in Wyncote, a newly developing residential enclave just south of the Reading Railroad's Jenkintown Station. Containing ten rooms, with a porch that wrapped around the front and one side of the house, and a closed porch at the rear, the house was characterized as a "model of convenience, light and cheerful in appearance." The tight, original entrance hall was soon expanded by the addition of a large, two-story bay and fireplace. Parker's signature on a rendering for the project confirms her early involvement in the design [SEE FIG 8, P. 35]. Ashmead's fortunes took a turn for the worse when the Spring Garden National Bank failed. By 1897 the house had been sold, and Ashmead relocated to Connecticut.

Ashmead House, 2022

170 Fernbrook Avenue, Wyncote, Pennsylvania
Still standing.

REFERENCES

PRERBG 3, no. 7 (February 20, 1888): 77.
Builder and Decorator 6, no. 3 (May 1888): supplement.
PRERBG 3, no. 24 (June 18, 1888): 282.
HABS No. PA-6828

03

Max M. Suppes House, The Rocks

1888

This large, two-story frame house—Parker's earliest documented independent work—was situated on a rock outcrop overlooking a bend in the Stonycreek River at Moxham, a neighborhood on the south side of Johnstown. Max M. Suppes (1856–1916), a master mechanic and manager of the Johnson Steel Rail Company mill complex, commissioned the house in anticipation of returning to his native Johnstown. He lived there with his wife Annie (1859–1910) until 1894, when he became general manager of the Lorain Steel Company in Lorain, Ohio. The house, named for the nearby sunlit, stony fringe of the river, was then transferred to his sister, Alice May Suppes (Mrs. John H. Waters), and remained a family residence until 1913.

"The Rocks" on Stonycreek River

Osborne Street (east of Linton Street), Johnstown, Pennsylvania

Demolished.

REFERENCES

PRERBG 3, no. 16 (April 23, 1888): 187.
Memories of Four Score Years: Suppes, Waters, Unger, Wagoner, Jones, 1889-1968. 1968. Privately published booklet. Collection of the Historical Society of Pennsylvania (FA 929.2 S959w 1968).
Photographs: Johnstown Area Historical Association

Suppes House, ca. 1900 (as-cropped in image source)

04 George W. Christy House

1888-89

Christy House, 1890

210 North Essex Avenue, Narberth, Pennsylvania

Still standing but severely altered.

Featured in the December 1890 issue of the *Scientific American, Architects and Builders Edition*, the large house Parker designed for George W. Christy (1852–1910), an Old City liquor dealer and restaurateur, was reported to have cost $18,000. With a plan measuring 43 by 53 ½ feet, the house featured a first story built of stone, with upper floors of wood sheathed in shingles painted in "pearl gray, with bottle green trimmings," and a roof covered in Bangor slate. The vestibule and hall were trimmed with ancient oak and finished with hardwood floors and a paneled wainscoting. The hall featured an elaborate staircase, with carved newel and candelabra. The windows in the upper and lower halls were glazed with stained glass. Parlors were trimmed with cherry, dining room with oak, and the kitchen and pantries with yellow pine, oil-finished, the latter wainscoted and furnished with the latest appliances. Fireplaces included tiled hearths, hardwood mantels, and beveled glass mirrors. Bedrooms were trimmed in cherry, oak, and ash, while bathrooms were floored and wainscoted with white "English" tiling. Christy sought to expand his investments in the area as vice-president of the Elm Land and Improvement Company [SEE CAT. NO. 15]. He sold this house in October 1891, possibly to finance the new venture. By the turn of the century, however, he was living in rented quarters in Philadelphia. Christy's house—far larger than its neighbors—was subdivided into apartments and is now altered beyond recognition.

REFERENCES

PRERBG 3, no. 47 (November 26, 1888): 563.
Philadelphia Inquirer, August 19, 1889.
Philadelphia Record, May 3, 1890.
Scientific American, Architects and Builders Edition 10, no. 6 (December 1890): 90, 96–97.
Photograph: Lower Merion Historical Society

THE ARCHITECTURE OF MINERVA PARKER NICHOLS

Christy House, south and west facades, 1890

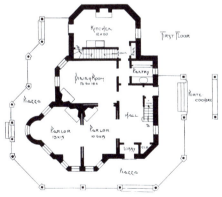
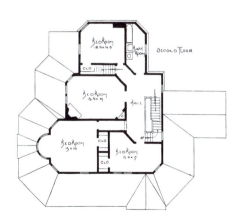

Christy House, plans

05 Frank L. Archambault House

1889

32 North Lansdowne Avenue,
Lansdowne, Pennsylvania

Demolished after 1945.

Frank L. Archambault (1852–1934) was a jeweler with a business located at 200 Market Street in Philadelphia. He commissioned the office of Edwin W. Thorne to design a stone residence in Lansdowne in January 1889. Contracted for $6,000, the house was completed by the fall. Archambault's residency appears to have been brief—an 1892 real estate survey identifies the residents as the Thomas family. The case for Parker having led this commission is based on its strong similarities to her designs for the Painter, Jones, and Munn houses [SEE CAT. NOS. 24, 38, AND 40].

REFERENCES

PRERBG 4, no. 4 (January 30, 1889): 38.
PRERBG 4, no. 14 (April 10, 1889): i.
Home-Maker 7, no. 3 (December 1891): 756–57.
Photograph: Media Historic Archives Commission

06 Amanda M. Maxwell House

1889

Chestnut Avenue, Cheltenham Township, Pennsylvania

Not built.

Possibly regarding her purchase as a real estate investment, Amanda Maxwell (1836–1921), the mother of the architect, bought two lots from the newly established Oak Lane Land Company in August 1889. The company was capitalizing on newly expanded rail routes in the vicinity and on the abundance of open land at the city's northern edge. Design work preceded the land purchase, the architect reporting in May 1889 that she had "completed the drawings for a $4,000 frame and stone house" of two stories with a basement. Work was anticipated to begin in the fall but Maxwell never built, and the lots were sold in 1907.

REFERENCES

PRERBG 4, no. 20 (May 22, 1889): 243

Archambault House (with turret), c. 1895

07
Lewis T. Brooke House

1889-91

Biddulph Road,
Radnor, Pennsylvania

Altered in 1893; demolished by 1961.

Lewis Trimble Brooke (1836–1892) was a real estate speculator with a specialization in developing former agricultural land and farms into residential estates—possibly beginning with his father's lands in Radnor. He maintained an office at 14 South Broad Street, in the same building where Parker worked and where she eventually opened an independent office (by which time Brooke had moved his office to 18 South Broad). His early patronage seems to have been an important catalyst for launching Parker's career but it is unclear whether construction of the Radnor house was completed under her direction. The description of her plans for the house noted: "a large reception hall, with oak rafters and paneled with the same wood, a stone fireplace of unique design [that] adds beauty to this hall, from which open an office, parlor, dining room and library."

By May 1891 Brooke was bankrupt, and his assets were sold off by sheriff's sale. The sale records describe a piece of land upon which, "there is being erected a three story stone dwelling." By October 1892, when the nearly five-acre property was purchased by Martin Luther Kohler (for $15,000), the transaction included a "stone messuage or tenement thereon erected" (Delaware County Sheriff's Sale Records, Book E, p. 296–97 and Deed Book D08, p. 396). The following month, Kohler commissioned architects Hazelhurst and Huckle to prepare plans for the property, including a substantial stable built of local stone with a shingle roof. While published notices suggest that this was to be all new construction, a period photograph of Kohler's estate suggests that it was instead an alteration to an existing structure. Notable differences between the front volume (assumed to be Parker's design) and the rear volume (assumed to be the work of Hazelhurst and Huckel) include the detailing of the window headers (cut limestone as opposed to flat jack arches), the selection of roofing tiles (Bangor slate versus Ludowici

Brooke House after 1892-93 alterations

Celadon-type tiles), the stone used in the stepped gable and the prominence of the mortar joints (suggesting an alteration to the roof gable at that location), and the shaping of the water tables at the third level (squared in the front and shaped at the rear). All suggest a later building campaign, offering evidence of a composition brought about by the intervention of new ownership and different agendas.

Brooke died in November 1892, in Philadelphia, at the Center City home of his second wife, Emma Williams Brooke (ca. 1844–1925), a physician trained at the Women's Medical College of Philadelphia and a longtime member of the New Century Club of Philadelphia.

REFERENCES

PRERBG 4, no. 18 (May 8, 1889): 210.
Philadelphia Record, February 22, 1890.
AABN 27, no. 739 (February 22, 1890): xvii.
Philadelphia Record, March 21, 1890.
PRERBG 5, no. 12 (March 26, 1890): i.
PRERBG 7, no. 45 (November 9, 1892): 1585.
Samuel Fitch Hotchkin, *Rural Pennsylvania in the Vicinity of Philadelphia* (Philadelphia, PA: G.W. Jacobs & Co., 1897), 225-229, 243.
Photograph: Radnor Historical Society

08
William R. Wright House

1889

As a salesman for masonry building supplies, William R. Wright (1855–1920) likely became aware of Parker through professional circles. In December 1888 he purchased a corner lot on a rise overlooking the commercial district of Narberth. A few months later, his elder sister, Sarah, purchased the adjacent lot [SEE CAT. NO. 9]. They commissioned Parker to design their houses the following May. Parker sited Wright's two-story frame house close to their shared property line to provide ample room for a side garden along Haverford Road—with vistas to south Narberth. This garden was accented by a bay window topped with a conical roof. The house was sold in 1920, just days before Wright's death. Later, the interiors were subdivided into apartments.

Wright House, 2022

102 Grayling Avenue, Narberth, Pennsylvania

Still standing.

REFERENCES

PRERBG 4, no. 18 (May 8, 1889): 210.
Photographs: Lower Merion Historical Society
HABS No. PA-6824

09
Sarah E.W. Bewley House

1889

Bewley House, 2023

104 Grayling Avenue,
Narberth, Pennsylvania

Still standing.

Sarah Elizabeth Wright Bewley (1850–1918), elder sister of William Wright, was a longtime purchasing agent specializing in home furnishings and "varieties." As someone with her own sources of income, she may have seen the house as an investment—owning it until 1913 while continuing to be listed in the Philadelphia city directories. Bewley's lot was about half the size of her brother's [SEE CAT. NO. 8]. While the two houses are nearly identical in plan, Parker varied their roof lines, the gabled ends of the Wright house contrasting with the jerkinhead roofs over the main facade and dormers of the Bewley house. An early black-and-white photograph of the house reveals strong horizontal bands of shingles in a contrasting dark tone between the first and second floors, as well as in the third-floor gable ends.

REFERENCES

PRERBG 4, no.18 (May 8, 1889): 210.
Photographs: Lower Merion Historical Society
HABS No. PA-6825

10
F. Millwood Justice House

1889–90

Justice House, 2019

Justice House, detail of porch, 2022

1104 Montgomery Avenue, Narberth, Pennsylvania

Still standing.

Longtime Narberth resident F. Millwood Justice (1864–1935) married into a line of early American silversmiths that descended from Philip Syng (member of Benjamin Franklin's Junto). Justice was co-owner of A. R. Justice & Co., an importer and exporter of plated ware and cutlery located at 14 North Fifth Street, Philadelphia. In July 1889 Justice commissioned Parker to design a substantial frame and stone house measuring 36 by 42 feet. A large porch with fine detail led to a spacious hall. Rooms on the ground floor included a parlor, a library, and a dining room, along with the kitchen and pantry. Ample bedrooms—with communicating doors between the parents' room and some children's rooms—occupy the second and third floors. The house remained a family residence until the late 1960s and is among the most intact and distinguished surviving examples of the architect's work.

REFERENCES

PRERBG 4, no. 27 (July 10, 1889): 320.
HABS No. PA-6817

THE ARCHITECTURE OF MINERVA PARKER NICHOLS

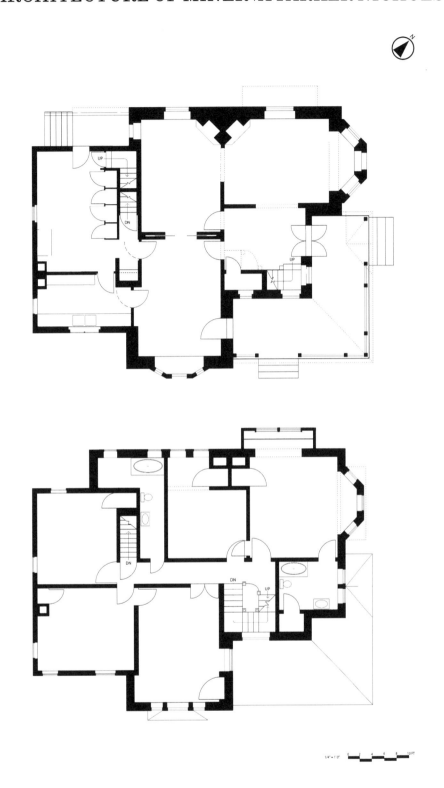

Justice House, first and second-floor plans (Gabriel Albino, Jhon Velazco, and Changfeng Luo, delineators, 2023)

CATALOGUE RAISONNÉ

Justice House, entrance hall from parlor, 2019

11

Projects for the Parksley Land and Improvement Company

ca. 1889–92

Parksley, Virginia
Probably not built.

In an early effort to invest in her daughter's future as an architect, Amanda M. Maxwell purchased one hundred thirty shares in the Parksley Land and Improvement Company, in February 1885. The company was established to develop the town of Parksley, Virginia, a station on the New York, Philadelphia and Norfolk Railroad. The line had been founded in 1884 to develop the agricultural potential of the fertile land and rich seafood resources of the Delmarva Peninsula.

Maxwell was among the company's founding shareholders (a street in Parksley is named after her), and her board colleagues were all northerners: Henry R. Bennett and his brother-in-law Samuel T. Jones from Dover, Delaware (the former's shares were in the name of his mother, Catherine); William C. Wilson of Philadelphia (a descendant of Betsy Ross); and the "leading spirit" of the organization, Elizabeth Stanton Chadbourne, an elocutionist, from Savin Hill, Boston. Maxwell's share of the company, like those of her colleagues, was valued at $13,000. How this group of investors initially met remains unknown.

By April 1889, news reports of a building boom were circulating, with fifty new houses to be built that spring, along with a hotel building estimated to cost $20,000, the latter from designs by "Miss Minerva Parker." The three-story structure was to contain fifty rooms, with amenities that included an elevator, steam heat, and open fireplaces in every room. The following year, it was reported that Parker had "made plans for a brick and shingle house, two-and-a-half stories high, for Henry R. Bennett... to have hard-wood finish, wood mantels, open fire-place, and all modern improvements." She also provided plans to the Parksley Land and Improvement Company for two-, four-, and six-roomed frame houses in several variations.

The actual extent of Parker's built work in Parksley remains frustratingly elusive. While it is certain that the hotel design was not realized (another speculator had opened a facility soon

Plan of Parksley, Virginia, c. 1888

after the railroad began service), it is unclear if any individual houses were, in fact, built (one possibility is the Pate House, CAT. NO. 29). Perhaps the house designs were commissioned in anticipation of a building boom that never came. It seems that the anticipated influx of northerner investors seeking winter retreats never materialized. Deed research has shown that the bulk of the existing houses in town were constructed after 1898, and most intensively during the period 1902–12.

REFERENCES

Baltimore Sun, January 28, 1889.
Norfolk Virginian, January 29, 1889.
Washington Post, January 29, 1889.
Richmond Dispatch (VA), February 26, 1889.
Norfolk Virginian, March 10, 1889.
Norfolk Virginian, April 17, 1889.
PRERBG 4, no. 33 (August 21, 1889): 391.
Baltimore Sun, April 29, 1890.
PRERBG 5, no. 26 (July 2, 1890): 385.
Philadelphia Record, July 4, 1890.
Parksley Land and Improvement Company Records: Eastern Shore of Virginia Heritage Center

12 Edward J. Davis House

1889

Little is known about the owner of this modest house and stable, except that he purchased the property in April 1889 and soon afterward contracted with builder E. S. Sentman to erect the house. Shorn of its front porch, the house is now significantly altered.

Davis House, 2022

104 Dudley Avenue, Narberth, Pennsylvania

Still standing but altered.

REFERENCES

PRERBG 4, no. 29 (July 24, 1889): 343.
PRERBG 5, no. 12 (March 26, 1890): i.
HABS No. PA-6829

13 James A. Patterson House

1889–90

6100 West Columbia Avenue, Philadelphia, Pennsylvania
Demolished in 1927.

James Addison Patterson (1856–1935) was a real estate investor associated with the Overbrook Land and Improvement Company, a source for several of Parker's early commissions [SEE CAT. NOS. 39 AND 40]. A native of Charlottesville, Virginia, and a graduate of the United States Military Academy at West Point, Patterson had offices on the ground floor of 14 South Broad Street; Parker's office was on the third floor.

The house, built of local stone, was described by Parker as being, "so plain that it depends entirely upon the outline of the building and the beauty of the landscape for its attractiveness." Front doors of oak and beveled glass gave onto a vestibule wainscoted in oak with a built-in seat for storing overshoes. Rafters in the vestibule and hall were evenly spaced, while floors in the hall were of narrow oak boards; wainscoting matched that of the vestibule. The leaded glass windows featured a "border of delicate rainbow colors," answering, as Parker suggested, "all the necessary purposes of decoration, light and color." The plaster above the wainscoting was sand finished and painted a dull blue-gray to match the long tiles in the hearth and mantel under the stairs.

The library—set off from the hall and with a rear entrance—was designed for possible use as a home office. It was finished in walnut, with a broad, open fireplace faced in light copper-colored tile. The gaslight fixtures had a copper finish, while the central light globe was a dull yellow as were the walls, which had a frieze in shades of brown and copper. Parker expressed her preference for bookcases that were low and open, "so that a book may be taken possession of without any preliminary unlocking of doors." The parlor was finished in white and gold with light amber tile used on the hearth, while the dining room was trimmed in oak with an antique finish with a broad window seat in the bay. The four bedrooms were finished in, "old rose, pale blue, Nile green, and a primrose yellow; the wood-work painted to match, the colors all very delicate in tone."

THE ARCHITECTURE OF MINERVA PARKER NICHOLS

Patterson House, 1902

Patterson House, plan

A stable designed by Parker was built in 1890. Patterson sold the house in March 1892. The large property, which was surrounded by rowhouses by 1927, was demolished to make way for a church.

REFERENCES

Philadelphia Inquirer, May 23, 1889.
PRERBG 4, no. 35 (September 4, 1889): 416.
PRERBG 5, no. 7 (February 19, 1890): 83.
PRERBG 5, no. 12 (March 26, 1890): i.
Northwestern Architect 11, no. 4 (April 1891): plate.
Home-Maker 6, no.1 (April 1891): 63–66.
PRERBG 7, no. 12 (March 23, 1892): 1048.
Photographs: Philadelphia City Archives; AAUP

CATALOGUE RAISONNÉ

Patterson House, entry hall from *Northwestern Architect*, c. 1890

14
J. Frank Beale House

1889

James Frank Beale (1843–1921) was a druggist in Philadelphia with a partnership at Fifth and Market Streets operating under the name Dotts, Beale & Lambert. He and his wife, Anne (1847–1923), lived in the Spring Garden section of the city, not far from Parker's home, and may have known her through their social circles. The two-and-a-half-story frame house, built in Berwyn—then a sleepy stop on Philadelphia's Main Line—originally measured 30 by 32 feet and featured a substantial porch on three sides, as well as an entrance hall with a corner fireplace and carved wooden mantel. The Beales resided there until 1903.

Beale House, 2022

746 Conestoga Road, Berwyn, Pennsylvania
Still standing.

REFERENCES
PRERBG 4, no. 42 (October 23, 1889): 499.
HABS No. PA-6830

15

Houses for the Elm Land and Improvement Company

ca. 1890–93

Elm Land and Improvement Co. House, 2022

232 North Essex Street, Narberth, Pennsylvania

Still standing.

With his house at 210 North Essex Street completed in the summer of 1889 [CAT. NO. 4], it appears that George W. Christy commissioned Parker to prepare plans for a second stone and frame house, featuring interiors of "cherry and quartered oak, with considerable tile work, and a number of handsome stained glass windows." At the time, Christy was an investor with the newly established Elm Land and Improvement Company, and the board favored a higher level of housing density in the neighborhood being developed on their fourteen-acre tract.

If Parker's second design for Christy was built, it can be plausibly identified as the house at 232 North Essex Street, since it strongly resembles several of her contemporaneous designs in its details. In particular, its jaunty front door, closely relates to the front doors of her houses for William R. Wright and Frank Wallace Munn [CAT. NOS. 8 AND 38] and there is, as well, a volumetric resemblance between it and the Pate House in Parksley, Virginia [CAT. NO. 29]. The house at 232 North Essex Street was built sometime between January 1891 and August 1893. It was purchased by James Cooper Simpson (son of J. Alexander Simpson—an investor with Christy in Elm) and served as the Simpson family's residence until 1937.

REFERENCES

Philadelphia Record, February 11, 1890.
PRERBG 5, no. 6 (February 12, 1890): 67.
AABN 27, no. 739 (February 22, 1890): xvii.
PRERBG 5, no. 12 (March 26, 1890): i.
PRERBG 5, no. 20 (August 20, 1890): 498.
HABS No. PA-6823

16

John M. Kennedy House

1889

Unidentified location,
Narberth, Pennsylvania

Probably built.

References to Parker designing a house for John M. Kennedy suggest that it was built in Narberth—although there is some ambiguity on that point. Kennedy's name is not found among the Montgomery County deed records describing properties in the borough, although a developer by that name, operating in the Philadelphia region, may have been Parker's client.

REFERENCES
PRERBG 5, no. 12 (March 26, 1890): i.
Woman's Progress 1, no. 2 (May 1893): 58.

17

Eliza C. Hartel House and Store

1889-90

1–3 North Lansdowne Avenue,
Lansdowne, Pennsylvania

Demolished after 1955.

From 1891 to 1947, Eliza C. Hartel (1861–1947) lived in the three-story, granite stone house that Parker designed for her. Located at a prominent intersection just north of the Lansdowne station, the south side of the building included a grocery store that Hartel operated for several decades. The family dwelling was in the north-facing part of the structure and featured a large bay surmounted by a turret; there was likely a balcony on the third floor, overlooking a garden. Decidedly residential in character into the 1920s, the building was extended to the property lines and new wood-framed store facades were installed with a large, covered balcony above, echoing the original structure's Queen Anne details.

REFERENCES
PRERBG 4, no. 42 (October 23, 1889): 499.
Philadelphia Record, February 11, 1890.
PRERBG 5, no. 6 (February 12, 1890): 67.
AABN 27, no. 739 (February 22, 1890): xvii.
Photographs: Media Historic Archives Commission

CATALOGUE RAISONNÉ

North Lansdowne Avenue at Baltimore Pike. Hartel Store and house visible at upper left corner, 1955

18

Elizabeth E. Gallagher House

1890

The daughter of Irish immigrants, Elizabeth E. Gallagher (ca. 1855–1943) appears to have built a successful life for herself from humble beginnings. She came to own several commercial buildings in Philadelphia, including 1619 Chestnut Street, where she operated a millinery business for over twenty years. At the time of her death, her estate was valued at more than $100,000.

Gallagher commissioned Parker to design a house at Moore's Station (now Prospect Park) two years after acquiring the large property. Gallagher ultimately subdivided her parcel into at least five building lots and maintained ownership of them into the late 1910s. She erected the brick and frame house at the corner of Tenth and Lafayette Avenues; its footprint is known through a 1919 Sanborn map. The plan so closely resembles a design that Parker published in May 1892 as "built near Philadelphia" that one may assume she was describing Gallagher's house.

The published plan featured a central hall opening to a parlor with a substantial circular bay. This room featured a built-in seat under the window; beyond the parlor was a library with a corner fireplace. The dining room gave easy access to a substantial porch. Parker indicated that this could be enclosed during colder months as a conservatory.

Lafayette and Tenth Avenues, Prospect Park, Pennsylvania

Demolished before 1970.

REFERENCES

Philadelphia Record, March 15, 1890.
PRERBG 5, no. 11 (March 19, 1890): 146.
PRERBG 5, no. 12 (March 26, 1890): i.
Home-Maker 8, no. 2 (May 1892): 133–34.

CATALOGUE RAISONNÉ

Gallagher House, perspective from the *Home-Maker*, May 1892

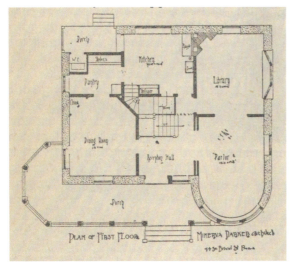

Gallagher House, plan

REFERENCES

Philadelphia Record, March 15, 1890.
PRERBG 5, no. 11 (March 19, 1890): 146.
PRERBG 5, no. 12 (March 26, 1890): i.
Home-Maker 8, no. 2 (May 1892): 133–34.

19 Edward Y. Taylor and Harriet Potts Taylor House

1890

Harriet Potts Taylor (1842–1935), a "steadfast member of the Unitarian church," was the second child of Thomas I. Potts and Mary F. Potts. In 1883, after the death of her first husband, she married a real estate broker, Edward Yard Taylor (ca. 1845–1907), and continued to raise two teenaged children from her first marriage.

Although Harriett Taylor could have come into contact with Parker through shared Unitarian connections, Taylor's husband could have been the link between them. His offices (Taylor & Miles) were located at 1305 Arch Street, where Parker's former employer, Edwin W. Thorne, had moved his offices in August 1889. Thorne is known to have played a role in the design and construction of this house and the one built for Taylor's sister, Mary Potts [CAT. NO. 20]—perhaps as a joint venture with Parker at a time when she was inundated with new work.

The Taylor house—like the one built for Mary Potts—was built of stone with half-timbering in its gable ends. A curved bay on the south side of the house is capped by a conical roof with a balcony on the third floor, marking the location of a children's playroom. Compact and efficient in plan, the house was organized around an entrance hall, with a service passageway connecting the hall to the kitchen. With their southern exposure, the parlor and dining room enjoyed ample sunlight. Three bedrooms, a bath, and a sewing room, plus balcony (enclosed in 1922 for use as a bathroom) were on the second floor.

In 1898 Taylor appears to have become estranged from her husband and moved to Redlands, California, where she spent the rest of her life with her daughter, Anna Kingsbury, and Anna's family.

533 West Hortter Street, Philadelphia, Pennsylvania
Still standing.

CATALOGUE RAISONNÉ

Taylor House, first- and second-floor plans
(Gabriel Albino and Jhon Velazco, delineators, 2023)

Taylor House, ca. 1890

REFERENCES

PRERBG 5, no. 12 (March 26, 1890): 162.
PRERBG 5, no. 16 (April 23, 1890): i.
Builder, Decorator and Wood-Worker 14, no. 3 (May 1890): 3.
Woman's Progress 1, no. 2 (May 1893): 58.
Frank Leslie's Popular Monthly 50, no. 2 (June 1900): 199–200.
PRERBG 37, no. 8 (February 22, 1922): 121.
San Bernadino County Sun, March 23, 1935.
Photograph: AAUP
HABS No. PA-6827

20
Mary Potts House

1890

Potts House, 2022

535 West Hortter Street, Philadelphia, Pennsylvania

Still standing but altered.

Mary Potts (1857–1927) a longtime member of the New Century Club of Philadelphia, was the youngest daughter of Thomas I. Potts, owner of a successful iron foundry in the city with an estate valued at over $100,000 in 1860, and his wife, Mary F. Potts (1819–1900). After the death of Thomas in 1865, their son, Horace T. Potts, took over the foundry. Daughter Mary appears to have continued living with her widowed mother, and a cousin, Virginia K. Maitland. The house was commissioned from Parker by Mary Potts, and it became the residence of her mother, Mary F. Potts, for the last decade of her life. Funds for this house and the Taylor house next door [CAT. NO. 19] may have been generated by Mary F. Potts's sale of the family house on Arch Street for $20,500. Mary Potts and her cousin lived together for many years, traveling to Europe together in 1910. When Mary died, she left the bulk of her estate to Maitland.

It is likely that Potts met Parker through their associations with the Unitarian Church—the Potts family had strong ties to the First Unitarian Church in Philadelphia. Parker's design was for a three-story stone house, with half-timbered gable ends, in a Queen Anne style. The distinctive entrance, through a compact turret, led to the stair hall and parlor. Three bedrooms and baths were on the second floor; a further two bedrooms and a playroom were on the third. In 1915 Potts commissioned Horace Wells Sellers to design alterations to the house, including a volume that replaced the turreted entrance and porch, and an extension to the rear. Potts sold the property in 1924.

REFERENCES

PRERBG 5, no. 15 (April 16, 1890): 209.
PRERBG 5, no. 16 (April 23, 1890): i.
Builder, Decorator and Wood-Worker 14, no. 3 (May 1890): 3.
Woman's Progress 1, no. 2 (May 1893): 58.
Times (Philadelphia), September 7, 1895: 6.
Frank Leslie's Popular Monthly 50, no. 2 (June 1900): 199–200.
PRERBG 30, no. 28 (July 14, 1915): 440.
Photograph: AAUP
HABS No. PA-6826

THE ARCHITECTURE OF MINERVA PARKER NICHOLS

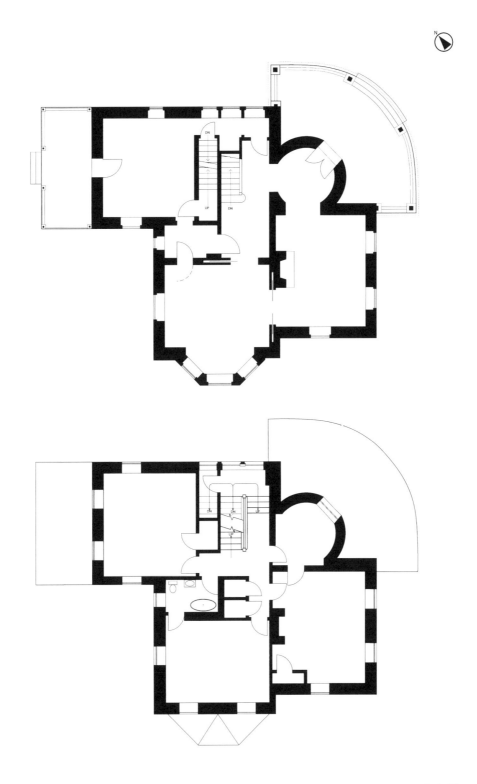

Potts House, first- and second-floor plans (Gabriel Albino, Jhon Velazco, and Chengfeng Luo, 2023)

21
Buildings for the Pennsylvania Central Railroad

1890

Initial notice of this design comes from a biographical profile of the architect that originated in a Philadelphia newspaper that was syndicated across the United States (from Boston to tiny Williamsport in the northern part of the Dakota Territory). The article in the *Philadelphia Record* of February 17, 1890, begins: "In a very tiny room on the third floor Miss Parker was found drafting the floor plan of a large building for a railroad company," and goes on to note that she was also working on the design of "a railroad bridge."

While the article makes no mention of a specific client or location, three months later her former employer, Edwin Thorne, noted that he was preparing plans for, "a three-story fire-proof [building with] . . . an engine house attached," for the Pennsylvania Central Railroad (PCRR), established in 1889 to connect Bellefonte with Mill Hall via the Nittany Valley. The same publication referred to his collaboration with Parker in realizing the designs of the Taylor and Potts houses [CAT. NOS. 19 AND 20]. It is conceivable that his work for the PCRR could have been a collaborative effort with her too. The railroad's engine house was located north of Bellefonte, near the Spring Creek; the bridge location is unknown.

Possibly near Bellefonte, Centre County, Pennsylvania
Demolished.

REFERENCES

"A Lady Architect." *Philadelphia Record*, February 17, 1890.
Builder, Decorator and Wood-Worker 14, no. 3 (May 1890): 3.

22 Sketch for a Cottage

1890

Location unknown.
Undetermined.

According to the June 20, 1890, issue of *California Architect and Building News*, "a preliminary sketch for a cottage designed by Miss Parker appear[ed] in the May number of the *Journal of Building*." The *Journal*, a semi-monthly magazine with offices at Pittsburgh's Builders' Exchange, was established in 1889. By 1897 it had thirty-four hundred subscribers but it disappeared shortly thereafter. Volumes of the magazine remain elusive.

REFERENCES

Journal of Building (Pittsburgh) 1 (May 1890).
California Architect and Building News 11, no. 6 (June 20, 1890): 66.

23 Elizabeth Newport House

1890

South Eighteenth Avenue, Longport, New Jersey
Demolished.

This modest two-and-a-half story frame cottage was designed for Elizabeth Newport (1829–1897). It measured 30 by 36 feet and included a wraparound porch, modern conveniences, and hot air heating. Little is known about Newport or her connections to Parker.

REFERENCES

PRERBG 5, no. 21 (May 28, 1890): 306.
Philadelphia Record, May 29, 1890.

24 William P. Painter House

1890

Physician William Pierce Painter (1842–1919) graduated from the Jefferson Medical College in 1875. He practiced in Delaware County, Pennsylvania, and in California and Arizona, serving two years at Fort Yuma as the post surgeon. He married Margaret Middleton (1845–1900) in 1886 and four years later commissioned Parker to design their house. Dr. Painter and his wife resided in the house until their deaths in 1900 and 1919.

Parker used the commission to explore a plan type she used elsewhere, including for the Archambault, Jones, and Munn houses [SEE CAT. NOS. 4, 38, AND 40].

Painter House, 2022

1016 Main Street, Darby Borough, Pennsylvania
Still standing.

REFERENCES
PRERBG 5, no. 16 (April 23,1890): i.
Home-Maker 7, no. 3 (December 1891): 756–57.
HABS No. PA-6821

25

Row Houses for James H. Carter

1890–91

James H. Carter was a real estate speculator and builder with business ties to John M. Kennedy, a fellow speculator for whom Parker had designed a house in 1889 [CAT. NO. 16].

Parker prepared plans for a development that consisted of fourteen three-story houses, each with a frontage of sixteen feet, to be located on the south side of Market Street, east of Forty-Ninth Street. A further sixteen houses planned for the north side of Ludlow Street, were to be two stories with a fourteen-foot frontage. All lots were reported to be approximately one hundred feet deep, with each house "set back from the street enough to provide for large porches and lawns in the front." Houses would be built of brick with brownstone trimmings, stained glass, and hot air heating. Although surveyors were on site to lay out the property in March 1891, the project was abandoned. By 1893 Carter's name had disappeared from Philadelphia directories.

It is worth noting that Carter broke ground on a row of sixteen houses on the north side of Walnut Street, west of Fifty-Second Street, in April 1890, shortly before the first news accounts of the Market Street development appeared. Whether Parker had any role in the design of the Walnut Street houses remains unclear, but they closely match the description of those planned for Ludlow Street: two stories, fourteen-foot frontages, with large porches and lawns in front of the houses.

Market, South Forty-Ninth, and Ludlow Streets, Philadelphia, Pennsylvania

Not built.

REFERENCES

Philadelphia Inquirer, April 26, 1890.
PRERBG 5, no. 21 (May 28, 1890): 306.
Philadelphia Record, May 29, 1890.
Philadelphia Record, June 27, 1890.
Evening Star (Washington, D.C.), February 28, 1891.
Philadelphia Inquirer, March 20, 1891.
Philadelphia Record, March 27, 1891.
Philadelphia Record, April 8, 1891.
Philadelphia Inquirer, April 28, 1891.

26 George Beerman House

1890

Location unknown.
Undetermined.

This project is known only from a news account that noted Parker had plans on the boards for "a suburban house for George Beerman, the site for which has not been decided upon yet." Nothing is known about the client or if the project proceeded beyond preliminaries.

REFERENCES
Philadelphia Record, May 29, 1890.

27 F. B. Crooke House

1890

Location unknown.
Undetermined.

F. B. Crooke hired Parker in the spring of 1890 to design, "a handsome dwelling" that he intended to build during the summer. The house was described as a two-story, brick structure with stone trimmings and slate roof, measuring 20 by 55 feet in plan.

REFERENCES
PRERBG 5, no. 24 (June 18, 1890): 354.
Philadelphia Record, June 20, 1890.

28
C. F. Johnson House

1890–91

Near Beaumont, Texas.
Undetermined.

The client's identity remains elusive. No transfers with this name have been identified in the Jefferson County, Texas, deed records. To date, the possibilities that Charles F. Johnson was the son of Parker's client Maria Nye Johnson [SEE CAT. NO. 57], or that he was a cousin of Miss Mary Potts [SEE CAT. NO. 20], whose mother was a Johnson, have been pursued; neither line of inquiry has produced results. The structure was characterized as a bungalow and may have been intended to serve as a winter retreat along the Gulf Coast.

REFERENCES

PRERBG 5, no. 24 (June 18, 1890): 354.
Philadelphia Record, June 20, 1890.

29
Edward C. Pate House

1890–92

24000 block of Bennett Street, Parksley, Virginia
Demolished.

The extent of Parker's work in Parksley, Virginia, has been difficult to establish. The attribution to Parker of one built work there, the Edward C. Pate House, is based on similarities in its appearance to her designs for the Elm Land and Improvement Company [CAT. NO. 15]. Pate (1861–ca. 1911) a successful merchant in Parksley, purchased two lots on Bennett Street around the time Parker is known to have been preparing designs for the Parksley Land and Improvement Company. Construction was anticipated to begin in the spring of 1891 but was delayed until the following year. The house remained in the family's ownership into the 1950s.

REFERENCES

Peninsula Enterprise (Accomac, VA), November 29, 1890.
Peninsula Enterprise (Accomac, VA), January 3, 1891.
Peninsula Enterprise (Accomac, VA), April 2, 1892.
Peninsula Enterprise (Accomac, VA), August 13, 1892.
Photographs: Town of Parksley, Virginia

CATALOGUE RAISONNÉ

North side of Bennett Street in Parksley, Virginia showing the Pate House, ca. 1920

30 Macaroni Factory for Emmanuel Guano and Antonio Raggio

1890-92

This macaroni factory, a brick structure trimmed with stone, owned by brothers-in-law Emmanuel Guano (1852–1926) and Antonio Raggio (1851–1933), stood at the southwest corner of South Seventh and Montrose Streets, two blocks from Philadelphia's Italian Market. Built in two phases, the factory consisted of a five-story building (built in 1890) and a four-story structure measuring 48 by 70 feet (completed in 1892).

South Seventh and Montrose Streets, Philadelphia, Pennsylvania

Demolished before 1917.

REFERENCES

Philadelphia Inquirer, July 14, 1890.
PRERBG 5, no. 28 (July 16, 1890): 418.
Philadelphia Record, July 18, 1890.
PRERBG 5, no. 30 (July 30, 1890): 450.
PRERBG 5, no. 35 (September 3, 1890): 530.
PRERBG 6, no. 37 (September 16, 1891): 591.
PRERBG 7, no. 22 (June 1, 1892): i.
Philadelphia Record, June 4, 1892.
Philadelphia Record, June 16, 1892.
Richard N. Juliani, *Building Little Italy: Philadelphia's Italians Before Mass Migration* (University Park, PA: Pennsylvania State University Press, 1998), 261–63.

31
Sarah A. Stewart House

1890

An important force in establishing public kindergartens in the Philadelphia school system, Sarah A. Stewart (1839–1925), founded the International Kindergarten Union in 1893 and remained a proponent of the pedagogical methods of Friedrich Fröbel throughout her long career. She was recruited to Philadelphia in the fall of 1886 to establish a laboratory school for kindergarten teachers.

Stewart, who likely came to know about Parker through her membership in the New Century Club of Philadelphia, commissioned the architect to design a cottage on the New Jersey shore at Avon-by-the-Sea. The two-story frame construction featured wood mantels, as well as stained glass and a generous porch. Stewart took up full-time residence at the house in 1895 and remained there for the next twenty-five years.

107 Norwood Avenue,
Avon-by-the-Sea, New Jersey

Still standing.

REFERENCES

PRERBG 5, no. 34 (August 27, 1890): 514.
Philadelphia Record, August 29, 1890.
HABS No. NJ-1269

THE ARCHITECTURE OF MINERVA PARKER NICHOLS

Stewart House, 2022

32 Presbyterian Church at Oak Lane

ca. 1889

Parker produced this preliminary sketch for a competition to design a Presbyterian church in the vicinity of the Oak Lane station, sometime between 1889 and December 1891. The proposal was for a stone building of modest size with a dedicated space for a Sunday school off the main vestibule. This space could be opened to the sanctuary by means of a sliding partition.

Philadelphia, Pennsylvania

Probably not built.

REFERENCES

Drawing: Adelaide Nichols Baker Papers, Schlesinger Library, Harvard Radcliffe Institute

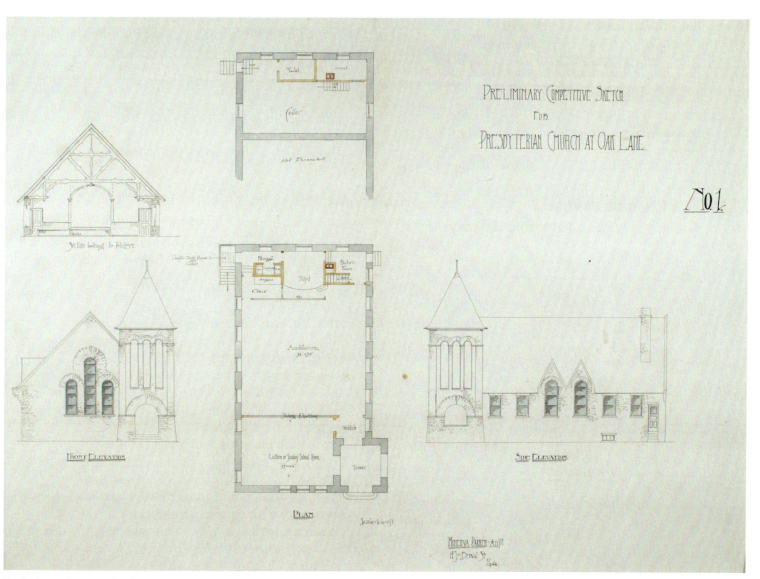

Preliminary Competitive Sketch for Presbyterian Church at Oak Lane, ca. 1889 (Minerva Parker, delineator)

33 Minerva Parker House

1890

Chestnut Avenue,
Cheltenham Township, Pennsylvania
Not built.

Designed for Parker's own use, to be built on property owned by her mother, Amanda Maxwell, who had considered building on it herself [SEE CAT. NO. 9], the house was characterized as being "stone and pebbled ash [sic], two story." Its interiors were to be finished with "hard wood . . . and all accommodations modern." Parker did not pursue the project.

REFERENCES
PRERBG 5, no. 36 (September 10, 1890): 545.
Philadelphia Record, September 12, 1890.

34 Mrs. Baugh House

1890

Lansdowne, Pennsylvania
Probably not built.

While it appears that this project remained unbuilt (there are no deed transfers associated with the Baugh surname at the time), the commission may have been associated with the family of industrialist Daniel Baugh (1839–1921), whose wife, Anna Wills Baugh (1839–1922), or his mother, Hannah Krauser Baugh (1803–1896), may have been pursuing an interest in building as a speculative investment. As president of the Philadelphia School of Design for Women, Daniel Baugh was in close contact with Emily Sartain, its principal during his tenure (1900–1901). Parker, who maintained close ties to Sartain and taught at the school from 1891 to 1895, lived a few blocks away from the Baughs, whose address was 1906 Spring Garden Street.

REFERENCES
PRERBG 5, no. 41 (October 15, 1890): 626.
Philadelphia Inquirer, October 18, 1890.
Philadelphia Record, November 3, 1890.

35
Rachel Foster Avery House, Mill-Rae

1890–91

Avery House, 2021

Avery House, east facade, ca. 1915

13475 Proctor Road,
Philadelphia, Pennsylvania

Still standing.

At the end of October 1891, the *Philadelphia Times* reported that Parker was completing plans for a "very handsome suburban dwelling at Somerton, to be built for Mrs. Rachel Foster Avery, secretary of the National Suffrage Association. The dwelling, which will be the home of Mrs. Avery, is to be three stories high, of stone throughout, embodying the colonial style of architecture. In dimensions it will be of an unusual shape, having a front of 70 feet and a depth of but 40 feet. Large open promenade porches will surround the house and will be made a distinctly ornamental feature of the dwelling. The large antique entrance door, of old English design, will open into a wide colonial hall, this in turn connecting with a large reception hall, with open fireplace and many other artistic features. Especially indicative of the owner's philanthropic ideas is a fully-equipped kindergarten school in the lower portion of the dwelling, which, in addition to use by the youthful Averys, will confer its advantages upon the children of the surrounding neighborhood."

CATALOGUE RAISONNÉ

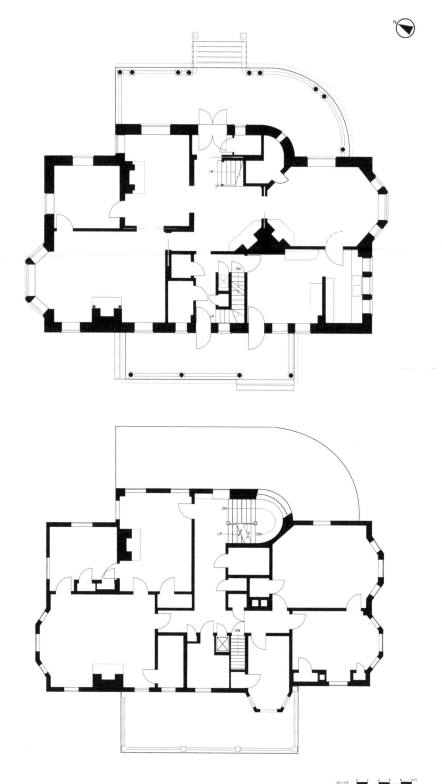

Avery House, first- and second-floor plans (Gabriel Albino and Jhon Velazco, 2023)

THE ARCHITECTURE OF MINERVA PARKER NICHOLS

Avery House, detail of porch, 2021

Avery House, stair, 2021

Avery (1858–1919), a member of the New Century Club of Philadelphia, served on the Sunday School Committee of the Spring Garden Unitarian Church alongside Parker and lived at 748 North Nineteenth Street, just a few blocks away from the architect. The timing of the commission coincided with the death of Avery's sister, Julia T. Foster (1843–1890), from whom she inherited an estate valued at almost $60,000 (including a significant portion of the Pittsburgh Dispatch Building—their father having founded the newspaper in 1846). Avery lived in the house at Somerton until 1900, owning the property for another five years before selling it. During her tenure, the house, with its large interconnected public spaces and its second- and third-floor bedrooms, served as a placc for women to gather and plan suffrage events and conferences. Susan B. Anthony—a close friend of the Foster family and a mentor to Rachel Foster Avery—was a guest at the house.

In 1906 the property was purchased by Joseph C. Trainer, who renamed it Cranaleith. His family owned it for more than a century and donated it to the Cranaleith Spiritual Center. The house is listed on the National Register of Historic Places.

REFERENCES

PRERBG 5, no. 44 (November 5, 1890): 685.
Philadelphia Record, November 14, 1890.
Philadelphia Record, January 10, 1891.
Times (Philadelphia), September 13, 1891.
Times (Philadelphia), October 30, 1891.
Times (Philadelphia), September 10, 1892.
Photographs: Cranaleith Spiritual Center
HABS No. PA-6818

36 Queen Isabella Association Pavilion

1890–91

Queen Isabella Association Pavilion, elevation, ca. 1890

Chicago, Illinois
Not built.

The Queen Isabella Association was established in 1889 to promote the importance of women's work on the occasion of the World's Columbian Exposition of 1893 in Chicago. The association's membership was largely professional women, many of whom were suffragists.

To honor Queen Isabella of Spain and her role in dispatching Christopher Columbus to the Americas, the organization announced that they intended to erect a large statue at the fair, along with a building for exhibitions and events. In June 1890 Parker offered to prepare plans for the building pro bono and suggested that its architecture be "as distinctively characteristic as possible of the time of the Queen and the Spanish style." Design work commenced in August. By that time Parker had investigated the "highest type of Spanish architecture," choosing as the basis for her design the Alhambra in Granada, particularly the fourteenth-century Palace of the Lions.

Symmetrical in plan, Parker's design provided a large entry hall to house the sculpture of Queen Isabella. Beyond it, an auditorium with seating for five hundred included a pit for stenographers at the foot of the stage—presumably to enable transcription but also, via the pavilion's telegraph station, to rapidly spread news about the association's events. Parker's design provided extensive spaces for meetings and exhibitions; apartments to accommodate women were to be provided on the second floor. "One extremely novel feature of the undertaking," the *Inter Ocean* reported, was "an arrangement by which infants whose parents are visiting the Fair can be checked and left in charge of trained nurses and female physicians at the Pavilion until called for at the close of the day." Another feature was a sewing room, with seamstresses on hand in case of need.

Parker presented her designs at the Association's November 1890 meeting in Chicago. Although the Isabellas voted unanimously to approve the design, it was sidelined in favor of those of the Exposition's Board of Lady Managers

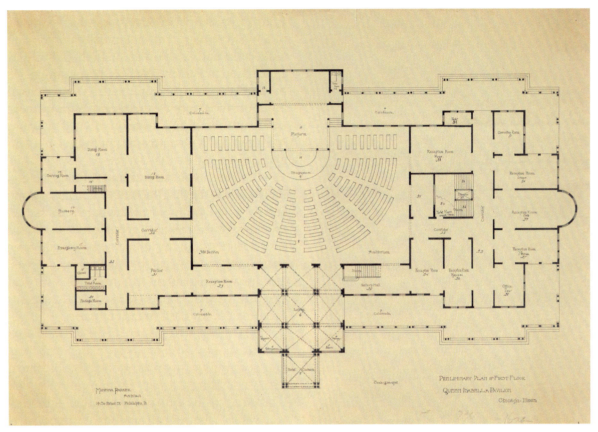

Queen Isabella Association Pavilion, plan, ca. 1890

for a separate Woman's Building. Politics played a role: the Lady Managers, who exerted final control over the Woman's Building and exhibition activities, did not look favorably on the supposedly radical perspectives of some of the association's members. Ultimately, the Queen Isabella Association abandoned Parker's design and constructed a separate, smaller building outside the fairgrounds.

REFERENCES

Inter Ocean (Chicago), June 27, 1890.
PRERBG 5, no. 34 (August 27, 1890): 514.
Pittsburgh Dispatch, September 7, 1890.
Philadelphia Inquirer, September 29, 1890.
PRERBG 5, no. 44 (November 5, 1890): 685.
Philadelphia Inquirer, November 8, 1890.
Inter Ocean (Chicago), November 23, 1890.
Women's Penny Paper (London), December 6, 1890.
PRERBG 5, no. 50 (December 17, 1890): 784.
Philadelphia Record, December 19, 1890.
PRERBG 6, no. 6 (February 11, 1891): i.
Evening Star (Washington, D.C.), February 26, 1891.
Melbourne Herald, March 10, 1891.
PRERBG 6, no. 10 (March 11, 1891): 145–46.
Drawings: Adelaide Nichols Baker Papers, Schlesinger Library, Harvard Radcliffe Institute

37
Francis Jordan Jr. House

1890–93

Jordan House, perspective, ca. 1892

320 Cynwyd Road,
Bala Cynwyd, Pennsylvania
Still standing.

Francis Jordan Jr. (1843–1911) was co-owner of a wholesale grocery business that had been associated with his family since the 1780s. His connection to Parker may have been through his brother William, who appears to have purchased a lot from the Overbrook Land and Improvement Company directly opposite one owned by James A. Patterson. William seems not to have built on his plot [SEE CAT. NOS. 13 AND 39].

The Jordan house was built in the Colonial Revival style, the first floor faced with local stone and the walls above finished with pebble dash. A spacious, central reception hall provided for an easy flow between the light-filled parlor, library, and dining room—each of which was equipped originally with a distinctive fireplace. A vertical expanse of brilliantly colored stained glass accented the rise of the main staircase.

"The thing most desired on the second floor," a contemporary account of the plan noted, "was four communicating rooms, to accommodate a family consisting of small children, and if a look is taken at the location of the beds and the doors you will see what a small amount of space is traveled from the mother's room, in the center, to each child."

Entries in the Philadelphia city directories list the family as living in Bala Cynwyd through 1898. In 1899 they were living at 2228 Spruce Street, and transferred ownership of the home in 1901.

REFERENCES

PRERBG 5, no. 44 (November 5, 1890): 685.
Philadelphia Record, November 14, 1890.
PRERBG 7, no. 49 (December 7, 1892): 1651.
AABN 39, no. 894 (February 11, 1893): 95.
Drawing: Adelaide Nichols Baker Papers, Schlesinger Library, Harvard Radcliffe Institute
HABS No. PA-6831

THE ARCHITECTURE OF MINERVA PARKER NICHOLS

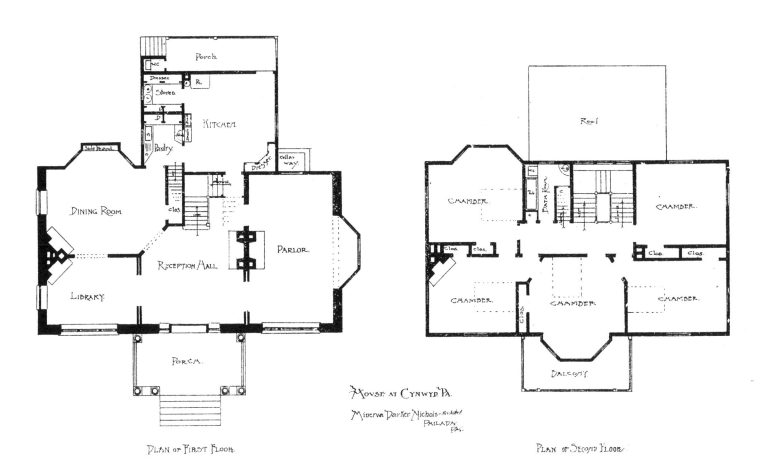

Jordan House, plans, ca. 1892

38
Frank Wallace Munn House

1890–91

Munn House, 2022

1014 Oak Lane Avenue, Philadelphia, Pennsylvania

Still standing.

Owner and operator of a fleet of steam tugboats, Frank Wallace Munn (1851–1919) resided in the house that Parker designed for him until his death in 1919. His wife, Martha (1857–1938), continued to live there until her own death in 1938. The couple's daughter, Florence, was a flower girl at the architect's wedding.

Parker published this design in the December 1891 issue of the *Home-Maker*. She noted that the design had been "built several times with slight alterations." In this case, it was built of local stone with ridge pointing. The front entrance featured a large oak door with custom strap hinges and latch and a handsome beveled glass window set on a diagonal—a signature element in several of Parker's designs.

The reception hall rafters were cased in oak while the hall windows were of leaded glass, white fluted, with a design in amber. Reached from the hall through pocket doors, the parlor was finished in natural cherry and had a corner fireplace with tiled hearth and jambs. The room's palette was pink and light fawn. The library and dining room were finished in oak; their walls were covered in blue-gray wallpaper, with gold accents in the case of the library.

The second-floor bedrooms were finished in cypress and papered in colors: pale blue in the front bedroom, and pink, white, and light yellow in the others. The room over the kitchen served as a play-area and sewing room. On the third floor there were three rooms, including one that opened onto a balcony.

REFERENCES

PRERBG 5, no. 50 (December 17, 1890): 784.
Philadelphia Record, December 19, 1890.
Builder, Decorator and Wood-Worker 15, no. 6 (February 1891): 2.
Home-Maker 7, no. 3 (December 1891): 756–57.
HABS No. PA-6819

Munn House, perspective and plans from the *Home-Maker*, ca. 1891

CATALOGUE RAISONNÉ

Munn House, Detail of entry, 2021

39 Projects for the Overbrook Land and Improvement Company

1890–93

North Sixty-First Street and Columbia Avenue, Overbrook, Philadelphia, Pennsylvania

Not built.

Parker's involvement with the Overbrook Land and Improvement Company stems from her connections to realtors Lewis T. Brooke (1836–1892) and James A. Patterson (1856–1935), both of whom had significant involvement in the Overbrook development [SEE CAT. NOS. 6 AND 13]. Both men also maintained offices at 14 South Broad Street, where Parker had hers—Brooke moved his to 18 South Broad in 1890. The syndicate purchased fifty-five and a half acres from Lewis Jones in July 1889 for $109,000. The parcel had been part of Shady Nook, the Jones family farm, for decades. The company initially considered developing a "summer hotel" on part of the land and teased that Parker would be its architect, but it was soon reported that she was preparing plans for a "large number of houses to be erected on the property of the Overbrook Land Company." These were to be "of different dimensions and erected of stone, native to the locality and gray in color ... finished in the best style and with every modern comfort and convenience, two-and a-half and three stories high, the cost will be about $7,000 to $10,000 each." Ultimately, only the James A. Patterson and Lewis Jones houses were built to her designs [SEE CAT. NOS. 13 AND 40]. By 1895 development of Overbrook Farms by rival builders Wendell and Smith had eclipsed Overbrook Land and Improvement Company's holdings. The Overbrook Farms development was ideally located on land flanking the Overbrook train station. Subsequent development of the Overbrook Land and Improvement Company parcel came at the end of the decade and took the form of attached or duplex houses, the design of which were given over to other architects.

REFERENCES

Philadelphia Inquirer, May 23, 1889.
Philadelphia Record, September 6, 1890.
Philadelphia Inquirer, September 12, 1890.
Philadelphia Record, November 14, 1890.
PRERBG 5, no. 47 (November 26, 1890): 735.
Philadelphia Record, November 29, 1890.
Philadelphia Inquirer, December 2, 1890.

40 Lewis Jones House

1890–91

A major investor in the Overbrook Land and Improvement Company, Lewis Jones (1835–1917) commissioned Parker to design a model house for the development. The design closely follows that of the Frank Wallace Munn House but differs in the placement of the porch and the orientation of the stair in the reception hall [SEE CAT. NO. 30]. Jones seems not to have taken up residence in the house; he continued to live at Shady Nook, the farmhouse (still standing) that he built for himself in the 1860s.

Jones House, 2022

1113–1115 North Sixty-Third Street, Philadelphia, Pennsylvania

Still standing.

REFERENCES

PRERBG 5, no. 44 (November 1, 1890): 685.
Times (Philadelphia), September 13, 1891.
Home-Maker 7, no. 3 (December 1891): 756–57.
HABS No. PA-6822

THE ARCHITECTURE OF MINERVA PARKER NICHOLS

Jones House, west and south facades, 2022

41

Spring Garden Unitarian Church

ca. 1890–91

North Broad and Brandywine Streets, Philadelphia, Pennsylvania

Not built.

Parker was a congregant and Sunday school teacher at the Spring Garden Unitarian Church, where she met her future husband. An undated drawing shows proposed alterations to the facade of the church, but no further documentation has been found. Although nothing came of her proposal for the Spring Garden Unitarian Church building, sold by the congregation in 1896, it is possible that the project led to Parker's New Century Club of Philadelphia commission [SEE CAT. NO. 4] In developing the Spring Garden church project, Parker would have worked with Anna W. Longstreth, who was the longtime president of the congregation's board of trustees and was president of the New Century Club, when its new clubhouse opened.

REFERENCES

Philadelphia Press, February 26, 1894.
Photograph: AAUP
Drawing: Adelaide Nichols Baker Papers, Schlesinger Library, Harvard Radcliffe Institute

42

Sylvester J. Baker Jr. House

1891

Corner of Haverford and Iona Avenues, Narberth, Pennsylvania

Demolished before 1948.

In February 1891 Parker referred to completing plans for a "dwelling at Merion, cor. Haverford and Iowa [sic] avenues, to be stone and frame, finished in hard wood, with all the latest improvements, the cost will be from 10,000 to $12,000." There is no Iowa Street in Merion, but the similarly named Iona Street crosses Haverford Avenue in Narberth. A plot at that intersection was sold to Sylvester and Keturah Baker in July 1890. The fact that Parker did not name the clients may suggest that the land developer played a hand in the commission. Little else is known of the commission and the house was demolished sometime before 1948.

REFERENCES

Builder, Decorator and Wood-Worker 15, no. 6 (February 1891): 2.

43
New Century Club of Philadelphia

1891–92

New Century Club, facade detail, 1973

New Century Club, south facade, 1965

124 South Twelfth Street, Philadelphia, Pennsylvania

Demolished in 1973.

Anna W. Longstreth (1840–1899), president of the board of Spring Garden Unitarian Society of Philadelphia, was in close contact with Parker several years before the New Century Club of Philadelphia began planning for a clubhouse. Longstreth was a founding member of the club and its building was dedicated during her term as president, 1892–95.

As reported in the *Philadelphia Record*, "The Century Club, an outgrowth of the Centennial, which has done much to promote the interests of working women in Philadelphia by establishing the [New] Century Guild and the Legal Protection Society for Working Women, has secured permanent quarters and will soon transform the properties...into a club-house and headquarters for the work of the club and its affiliated bodies. The lot secured has frontage of 40 feet and extends back from Twelfth street a distance of 98 feet...The Century Club-house is to be of vitrified brick, with stone facings and many tasteful and decorative features. The first floor is to contain club-rooms, reception parlors and class-rooms, together with rooms to rent for Women's Exchange and other purposes. On the second floor is to be a Grand Assembly Hall, to be used as the New Century Drawing-room and for suppers, theatrical and like entertainments

… To further the financial building scheme for the club some of the ladies connected with it have formed a stock company, capitalized at $50,000, with 2,000 shares at $25 each. The outlook for deriving a large revenue from the rental of the building and its rooms and offices is so encouraging that the promoters of the company are confident good dividends will follow."

Bids were accepted beginning in April 1891. Contracts were awarded to J. E. and A. L. Pennock, with a reported cost of $35,000 (an additional $5,000 was spent on furnishings). Construction was substantially completed by the end of the year with formal dedication occurring on January 11, 1892. The auditorium in which the main festivities occurred, called the "drawing room" by members, seated seven hundred. It featured murals by Gabrielle de Veaux Clements (1858–1948) and a "starry sky" ceiling (enhanced by inset electric lights) that was the work of the architect.

New Century Club, entry and main stair, ca. 1892

New Century Club, main stair, ca. 1892

In 1907 architect Horace Wells Sellers made alterations to the stair hall and fourth floor (converting the latter from staff spaces to a tearoom). The club flourished into the 1950s, but declining membership resulted in the demolition of the building in May 1973.

REFERENCES

PRERBG 6, no. 2 (January 14, 1891): 18.
Philadelphia Record, January 16, 1891.
Builder, Decorator and Wood-Worker 15, no. 6 (February 1891): 2.
Philadelphia Record, February 9, 1891.
Builder, Decorator and Wood-Worker 16, no. 2 (April 1891): 2.
Philadelphia Record, April 3, 1891.
PRERBG 6, no. 14 (April 8, 1891): 209.
Philadelphia Record, April 22, 1891.
PRERBG 6, no. 16 (April 22, 1891): 242.
PRERBG 6, no. 44 (November 4, 1891): 709.
Philadelphia Inquirer, January 10, 1892.
Philadelphia Inquirer, January 12, 1892.
PRERBG 7, no. 2 (January 13, 1892): 875.
Louise Stockton, "The Story of the New Century Club," Home-Maker 8, no. 1 (April 1892): 4–16.
Woman's Progress 1, no. 2 (May 1893): 58.
Brooklyn Daily Eagle, May 13, 1894.
Boston Daily Globe, January 23, 1896.
Kansas City Journal, March 20, 1898.
Jennie Cunningham Croly, The History of the Woman's Club Movement in America (New York: Henry G. Allen, 1898), 1021–28.
PRERBG 22, no. 24 (June 19, 1907): 391.
PRERBG 22, no. 29 (July 17, 1907): 467.
Photograph: Free Library of Philadelphia
Drawings: Architectural Archives, University of Pennsylvania; Harvard University, Schlesinger Library, Adelaide Nichols Baker Papers
Photographs: Campbell & Perkins Scrapbook Collections, Historical Society of Pennsylvania
Annual reports: The New Century Club of Philadelphia, Historical Society of Pennsylvania

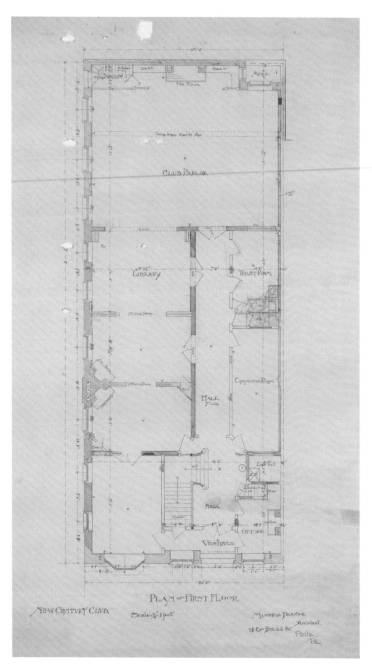
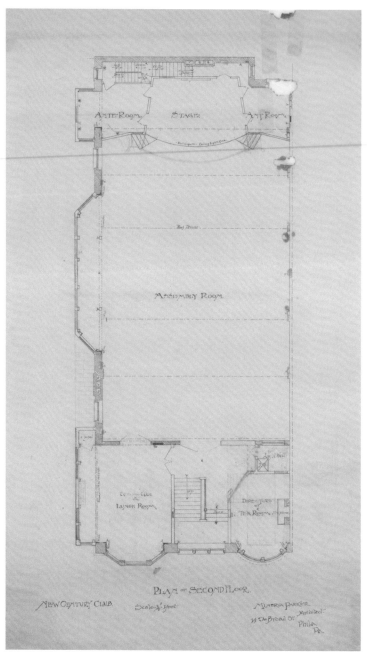

New Century Club, floor plans, 1891

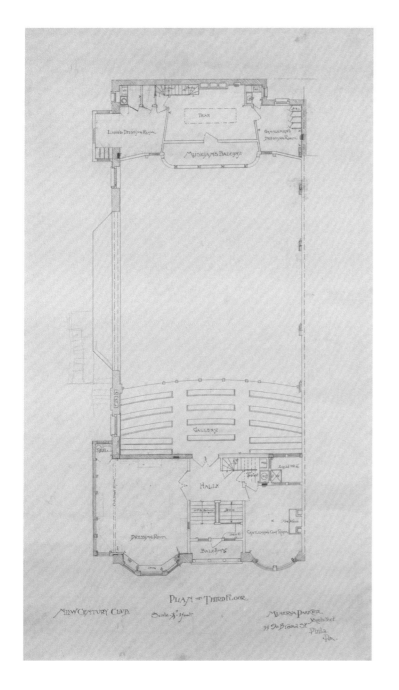
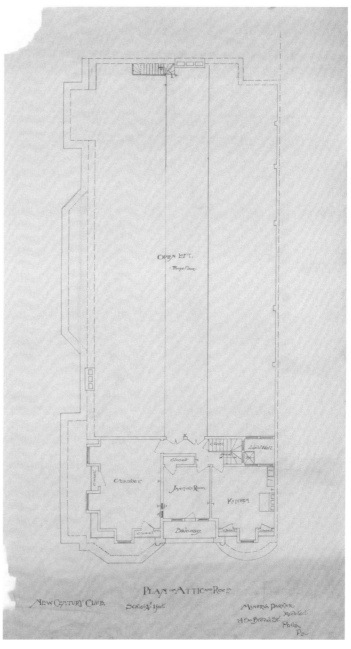

New Century Club "Drawing-room," ca. 1892

44 Abraham L. Pennock House

1891

The extent of Parker's work for nurseryman Abraham Liddon Pennock Jr. (1827–1917) remain unknown. The *Philadelphia Real Estate Record and Builders' Guide* noted "extensive alterations to the house of Abraham Pennock," suggesting that these were for his residence on Violet Lane. The surviving house, however, lacks any distinctive features associated with the architect's work, possibly indicating that the work was not built.

Pennock was the youngest son of a family known for its deep involvement in the Pennsylvania Anti-Slavery Society and for its advocacy of woman's suffrage and the temperance movement. He built his first greenhouse in Lansdowne in 1861 and remained a prominent florist in Philadelphia, operating the partnership of Pennock Brothers at 1514 Chestnut Street.

Violet Lane,
Lansdowne, Pennsylvania

Probably not built.

REFERENCES

PRERBG 6, no. 12 (March 25, 1891): iii.
Times (Philadelphia), March 30, 1891.

45
William J. Nicolls House

1891

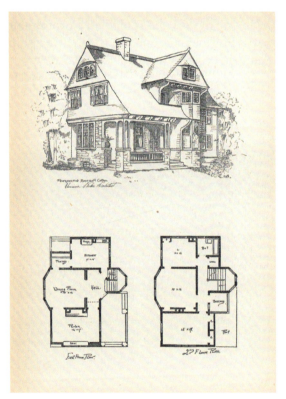

Page from the *Home-Maker*, 1890

337 East Curtin Street,
Bellefonte, Pennsylvania

Still standing.

William Jasper Nicolls (1854–1916) was a civil engineer who worked for the Reading Railroad as an assistant engineer and later with the Pennsylvania Steel Company as chief engineer. His wife, born Clara Valentine Lyon, resided in Bellefonte, Pennsylvania, at the time of their marriage in 1882. In 1891 the couple commissioned Parker to design them a summer house there, but they continued to maintain their primary residence in the Philadelphia region.

The design of the Nicolls house so closely mirrors the "little cottage" Parker illustrated in her essay "Practical Dwellings," published in January 1891 in the *Home-Maker*, that one can reasonably surmise that Clara Nicolls saw the design in those pages. She must have called on the architect quickly, because the published notice of this commission appears within two months of the appearance of the *Home-Maker* article.

Parker's plan for the house called for a compact rectangle featuring a porch extending from the southwest corner to a vertical bay containing the stair; a first floor organized around the stair hall and entry, with a kitchen and dining and sitting rooms; and a second floor with three bedrooms. Parker used locally quarried stone for the porch columns and for the base of the house, sheathing the frame walls in clapboard on the ground floor, with shingles above.

The house served as the setting for a romantic suspense thriller by Millie J. Ragosta entitled, *The House on Curtin Street* (1979).

REFERENCES

Home-Maker 5, no. 4 (January 1891): 443–45.
PRERBG 6, no. 12 (March 25, 1891): iii.
Millie J. Ragosta, *The House on Curtin Street* (Garden City, NY: Doubleday, 1979).
HABS No. PA-6832

Nicolls House, south facade, 2022

46 Emma de Crano McCammon House

1891

Gettysburg, Pennsylvania

Probably not built.

Emma de Crano McCammon (ca. 1835–1893) was the daughter of industrialist Frederick Mollar de Crano, a veteran of the Napoleonic Wars with investments in mining and railroads. Her brother, Felix F. de Crano, was a well-known Philadelphia artist. Emma was the mother of three sons by her husband David C. McCammon, operator of a tobacco trading house in Philadelphia, and an active player in progressive Republican politics.

Following David McCammon's retirement in 1872, the family moved to Gettysburg, where their sons attended the preparatory department of Pennsylvania College (now Gettysburg College). The family lived at 124 Carlisle Street in a house that Emma's brother purchased and placed in trust for the benefit of his sister and her children. When full ownership of the house was transferred to Emma in 1884 (five years after the death of her husband), she commissioned the renovation of the interiors and a substantial third-floor addition from architect John A. Dempwolf of York, Pennsylvania. Why McCammon commissioned Parker to design a new house seven years later is unknown. No land appears to have been purchased for the purpose and Emma was living at the 124 Carlisle Street house at the time of her death.

Parker's proposed design was described as "a large private residence," to be built of stone and shingle, two and a half stories high. Given the close involvement of Felix in Emma's affairs, it seems likely that the decision to hire Parker can be attributed to his Philadelphia connections.

REFERENCES

PRERBG 6, no. 16 (April 22, 1891): 241.
Philadelphia Inquirer, April 27, 1891.
Philadelphia Record, May 13, 1891.
Philadelphia Record, May 19, 1891.
Gettysburg Times (PA), February 9, 1943.
Deborah C. Pollack, *Felix F. de Crano: Forgotten Artist of the Flagler Colony* (Saint Augustine, FL: Lightner Museum, 2014).

47 Houses for Wendell and Smith

1891

St. Davids, Pennsylvania

Not built.

Among the most prolific and successful real estate developers in Philadelphia at the turn of the twentieth century were Herman Wendell and Walter Smith. Wendell received training at the Franklin Institute Drawing School (1869–70), and for the first decade of his career he worked as a carpenter-builder in the Frankford section of the city. He joined Walter B. Smith, one of his classmates from the Franklin Institute, in establishing a model for development that harnessed the skills of young architects who were on the rise professionally. Wendell and Smith were responsible for the development of Overbrook Farms and Pelham in Philadelphia, and the communities of Wayne and St. Davids along the Main Line.

While Parker was included in important publicity related to their St. Davids project, the firm's expenses ledger reveals her more limited role. On June 6, 1891, she received $23 under the heading of "sundry plans." By comparison, her contemporaries, William L. Price and Francis Price received $192.50, while William L. Bailey received $125. Disparities in rates of pay for men and women may account for most of this difference: the purse for the architect of the Woman's Building at the World's Columbian Exhibition of 1893 was one-tenth of what a man could expect and the proportion is comparable here. Bailey and the Prices—whose names appear dozens of times throughout the ledger—built extensively for the developers and expenses for their individual designs fill many of the subsequent ledger pages. Parker's name appears only here, suggesting that her designs did not advance beyond a preliminary stage.

REFERENCES

Carpentry and Building (September 1891): 207, 209–13.
Wendell and Smith Records: Athenaeum of Philadelphia

48 Twin Houses for the Campbell Sisters

1891–92

Twin Houses for the Campbell Sisters, ca. 1892

417–419 West School House Lane, Philadelphia, Pennsylvania

Still standing.

Sisters Mary A. Campbell (1840–1913) and Sarah Jane Campbell (1844–1928) were active in the suffrage movement through the Women's Suffrage Society of Philadelphia—Jane was its founder and president for over twenty years—and as publishers and editors of *Woman's Progress*, a magazine that Mary founded in 1893. As members of the New Century Club of Philadelphia, they would have been aware of Parker, as her plans for the clubhouse developed during the spring of 1891. They may have known her earlier than that: until 1886, the Campbell sisters owned a home at 2016 Green Street, a block from Parker's house.

The houses Parker designed for the Campbell sisters were an experiment in making two dwellings appear to be a single, larger house. Notably, the houses are set back from School House Lane, perhaps to avoid blocking southern light from reaching the house directly to the north, owned by their brother William and in which they lived. Colonial Revival in style, the brick and stone structure for the sisters featured parlors and dining rooms accessible from reception halls. Three bedrooms, along with a bath and sewing room, were located on the second floors of both houses, with four more bedrooms on the third. The sisters appear to have sold off the two houses by 1895.

REFERENCES

PRERBG 6, no. 18 (May 6, 1891): i
Philadelphia Record, May 9, 1891.
Times (Philadelphia), May 11, 1891.
Philadelphia Record, March 22, 1892.
Drawings: Athenaeum of Philadelphia
Drawings, specifications, and photograph: AAUP
HABS No. PA-6820

THE ARCHITECTURE OF MINERVA PARKER NICHOLS

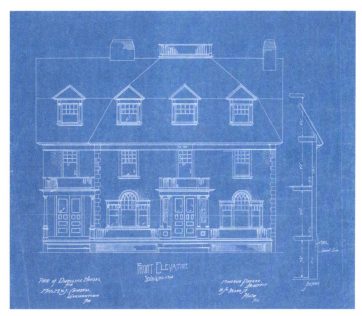

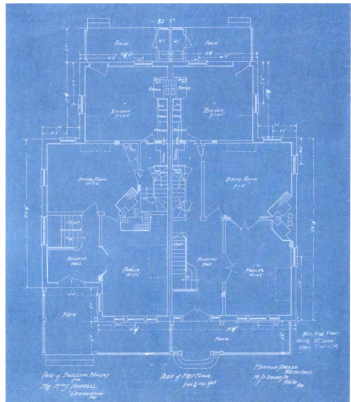

Twin Houses for the Campbell Sisters, elevation (top) and first-floor plan, 1891

49
Ida V. Stambach House

1891–93

Philadelphia native Ida V. Stambach (1853–1926), younger sister of John A. Stambach, a successful Philadelphia furrier, was a homeopathic doctor and graduate of the Hahnemann Medical College of the Pacific in San Francisco. An avowed supporter of women's suffrage, she became the second vice president of the California State Equal Suffrage Association in 1897. She hosted both the Reverend Anna Shaw and Susan B. Anthony at her Parker-designed house during their 1896 lecture tours of California. Aside from the fact that both Ida Stambach and Parker were successful professional women, it is unclear whether they had any direct connections that might have led to the commission in July 1891.

The frame and shingle house stood one and a half stories high. A bay window faced State Street and a porch extended across the building's front elevation. A detached structure used as Stambach's medical office and a water tower stood on the site. In 1893 Parker—by then married and working as Minerva Parker Nichols—provided plans for a four-room addition that roughly doubled the footprint of the house. The addition may have been commissioned in anticipation of Stambach hosting larger suffrage meetings. Around 1915 the house was divided into apartments and given the name Redwood Court. By 1956, what remained of the Stambach house was demolished to make way for an office building.

1509 State Street,
Santa Barbara, California

Demolished about 1956.

REFERENCES

Philadelphia Inquirer, July 22, 1891.
PRERBG 6, no. 29 (July 22, 1891): i.
Builder, Decorator and Wood-Worker 16, no. 6 (August 1891): 2.
Philadelphia Record, September 2, 1891.
PRERBG 8, no. 16 (April 19, 1893): i.

50
House for the Home-Maker

1891

Of her speculative design for a "small house of communication," Parker wrote that it was expected to "cost about $4,500, local stone to be used to the top of the second story joists, then shingled and ornamented as shown; the roof is of Bangor slate, cut square on the ends. Inside, the first floor hall is finished, including the open fireplace and stairs, in red oak. The library, with its low book-cases, is scarcely more than an alcove opening out of the parlor or living room. The hall, parlor, library, and dining room can all be thrown together, so that they form one apartment. The advantage of entertaining in a small house so arranged can hardly be over-estimated. The dining room is extended at will to accommodate the home gatherings at the holiday season."

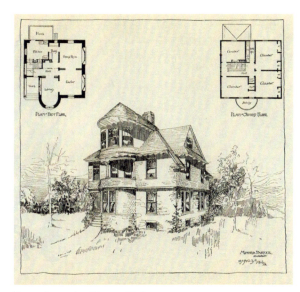

Page from the *Home-Maker*

Location unknown.
Probably not built.

REFERENCES

Home-Maker 6, no. 6 (September 1891): 514–16.

51
Eagle Iron Foundry

1891–92

Ruffner Street (near Blaine Street), Philadelphia, Pennsylvania

Demolished by 1938.

Established in 1835, the Samuel J. Cresswell Ironworks was a major producer of architectural metalwork in Philadelphia, remaining in business until 1969. The firm operated several facilities in Philadelphia, including the Eagle Iron Foundry at 812–820 Race Street. It was destroyed by fire in March 1891, prompting a search for a new location at which to renew and expand their operations.

By then David S. Cresswell (1845–1911), son of the company's founder, was in control of the company. He selected a site in the Nicetown section of the city, next to a major junction of the Philadelphia and Reading Railroad. Parker prepared drawings for a three-story machine shop and a large foundry building that covered an area of 60 by 184 feet. The facility, built of brick and iron, was touted as "one of the most complete of the kind in the country." Why Cresswell chose Parker to make the plans is unknown, although there may have been a connection through another patron of Parker, Miss Mary Potts, whose brother, Horace T. Potts, was Cresswell's contemporary and an iron and steel merchant [SEE CAT. NO. 20].

REFERENCES

PRERBG 6, no. 13 (April 1, 1891): 194.
Philadelphia Record, October 7, 1891.
PRERBG 6, no. 41 (October 14, 1891): 656.
PRERBG 6, no. 46 (November 18, 1891): 747.
Philadelphia Record, January 13, 1892.
Philadelphia Record, January 18, 1892.
Moses King, *King's Views: Philadelphia* (New York: Moses King, 1900), 40c.
Workshop of the World: A Selective Guide to the Industrial Archeology of Philadelphia (Wallingford, PA: Oliver Evans Press, 1990), 6.6.
Photograph: Warren-Ehret Company photograph albums. Hagley Museum and Library

THE ARCHITECTURE OF MINERVA PARKER NICHOLS

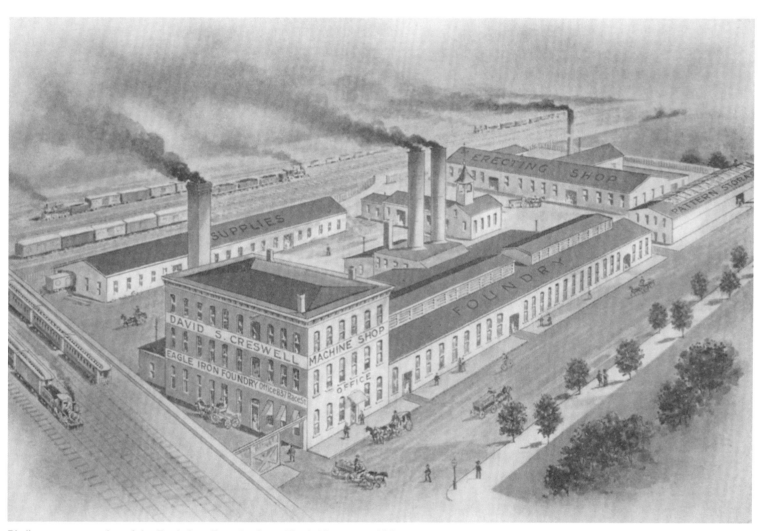

Bird's-eye perspective of the Eagle Iron Foundry from *King's Views*, ca. 1900, showing site with later additions

52
Esther R. Gaskell House

1891–92

1807–1809 Cleveland Avenue NW,
Canton, Ohio

Probably not built.

Esther R. Gaskell (1862–1936) was the daughter of a successful furniture maker, John Danner, who made his fortune on patents for revolving bookcases (sold through the John Danner Manufacturing Company). Her husband, Silas S. C. Gaskell (1859–1929), began his career as a salesman for her father's company. Together, Silas and Esther Gaskell established an art supply store in Canton under the name Dresden Color Company (later changed to Gaskell Art Shop). City directories note Esther's work as a china artist. Esther and Silas Gaskell built on the site and moved to that address in 1895. They lived there until their deaths in 1929 and 1936. Whether they used Parker's design is unknown.

REFERENCES

PRERBG 6, no. 46 (November 18, 1891): 747.
Times (Philadelphia), November 20, 1891.

53
First Unitarian Church of Wilmington

1891–93

807 West Street,
Wilmington, Delaware

Demolished after 1960.

Parker prepared plans for an addition to house a Sunday school (likely one story, wood frame) as an addition to the original brick church built in 1868. She also made alterations to the sanctuary. A city paper reported that its quality had "been greatly improved by the lowering and broadening of the pulpit platform and the placing of a twin window back of the pulpit." Giving further details of the window, the paper noted: "The glass is amber-colored ondoyant, leaded frames, with cut glass jewels at each point of the diamond shapes."

REFERENCES

PRERBG 6, no. 46 (November 18, 1891): 747.
Philadelphia Inquirer, November 19, 1891.
Philadelphia Record, November 20, 1891.
News Journal (Wilmington, DE), January 25, 1892.

54 New Century Club of Wilmington

1892–93

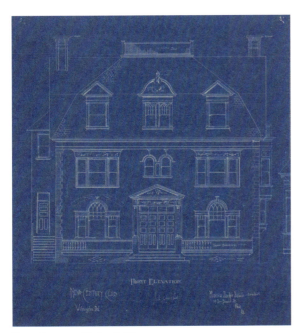

New Century Club, 1892

1014 Delaware Avenue, Wilmington, Delaware

Still standing.

In 1892 the New Century Club of Wilmington purchased land to build a clubhouse on the south side of Delaware Avenue between Jackson and Van Buren Streets. In its annual report, the club noted that the idea for the building came in early 1891, after the president of the New Century Club of Philadelphia described the plans for that chapter's new club home [SEE CAT. NO. 43]. The Wilmington New Century Club stated that "Rough sketches were submitted to several architects, who in turn, submitted their plans. It was decided to accept those of Mrs. Minerva Parker Nichols. We were more than pleased to find that we could employ a woman to do this work, and the wisdom of our choice is so apparent it is not necessary to comment upon it."

The commission was described in the *Philadelphia Real Estate Record and Builders' Guide* as a structure, "three-stories high, of vitrified brick and stucco work, colonial style of architecture, also fitted for steam heat, electric bells, and light, speaking tubes, dumb waiters, assembly room upon first floor, also offices and committee room. A fully equipped stage will be placed in assembly room, which is 25 [by] 43 feet. Second floor will contain a reception room and banquet hall, while the third will be fitted for dressing and toilet rooms, etc. The entire building will have all modern conveniences." The interior finishes were reported to be of yellow pine, ash and cherry, with the plaster tinted in the "softest shades of terracotta and nasturtium."

Ground was broken on July 18, 1892, and the building formally opened on January 31, 1893. Reports show the building cost $35,153.05, and Nichols was paid $535 to furnish drawings including: plans of cellar and foundations, principal story, second story, and third story; elevation and principal front; side elevations; longitudinal section; and transverse section (two of these drawings survive and are housed in the collection of Harvard University's Schlesinger Library). She was paid an additional fee to superintend the

CATALOGUE RAISONNÉ

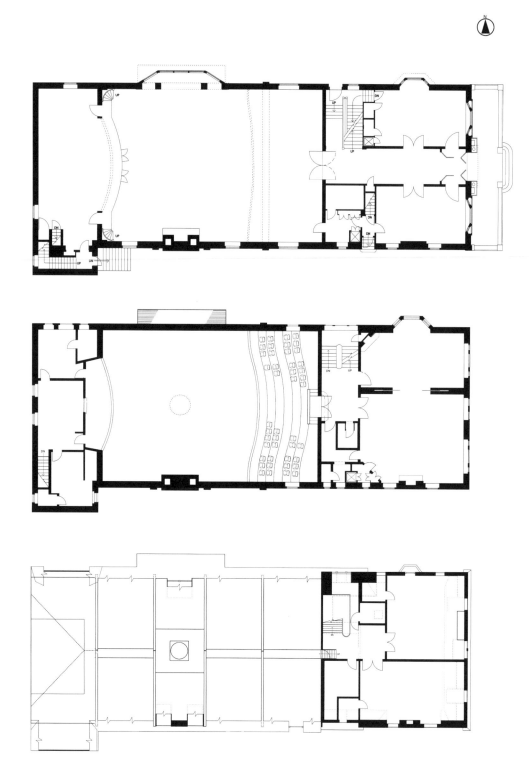

New Century Club, floor plans (Gabriel Albino, Jhon Velazco, and Changfeng Luo, delineators, 2023)

New Century Club, east and north facades, ca. 1893

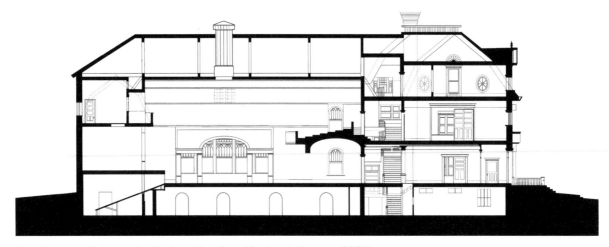

New Century Club, longitudinal-section (Igor Kiselev, delineator, 2023)

construction, at a rate of 2.5 percent, plus a per diem of $5 and travel expenses for each day she was on site.

In 1910, the Club built an addition to the auditorium, including new kitchens on the main floor and a new dressing room. An elevator was added in 1914 and additional alterations were made in 1930. The Club vacated the building in 1976 and it was sold the following year. Since October 1982, the building has been the home of the Delaware Children's Theater. The building is listed on the National Register of Historic Places.

REFERENCES

PRERBG 7, no. 16 (April 20, 1892): i.
Philadelphia Record, April 21, 1892.
PRERBG 7, no. 19 (May 11, 1892): 1147.
Philadelphia Record, May 13, 1892.
PRERBG 7, no. 22 (June 1, 1892): i.
Delaware Gazette and State Journal (Wilmington, DE), June 9, 1892.
PRERBG 7, no. 26 (June 29, 1892): i.
Delaware Gazette and State Journal (Wilmington, DE), November 17, 1892.
Marion Daily Star (OH), December 28, 1892.
Baltimore Sun, February 1, 1893.
New Cycle 6, no. 1–2 (February and March 1893): 290–301.
Woman's Progress 1, no. 2 (May 1893): 58–59.
Delaware Gazette and State Journal (Wilmington, DE), January 30, 1896.
News Journal (Wilmington, DE) March 21, 2012.
Photographs and papers: Delaware Historical Society
Drawings: Adelaide Nichols Baker Papers, Schlesinger Library, Harvard Radcliffe Institute
HABS No. DE-352

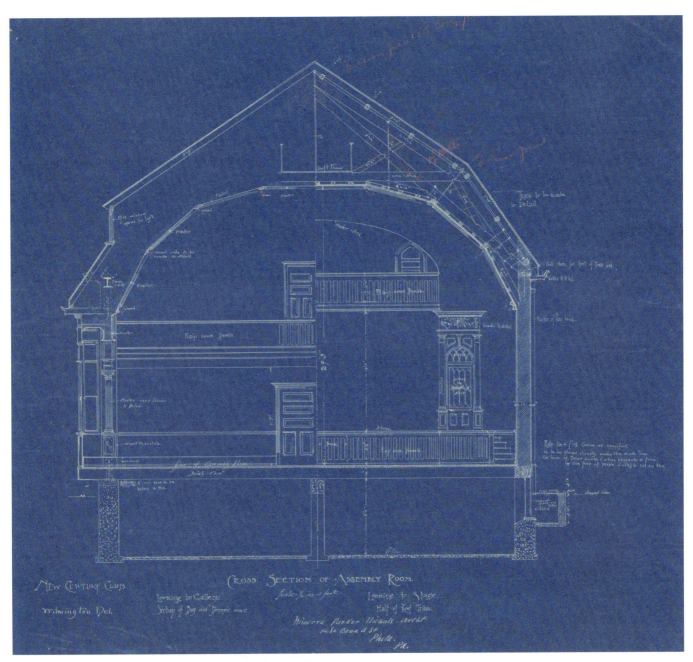
New Century Club, cross-section through auditorium, 1892

55
Margaret M. Barber House

1892–93

Barber House, ca. 1968

2308 North Broad Street, Philadelphia, Pennsylvania

Demolished in 2011.

Margaret Marr Barber (1845–1927) was a native of Lewisburg, Pennsylvania, and a graduate of Bucknell University. Her husband, Phineas M. Barber, amassed a fortune in the lumber trade, supplying building materials to the Philadelphia region through his firm, Barber, Alcott & Ross (divisions of which operated in Washington, D.C.; Asbury Park, NJ; Newbern, NC; and Dunkirk, NY—the latter with gross receipts of $500,000 annually). When her husband died suddenly in November 1891, Margaret Barber inherited a substantial portion of his estate. She supported the Women's Christian Temperance Union and endowed the establishment of the Barber Memorial Seminary, a school for African American girls in Anniston, Alabama.

Barber commissioned Nichols to design a substantial city house on North Broad Street costing $20,000, with a footprint measuring 20 by 85 feet. Containing eighteen rooms, the front of the building was constructed of Hummelstown brownstone, Lake Superior red sandstone, and Pompeiian brick. Inside, the halls and library were paneled in quartered oak, while the parlor was of white and gold finish. Bay windows overlooked a generous garden located on the south side of the house.

Sold by Barber in 1920, the house was converted to institutional use by the Reconstructionist Rabbinical College in 1968.

REFERENCES

Miltonian (Milton, PA), November 13, 1891.
PRERBG 7, no. 26 (June 29, 1892): i.
Philadelphia Inquirer, July 1, 1892.
Philadelphia Record, July 1, 1892.
Architectural and Building Monthly 5, no. 5 (August 1, 1892): 15.
PRERBG 7, no. 34 (August 24, 1892): i.
Times (Philadelphia), August 31, 1892.
Philadelphia Inquirer, September 14, 1892.
Woman's Progress 1, no. 2 (May 1893): 58.
Times (Philadelphia), September 7, 1895.
Philadelphia Inquirer, October 4, 1897.
Philadelphia Inquirer, August 5, 1920.
Photograph: AAUP
Photographs: Reconstructionist Rabbinical College Archives

56 Women's Reception Rooms, Pennsylvania Exhibition, World's Columbian Exposition

1892–93

Chicago, Illinois
Demolished at the conclusion of the fair.

Nichols was a member of the Philadelphia Ladies' Auxiliary Society, whose focus was on promoting women's work for the World's Columbian Exhibition in Chicago. Individual committees addressed education, public health, literature, science, and social economics. Sarah A. Stewart [SEE CAT. NO. 31] was in charge of the Education Committee, while the Art Committee, comprising Nichols and artists Alice Barber Stephens and Gabrielle de Veaux Clements, was headed by Emily Sartain. (Nichols and Stephens both taught at the Philadelphia School of Design for Women during Sartain's tenure as its principal.) The Art Committee coordinated the "furnishing [of] three apartments occupying about one-half of the first floor of the Pennsylvania State Building." The largest room was to be finished in bird's-eye maple, a wood native to the Commonwealth, with mural decorations by Margaret Lesley Bush-Brown, Clements, Sarah Paxton Ball Dodson, and Jeanne Rongier. A "carved Colonial mantelpiece," presumably designed by Nichols and positioned in a prominent corner of the room, was adorned with a statue by Charles Grafly and decorative panels by Mary E. Slater.

While twenty-seven male architects were represented in the Pennsylvania Building, Nichols's work was exhibited in the Woman's Building alongside work by Sartain and others. In addition to four of Nichols's architectural drawings (displayed in the Education Room), photographs of four of her buildings were exhibited, including the New Century Clubs in Philadelphia and Wilmington, the Campbell sisters' houses, and a "residence in Upsal"—presumably her Queen Anne design for Mary Potts.

REFERENCES

Philadelphia Record, April 11, 1892.
Times (Philadelphia), September 24, 1892.
Times (Philadelphia), September 23, 1893.
Robert L. Brownfield, ed., *Pennsylvania Art Contributions: State Building, Art Gallery and Woman's Building: World's Columbian Exposition* (Harrisburg, PA: Edwin K. Meyers, State Printer, 1893), 8–21, 59.

57 Maria Nye Johnson House

1892

San Francisco, California
Undetermined.

Maria Nye Johnson (1835–1926) was trained as a physician at the Hahnemann Medical College of Chicago, Illinois. She was a close family friend and confidant of the architect's mother and lived near the Parker family in Philadelphia. After Johnson left the city for San Francisco in the fall of 1891, she asked Nichols to prepare plans for a dwelling, but nothing seems to have come of the commission.

REFERENCES
PRERBG 7, no. 26 (June 29, 1892): i.

58 Office for the Architect

1893

1616 Mount Vernon Street, Philadelphia, Pennsylvania
Still standing but interiors altered beyond recognition.

In April 1893 Nichols reported that she had removed her offices from 14 South Broad Street to 1616 Mount Vernon Street and that she had "fitted up a handsome suite of rooms for draughting and an office."

REFERENCES
PRERBG 8, no. 16 (April 19, 1893): i.

59

House for the Moore Brothers

1892

Moore Brothers House, 2022

7350 Zimmerman Avenue, Pennsauken, New Jersey

Still standing.

Attributed to Minerva Parker Nichols, architect.

A notice that Nichols had "furnished all the plans in detail for the operation of the Moore Brothers during the present building season," appeared in the October 26 issue of the *Philadelphia Real Estate Record and Builder's Guide*. The structures were touted as being, "of quite a varied nature, introducing many new features of art, ornamentation and general comfort to dwelling houses." While the notice gives no location for the building activities of the Moore Brothers, there were eponymous operations in New Jersey in Atlantic City, Bridgeton, and the Camden area. Remarkably—given the ubiquity of the name Moore—there were no such activities to be found in Philadelphia. The crew working out of Camden appears to be the most likely to have been employing Nichols: that outfit is known to have been building a substantial development of row houses on Pearl Street in Camden (between Seventh and Eighth Streets), as well as several "fine new dwelling[s]" in the community of Delair (now Pennsauken) situated on a bluff overlooking the Delaware River.

The house built for Killam E. Bennett (1865–1933) at the corner of Zimmerman and Curtis Avenues was under construction in September 1892, just a month before the notice of Nichols's activities appeared. Bennett was the operator of a large lumber supply business in Camden and while no direct connection between Moore Brothers and Bennett has been firmly established, the builders were working on Curtis Avenue at the time. The house at 7350 Zimmerman and another on the corner of Zimmerman and Derousse Avenues are closely related in terms of massing and detail to several examples of Nichols's work, particularly the Nicolls House in Bellefonte, Pennsylvania [SEE CAT. NO. 45].

REFERENCES

PRERBG 7, no. 36 (September 7, 1892): 1436.
PRERBG 7, no. 43 (October 26, 1892): 1543.
HABS No. NJ-1271

60
John O. Sheatz House

1893

John Oscar Sheatz (1855–1922) began his working life at the Baldwin Locomotive Works. Before becoming the State Treasurer of Pennsylvania (1908–11), he was a coal dealer, real estate speculator, state representative, and mining executive. Sheatz hired Nichols to make modest alterations to an existing house on Hamilton Street, including the addition of a brick bay, Colonial Revival porch and new windows. The Sheatz family resided at the house until 1919 and maintained their ownership until 1933. In the intervening years, the house was a rental property.

3313 Hamilton Street,
Philadelphia, Pennsylvania

Still standing but altered.

REFERENCES

PRERBG 8, no. 12 (March 22, 1893): 185.
PRERBG 8, no. 16 (April 19, 1893): i.
Philadelphia Inquirer, September 21, 1919.
HABS No. PA-6840

THE ARCHITECTURE OF MINERVA PARKER NICHOLS

Sheatz House, south facade, 2022

61 New Century Guild of Working Women Guild House

1893

Educational programming by the New Century Guild of Working Women, an outgrowth of the New Century Club of Philadelphia, provided opportunities for women's self-improvement [SEE CAT. NO. 43]. Classes were offered in many subjects, from millinery and cooking to home nursing and childcare. Some classes were offered on Saturday nights, to accommodate the work schedules of its students. Enrollment was almost eight hundred students by 1891 and, in anticipation of future needs, the board of what was then constituted as the New Century Trust purchased a property on Arch Street, with the intention of building a dedicated clubhouse. Nichols, who became a member of the guild in November 1892, prepared plans for the structure; they were displayed on the walls of the New Century Club's assembly room at 1132 West Girard Avenue in an effort to "swell the building fund." The financial panic of 1893 drastically reduced the New Century Guild's membership and plans to build Nichols's design were permanently shelved.

1225–1227 Arch Street, Philadelphia, Pennsylvania

Not built.

REFERENCES

PRERBG 8, no. 23 (June 7, 1893): 349.
Times (Philadelphia), December 3, 1893.
New Century Trust Records, ca. 1854–2004 (Collection 3097): The Historical Society of Pennsylvania

62 Irwin N. Megargee House, Pen-y-Bryn

1893–94

1301 Rose Glen Road, Gladwyne, Pennsylvania

Main house demolished about 1909; cottage still standing.

Born into a family famous in the papermaking trade since the American Revolution, Irwin N. Megargee (1862–1905), commissioned Nichols to restore and expand an existing (probably eighteenth-century) stone farm into a summer retreat. Megargee called the project Folly Farm, a chronicler of local history noted, because the model dairy and stock farm he attempted to establish there proved unprofitable. Located in scenic Rose Glen, just outside Philadelphia, the farm comprised forty-five acres; the house was named Pen-y-Bryn—*top of the hill* in Welsh—for its location, with views overlooking the surrounding countryside. From there, it was noted, one could see the mill town of Roxborough, and at night, "the electric lights on the towers of Girard College."

Megargee's widow sold the property in 1909 and the main house was demolished soon after. The property is now publicly owned and open to the public as Rolling Hill Park. Remnants of the Megargee farm structures survive, including a small house known as The Cottage. While not confirmed to be built to Nichols's design, details of this structure echo other works by her, particularly the low dormer rising from a gambrel roofline over an entrance porch [SEE CAT. NOS. 45 AND 59].

REFERENCES

PRERBG 8, no. 42 (October 18, 1893): i.
Samuel Fitch Hotchkin, *Rural Pennsylvania in the Vicinity of Philadelphia* (Philadelphia: George W. Jacobs, 1897), 121.
Photographs: Lower Merion Historical Society
Photographs: Lower Merion Conservancy
HABS No. PA-6839

CATALOGUE RAISONNÉ

Megargee House, view of the Cottage at Folly Farm, 2022

63 John O. Keim House

1893–94

Nichols was hired by John Otto Keim (1855–1941), a Reading Railroad executive, to design substantial alterations to a house overlooking the Tacony Creek in Cheltenham Township. At the time, Keim and his wife, Mary Ella (1858–1924), were living at 1533 Green Street, just steps away from Nichols's office at 1616 Mount Vernon Street. The commission was reported to include the addition of, "fine porches, [and] colonial finish throughout the interior." Nichols reconfigured existing walls to accommodate a large reception hall that ran through the house, as well as the breakfast room, dining room, kitchen, laundry, pantry, sitting room, library, den, and parlor on the first floor. She used covered porches to connect a large playroom to the house. Upstairs, the bathrooms were redone, along with a nursery and bedrooms; a new stair led to the servants' quarters on the third floor.

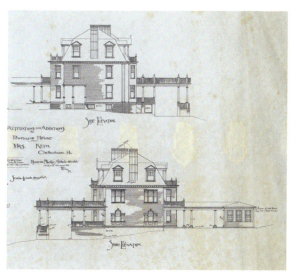

Keim House, elevations (detail), 1893

Jenkintown Road
(north of Tookany Creek Parkway),
Cheltenham Township, Pennsylvania

Demolished.

REFERENCES

PRERBG 8, no. 42 (October 18, 1893): i.
AABN 42, no. 932 (November 4, 1893): 3.
Drawings: Adelaide Nichols Baker Papers, Schlesinger Library, Harvard Radcliffe Institute

CATALOGUE RAISONNÉ

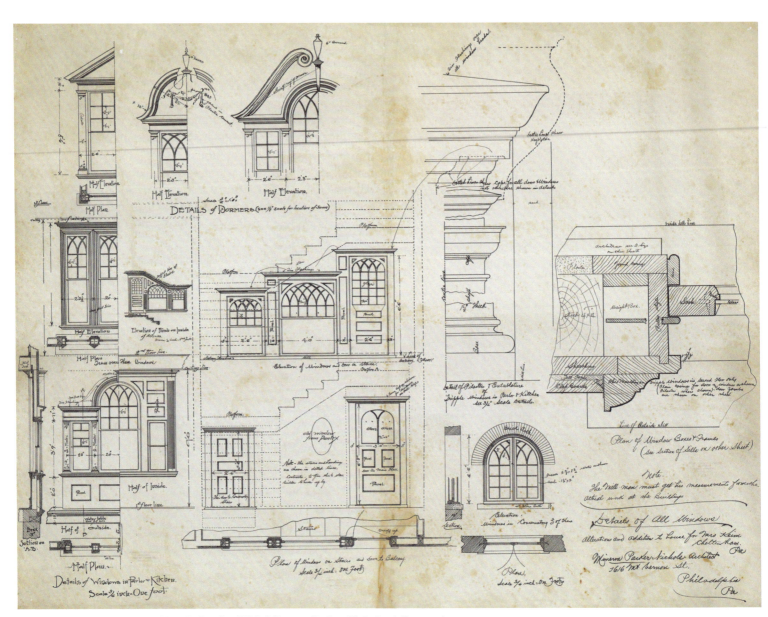

Keim House, window and millwork details, 1893 (Minerva Parker Nichols, delineator)

64
Unidentified House

1896

This design is known only through a stunning rendering (overleaf), likely in Nichols's own hand. The signature lists her residence as 53 Pineapple Street, Brooklyn, dating the design to the first six months of 1896.

Location unknown.
Undetermined.

REFERENCES

Drawing: Adelaide Nichols Baker Papers, Schlesinger Library, Harvard Radcliffe Institute

CATALOGUE RAISONNÉ

Perspective of the Unidentified House, ca. 1896 (Minerva Parker Nichols, delineator)

65 Browne and Nichols School for Boys

1896–97

Browne and Nichols School, ca. 1920s

20 Garden Street, Cambridge, Massachusetts

Demolished in 1968.

The Browne and Nichols School was established in 1883 by George Henry Browne (1857–1931) and Edgar Hamilton Nichols (1856–1910) as a private college preparatory school. Initially, instruction took place at two locations in Cambridge. In 1896, seeking to expand its facilities, Radcliffe College exchanged land with the boys' school, providing a site at 20 Garden Street on which to build a new school building. School leaders turned to Minerva Parker Nichols, who had just opened her office at 280 Prospect Place in Brooklyn, New York, to design their building. The architect was the sister-in-law of Edgar Nichols, her husband's younger brother.

Measuring 43 by 73 feet in plan, the design provided classrooms, a library, and administrative spaces on three floors, with a gymnasium and toilet facilities in the basement. Brick and limestone were used for the building's exteriors, with cast-iron columns and girders providing ample spans for interiors. Wainscoting was of "natural ash throughout," with the walls painted a "soft buff" color. Special attention was paid to the ventilation system: a gravity-type unit provided heating and cooling to rooms without use of a fan or blower, instead taking advantage of warm air's inherent buoyancy. Exhaust was by means of a galvanized iron chimney in the center of the roof.

In the late 1920s, expansion plans saw the acquisition of a site on Gerry's Landing Road in Cambridge although it would take twenty years to raise the funds to consolidate the campus. The building was sold in 1948 and used by other schools until 1968, when it was demolished.

REFERENCES

San Francisco Chronicle, April 14, 1901.
Lois Lilley Howe, "The History of Garden Street" in Vol. 33 of *Cambridge Historical Society: Proceedings for the Year 1949* (Cambridge, MA: Cambridge Historical Society, 1953), 47.
Photographs: AAUP
Photographs and records: Buckingham, Browne and Nichols School Archives
Drawings: Adelaide Nichols Baker Papers, Schlesinger Library, Harvard Radcliffe Institute

CATALOGUE RAISONNÉ

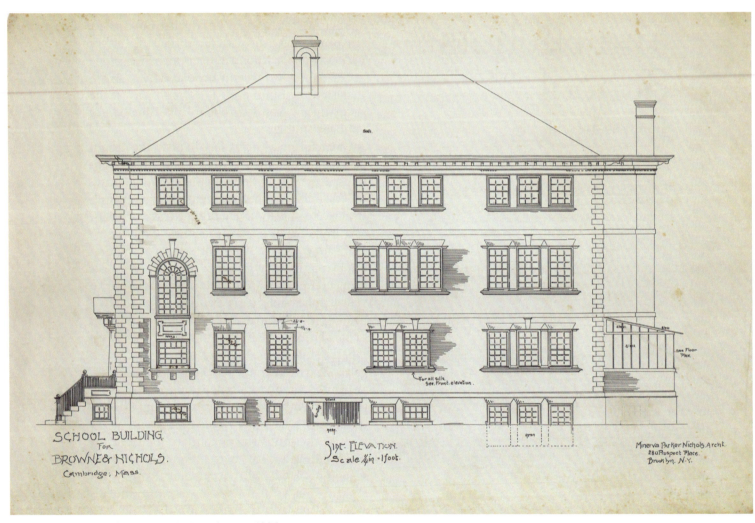

Browne and Nichols School, north elevation, ca. 1896

THE ARCHITECTURE OF MINERVA PARKER NICHOLS

Browne and Nichols School, conservatory

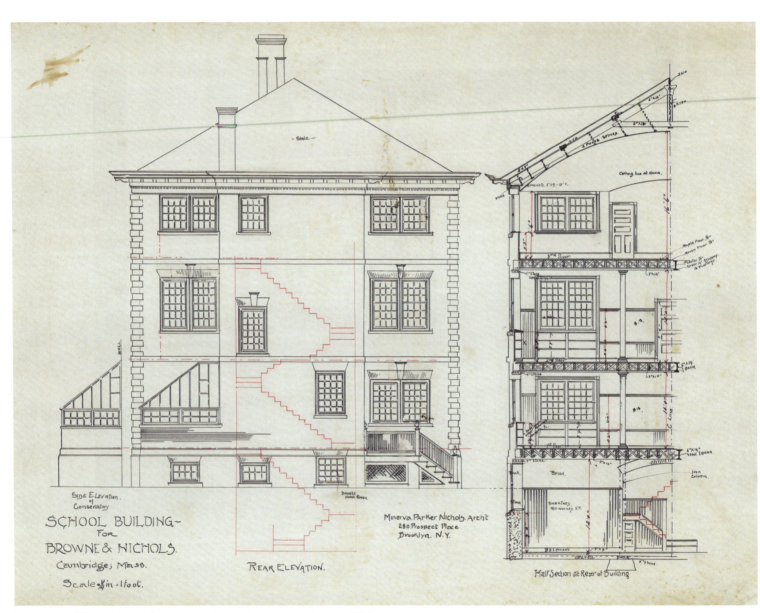

Browne and Nichols School, rear elevation and partial section, ca. 1896

66
Projects for the Hackley School

ca. 1900–1902

Established in 1899, the Hackley School was a boys' preparatory school, originally affiliated with the American Unitarian Association. Frances Hackley, a resident of New York City, donated her Tarrytown estate on Castle Ridge, overlooking the Tappan Zee of the Hudson River, along with the funds to make alterations for its use as a school and an endowment to support operations. Pressure to expand the school quickly resulted in the acquisition of a second estate, and additional donations were sought to build out what became known as the Hackley Quadrangle, the school's current location. The Upper School formally opened its doors in September 1900 for a class of twenty-five students; the Lower School—located in Hackley's former mansion—opened in October 1901. The extent of Nichols's additions is uncertain, but they appear to have encompassed a four-story structure built on the south side of Hackley's original house. The cupola surmounting the house was likely an addition denoting the structure's transition to institutional use.

Hackley Hall, ca. 1910

Union Avenue (above Marymount Avenue), Tarrytown, New York

Demolished.

REFERENCES

New York Tribune, August 26, 1899.
Boston Evening Transcript, October 20, 1900.
Yonkers Herald (NY), November 16, 1900.
San Francisco Chronicle, April 14, 1901.

67
First Unitarian Church of Gouverneur

ca. 1897

Trinity Avenue, Gouverneur, New York
Still Standing.

Nichols reported designing a "church for Gouverneur, N.Y." The project was likely an outcome of her involvement with the American Unitarian Association or her Unitarian ties in Philadelphia. Now a Masonic Temple, the one-story First Unitarian Church of Gouverneur was built of buff-colored brick with a prominent Palladian window facing Trinity Avenue.

REFERENCES
San Francisco Chronicle, April 14, 1901.

68
Prototype for a Nursery School

1893

Location unknown
Undetermined.

This undated drawing for a "small nursery school" may have been prepared by Nichols as a prototype structure for organizations associated with the Unitarian church and developed out of her design work for the day nurseries of the Brooklyn Bureau of Charities. The design's rustic character suggest that it may have been intended for rural areas.

REFERENCES
Drawing: AAUP

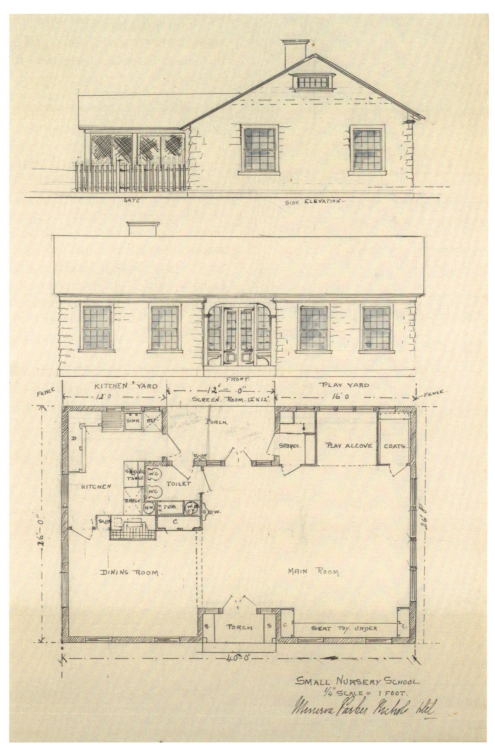
Prototype for a Nursery School, elevations and plan (Minerva Parker Nichols, delineator)

69

Brooklyn Bureau of Charities, Northern District Building

1900

The architect's husband, William I. Nichols, served as the General Secretary for the Brooklyn Bureau of Charities from 1896 to 1912. The bureau provided a range of social services and in 1899 purchased a house on Marcy and Division Avenues near the Brooklyn end of the Williamsburg Bridge, on a site opposite one that had been recently selected for a branch public library. "There is widespread poverty in this area," bureau board member Alfred T. White noted, and that fact, "coupled with a lack of relief agencies," required consolidation and expansion of the organization's facilities. This facility included woodyards that provided temporary employment for men, workrooms for unskilled women, laundry facilities, and day nurseries for the care of the children of working mothers. Nichols's alterations raised the roof of the building, providing clerestory lighting for internal classroom and activity spaces.

This is the last known instance of the architect's professional activities being reported on in professional circles.

191 Marcy Avenue, Brooklyn, New York

Demolished before 1940.

REFERENCES

New York Real Estate Record and Builders' Guide 66, no. 1704 (November 10, 1900): 651.
Brooklyn Bureau of Charities, *Twenty-Fifth Anniversary Meeting of the Brooklyn Board of Charities*, November, 1903.
Photographs: Harvard Art Museums, Fogg Museum

70 William I. Nichols Summer House

ca. 1903

Nichols's father-in-law, the Reverend John Taylor Gilman Nichols (1826–1900), raised his four sons in Saco, Maine, where he served the congregation of the First Unitarian Church for over fifty years. In 1884 he built a summer house in nearby Old Orchard Beach, as a family retreat. Following his death in 1900, the property passed to his eldest son, William, and his wife, Minerva. The latter, their daughter Adelaide recalled, "tactfully enlarged" the house, adding a two-story volume at the back and enlarging the original building with a large dormer on the street side. The barn and shed, also designed by the architect, served as children's play spaces. Summering in Maine proved impractical for the family, and the property was sold in 1906.

Nichols Summer House, 2022

6 Camp Comfort Avenue,
Old Orchard Beach, Maine

Still standing but severely altered.

REFERENCES

Papers: AAUP
Photographs: collection of William Whitaker

71
William and Minerva Parker Nichols House

1907–9

Nichols House, Wilton, rear facade, 2022

Nichols House, Wilton, 2022

36 Sharp Hill Road, Wilton, Connecticut

Still standing.

William I. Nichols's commitments to his Brooklyn charity work had prevented him from regularly visiting the family's summer house in Maine. In December 1907 he and his wife purchased a historic but dilapidated property in southern Connecticut, easily accessible from Brooklyn. In need of much work, particularly to remove late-Victorian touches, the mid-eighteenth-century house became the family's year-round retreat from the city.

Their son John Doane Nichols recalled that his mother, "though restrained from any drastic reconstruction both by financial necessity and respect for the integrity of the colonial character of the pre-Revolutionary house, was able to make deft improvements to bring light and space into the interior." She cut "wide doorways between rooms, partitioning the end of the old kitchen with its fireplace so that a smaller kitchen left the wide fireplace free as a center for a sunny dining room with French doors to a wide back porch."

To make a primary bedroom, Nichols transformed a windowless oak-beamed storeroom tucked behind the mass of the stone chimney, with two dormers, leaving the hand-hewn oak beams exposed. Bedroom closets were tucked in under the slope of the roof, or deftly pressed into the

Nichols House, Wilton, primary bedroom, 2022

eclectic hall space—dominated by the sculptural mass of the chimney. The ceiling of the southern bedroom was removed, opening the space up to the height of the roof ridge and allowing great amounts of sunlight to pour through the upper window. The barn was rehabilitated with new siding and a coat of green paint. Its lower level provided space for a horse stall, carriage, and workshop, while the second floor was converted into a playroom and a dormitory for summer visitors.

Nichols began living full-time in the house in 1922 and must have added central heating and indoor plumbing systems at that time (the cast-iron grates are still in place). The house was sold in 1931 but an account of the family's time there is provided in *Return to Arcady*, published in 1973 by the architect's daughter Adelaide Baker.

REFERENCES

Adelaide N. Baker, *Return to Arcady* (New York and Westport, CT: Lawrence Hill, 1973).
Photographs: AAUP
HABS No. CT-487

72
John W. T. Nichols House, The Kettles

ca. 1908–9

Aerial view of "The Kettles," ca. 1970

For her husband's second cousin, John White Treadwell Nichols (1852–1920), a successful dealer of cotton goods, Nichols designed a substantial summer house on a thirty-six-acre estate at Cove Neck, on property near to President Theodore Roosevelt's Sagamore Hill. The Kettles was situated on Cooper's Bluff, looking east toward Cold Spring Harbor. The three-story Dutch gabled entrance bay projected from the main facade and was supported on six stout columns. A substantial porch extended to the south, while the service wing was set to the curve of the entrance drive. The house featured a central hall that opened out onto a series of terraces overlooking the water. Living areas were located on the south end of the plan, with dining room at the north east corner of the main volume of the house—with direct access to the service wing and kitchen. At the second level, a loggia connected the main bedrooms, each with its own bay window.

"The Kettles," entry facade, ca. 1970

Cove Neck Road, Cove Neck, Oyster Bay, New York

Demolished about 1990.

REFERENCES

Photographs: collection of Peter D. Taylor
Robert B. Mackay, Anthony K. Baker, and Carol A. Trainer, eds., *Long Island Country Houses and Their Architects, 1860–1940* (New York: W. W. Norton, 1997), 307.

73
Cathedral of St. John the Divine

ca. 1909

References to Nichols's activities associated with the building of the Cathedral of St. John the Divine are unconfirmed but derive from the accounts of her grown children. This work was supposedly connected to a 1909 family trip to Europe, where the architect is reported to have made studies of English and French Gothic churches on behalf of the cathedral architects. No corroborating evidence has been discovered to elaborate on the scope or specifics of her role.

1047 Amsterdam Avenue,
New York, New York
Undetermined.

REFERENCES

Papers: AAUP

74
Housing Studies for Alfred T. White

ca. 1910

Brooklyn, New York
Undetermined.

Alfred Treadway White (1846–1921) was a close friend of the Nichols family and a co-founder of the Brooklyn Bureau of Charities, where the architect's husband was general secretary. A wealthy man through his successes in the fur business, White was for forty years a deacon of the First Unitarian Church of Brooklyn.

In 1867 White became involved in the church's settlement house, and in the years that followed, he became an outspoken and important housing reformer focused on improving living conditions among the urban poor. He was responsible for developing several model housing projects, including the Home and Tower Buildings in the Cobble Hill neighborhood of Brooklyn (William Field and Son, architects, 1877–79), and the 280-unit Riverside Buildings in Brooklyn Heights (William Field and Son, architects, 1890). Shared, central, semi-public court spaces were key amenities in both projects. The sale of liquor was prohibited at both, and their success was guaranteed by, "a strict moral and police supervision under a faithful janitor."

The extent of Nichols's work for White is unknown. A family source suggests a focus on the Riverside Buildings, twenty years old at the time. Perhaps Nichols explored pragmatic upgrades to the facilities tied to the need for day nurseries (or similarly useful facilities). Another possibility is that she embarked on a general study of successful housing types for the urban poor, in connection with a yet-to-be uncovered educational campaign.

REFERENCES

Christopher Gray, "The Riverside Buildings; a Model Tenement in Dickensian Style," *New York Times*, August 23, 1992: R7.
Christopher Gray, "Architectural Wealth, Built for the Poor," *New York Times*, October 12, 2008: RE7.
Papers: AAUP

75

First Church of Deerfield

1913

Following the installation of her husband as minister in March 1913, Nichols oversaw renovations to the church's interiors, as well as the installation of central heating and upgrades to electrical systems. She restored the character of the early interiors with a simplified color palette: white paint for the ceiling, soft pink for the walls, with the alcove behind the altar accented with a gold-leaf glaze. Pews were painted with a high-gloss white; cushions and rugs were a crimson red.

The work was described in a local newspaper as "simple but substantial and dignified in every particular. Few meeting houses have so fine a pulpit, since the varnish has been removed, the grain of the old San Dominican Mahogany shows forth. The pulpit is covered with a handsome silk brocade, crimson in color. The graceful bronze candelabrum...has been restored to its old place, suspended from the center of the ceilings and been electrified with six 100 watt lamps."

70 Old Main Street, Deerfield, Massachusetts

Still standing.

REFERENCES

Greenfield Gazette (MA), September 6, 1913.
Greenfield Gazette (MA), September 13, 1913.
Greenfield Gazette (MA), November 22, 1913.
Photographs: AAUP

76
William and Minerva Parker Nichols House

ca. 1916

In 1916 William Nichols expressed his desire to spend his remaining days at Hingham, Massachusetts, where he had started his career as a Unitarian minister. "Mother found a house for us to buy in Hingham," Nichols's daughter Adelaide recalled. "She restored a sedate white brick townhouse with her indomitable energy and skill," paying particular attention to its fine wainscoting and mantels. Nichols remained at the house after William's death in November 1917. She sold the property in May 1922.

346 Main Street,
Hingham, Massachusetts

Still standing but severely altered.

REFERENCES

Adelaide N. Baker, *Return to Arcady* (New York and Westport, CT: Lawrence Hill, 1973), 137–38.

77

John and Adelaide Baker House

1924–25

Baker House, ca. 1925

82 Clinton Avenue, Westport, Connecticut

Still standing.

Six months after their marriage in June 1924, Adelaide Nichols Baker (1894–1974) and John A. Baker (1887–1968) purchased a seventeen-acre tract on Clinton Avenue, overlooking the Saugatuck River. The property was close to the offices of the Dorr Company, where John Baker oversaw their research and testing activities, particularly the development of technologies and techniques for mining and mineral extraction of gold, silver, and other precious metals.

Nichols described her design for the Baker house as "early American and miner camp," drawing an association between her son-in-law's experience in the gold fields of the western United States and the early colonial architecture of southern Connecticut. "People should live in houses that are distinctly part of them," she asserted. She specified a chimney faced in white granite river stones—possibly sourced from the western United States—for the exterior, and chunky pink granite slabs for the interior fireplace surround. For the mantel, Jack Baker requested rough timber. The paneling in the entrance hall was wormy chestnut, harvested from Nichols's property in Wilton, Connecticut.

The Bakers lived in the house until 1928, when they moved into Guard Hill [SEE CAT. NO. 78]. In August 1930, the architect purchased the property from the Bakers and resided there until her death. The house was sold by her estate in February 1950.

REFERENCES

Philadelphia Inquirer, November 28, 1937.
HABS No. CT-485; Photographs: AAUP

CATALOGUE RAISONNÉ

Baker House, entry hall and living room, ca. 1925

78
John and Adelaide Baker House, Guard Hill

1929

"Guard Hill," 2022

78 Clinton Avenue,
Westport, Connecticut

Still standing.

Guard Hill was the name given to the Baker's property by a local historian with an interest in the American Revolution. The site was one of several high points where fires were built as a warning that the Redcoats had landed at Compo Beach and were marching on Danbury. The Bakers had purchased the property in 1924 and built a modest house designed by Nichols on the downhill side the following year [SEE CAT. NO. 77]. They lived in the house until 1929, when Guard Hill was completed.

The three-story house was built of stone and shingles, with its basement and garage built into the slope of the hill. The entrance hall, sheathed in wormy chestnut harvested from the architect's property in Wilton, Connecticut, opened through a double door into a two-story living room with a large fireplace and a ceiling with exposed timber beams. Originally, there were built-in bookcases and a window seat—a small window overlook from the second floor was a favorite lookout post for their grandchildren. The dining room opened out onto a three-tiered southern terrace; a sunporch provided a covered area for seating. The service area included a kitchen and pantry, as well as a servant's room. The children's playroom with low casement windows served as a nursery school in its first years and was later adapted for teenage gatherings. Upstairs were bathrooms, a primary bedroom, and four other bedrooms.

The Bakers raised three children in the house and it became a center for their nine grandchildren. The house was sold two years after Adelaide's death in 1974.

REFERENCES

"A True Family Home: Where the John A. Bakers Count Their Blessings," Fairfield County 14, no. 8 (August 1967): 14–15.
Elsie Thew, "The Baker Gardens on Guard Hill," *Westport News* (Westport, CT), July 25, 1973, sec. 2: 3.
Drawing and photographs: AAUP
HABS No. CT-484

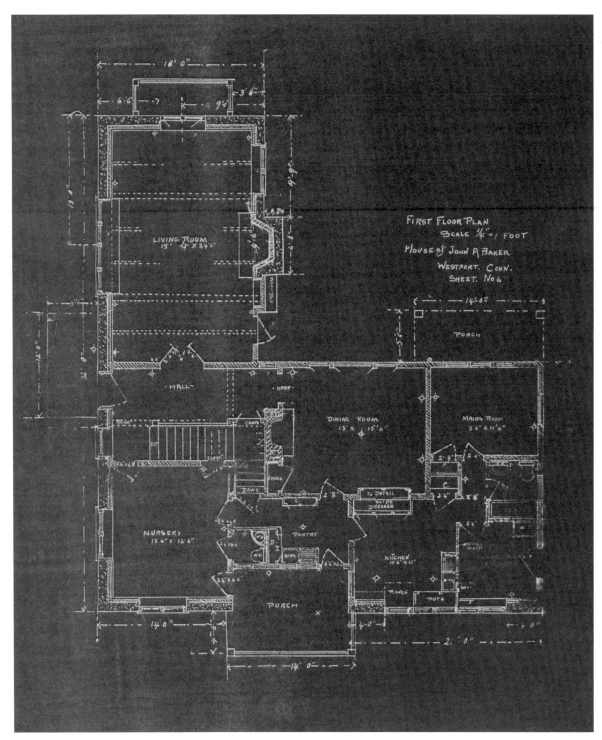

"Guard Hill," first-floor plan, 1929

THE ARCHITECTURE OF MINERVA PARKER NICHOLS

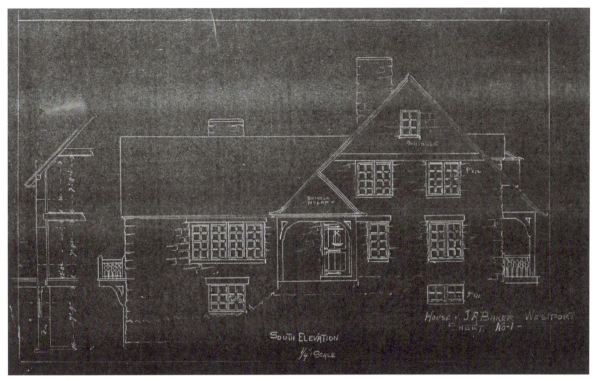

"Guard Hill," south elevation, 1929

"Guard Hill," terrace, ca. 1965

79 Unidentified House

ca. 1930s

This small cottage, perhaps a summer house, was captured in a pair of photographs found in a Baker family photo album. The house was likely designed by Nichols for a yet-to-be-identified family member. It closely recalls the family's Wilton house—in the detailing of the small windows under the eaves—and the Baker house—in the hand-hewn porch posts [SEE CAT. NOS. 71 AND 78].

Location unknown, probably Connecticut.

Undetermined.

REFERENCES

Photographs: AAUP

THE ARCHITECTURE OF MINERVA PARKER NICHOLS

View of the Unidentified House, ca. 1930s

80

Charles A. and Gertrude R. Lubrecht House

1936

Charles A. Lubrecht (1875–1963) was a physician and surgeon with a practice in Brooklyn, New York. He and his wife, Gertrude (1897–1995), purchased three acres on Clinton Avenue in Westport in June 1932. Westport deed records confirm that the property included an existing dwelling (located at 77 Clinton Avenue), and it was this house that served as their summer residence beginning in July 1932.

Gertrude Lubrecht took an active role in parent-teacher organizations and her name appears regularly in the Brooklyn society pages into 1937, while the US census of 1940 confirms that Brooklyn was their primary residence (as of April 1935). Their summers in Westport, no doubt, provided the couple with the opportunity to meet their neighbor Nichols—who had moved into 82 Clinton Avenue in 1930—and to familiarize themselves with the house that she had designed for Jack and Adelaide Baker in 1929 [SEE CAT. NO. 78]. These associations ultimately led them to commission Nichols to design them a new home sometime in 1935 or early 1936. Nichols reported having designed a house as late as 1936, and there is little doubt that she was referring to the Lubrechts' house.

Reflecting on the design of houses in 1937, Nichols expressed her belief in "purely functional houses, built to live in." She found much of value in simplification and found in Georgian and Colonial Revival styles an ideal of spareness. Nichols thought modern architects should take what is good out of every period, "letting fitness for use rule choice." The Lubrechts sold the house in 1957.

73 Clinton Avenue,
Westport, Connecticut

Still standing.

REFERENCES

Brooklyn Daily Eagle, June 8, 1932.
Philadelphia Inquirer, November 28, 1937.
HABS No. CT-486

THE ARCHITECTURE OF MINERVA PARKER NICHOLS

Lubrecht House, south and east facades, 2022 with later garage extension

CATALOGUE RAISONNÉ

Lubrecht House, entry hall, 2022

Lubrecht House, living room, 2022

81 Homes for Veterans

ca. 1945–47

In remarks in connection with the celebration of the seventieth anniversary of the New Century Club of Philadelphia, Nichols said that she "had recently been designing homes for veterans." Also reported on was the fact that Nichols had remained active as an architect well into her eighties (a fact corroborated by several family memoirs).

Nichols's clients in this period were probably exclusively her daughter Adelaide and son-in-law John "Jack" Baker. The couple had begun to develop former farms with an eye toward the returning veterans of World War II. The Bakers began with a parcel at their Westport property now known as 3 Guard Hill Road. That house, built just after the war using timbers salvaged from an old barn, was maintained as a rental property for several decades.

The Bakers were also developing land in the nearby town of Weston, with a focus on the thirty-acre former estate of Francis B. Coley, purchased in July 1945. The project involved renovations to the existing farmhouse and barn structures located at 28 Good Hill Road. By 1956 (seven years after Nichols's death), the larger parcel had been subdivided into ten properties and a new lane platted and named Hidden Hill Road. Numbers 4 and 13 Hidden Hill Road were extant by 1956.

The extent of Nichols's design work at these sites remains unclear, and it is unknown whether there were other areas on which her daughter and son-in-law sought her input, during this period.

Westport and Weston, Connecticut
Probably built.

REFERENCES

Philadelphia Inquirer, March 11, 1947.

Writings

MINERVA PARKER NICHOLS: THE AGENCY OF WOMEN IN BUILDINGS AND TEXTS

Franca Trubiano

THE AGENCY OF WOMEN IN BUILDINGS AND TEXTS

It is useless to enter the profession of architecture without a thorough training grafted upon a real love for the expression of art in building.

—Minerva Parker Nichols

WRITINGS

The first American woman to practice architecture independently, Minerva Parker Nichols was as adept with a pen as she was with a T-square—agents in her pursuit of architectural expression in the art of building. This essay is an invitation to ponder more closely her use of the written word between 1887 and 1896. By writing at a time when women were sparingly represented in all manner of publications, did she hope to gain new commissions, extend her client base, educate her suffragist sisters, or create a legacy of ideas about building? It was a radical proposition for women to build; it was barely less so for them to publish.

By the standards of late nineteenth-century America, Minerva authored a great deal in a short period. In nine years, she wrote dozens of articles and opinion pieces. She even had her own dedicated series on "practical dwellings and homes" in the women's monthly the *Home-Maker*, having published five different essays on the "merit of architectural work" in 1891 and 1892.[1] She may have spent many a day on the building site overseeing the construction of buildings, yet she considered it an essential part of her practice to publish. Why? Why did Minerva believe dissemination of architectural thoughts was as important as designing and building? And where did she learn to exercise the art of writing in service to her architectural practice? These questions are not easily answered but are worth exploring.

Architecture as an Art of Expression

In 1889, at the age of twenty-seven, Minerva made communicating the products of her labor an important aspect of her professional practice. That year, on November 16, her writing was published for the first time

---

Epigraph: Minerva Parker Nichols, "Women as Architects," 1896.

1   Minerva Parker, "Practical Dwellings," *Home-Maker* 5, no. 4 (January 1891): 443.

in the *Woman's Journal*, a newspaper dedicated, as advertised on its front page, to "the interests of Woman—to her educational, industrial, legal, and political Equality, especially to her right of Suffrage." The Pennsylvania Woman's Suffrage Association, with which the *Woman's Journal* was affiliated, had its offices at 1601 Mount Vernon Street in Philadelphia, and being but a few blocks from Minerva's home, it isn't surprising; perhaps it isn't surprising that she submitted her article to this mouthpiece for women's rights.[2] Stories of political import, reporting on the property rights of married women, and human-interest narratives of personal hardship were common in the *Woman's Journal*. We learn, for example, of a railway stewardess destined to a life in service even after having secured freedom from slavery and of the bravery of Charity Lambert, a "colored woman who distinguished herself by her courage and unselfishness during the wreck ... of the *Corona* on the Mississippi."[3] Less common were professional and intellectual pieces such as Minerva's "Architecture as an Art."

This was her first essay on the subject, yet it revealed the depths of her erudition and courage in wading through the waters of architectural theory. It is here that we are introduced to Minerva's understanding of and appreciation for the art historical concept of "expression" as developed in the term, "character." When speaking of a building's appearance, for example, she noted:

> Our houses, like our faces, may not be beautiful, but they shall, at least, have the firm and rugged lines that denote character. Looking over the splendid examples of the past, we find in each recognizable style the influence of the times and people. The sober, symbolic Egyptian; the purity and simplicity of Greece; the glory of Rome. The Normans and early English built homes like forts. The delicate

---

2   Minerva Parker lived at 1614 Green Street from 1885 to 1893, a few blocks from the Pennsylvania Woman's Suffrage Associate. See https://www.minervaparkernichols.com/life.
3   Minerva Parker, "Architecture as an Art," *Woman's Journal*, November 16, 1889, 362.

lines of Gothic, with its slender spires and pointed arches, speak eloquently of the elevation of the Christian Church.[4]

In her choice of words, Minerva clearly communicated to readers her knowledge of architectural history, her familiarity with the idea of style in art theory, and its alignment with character in the fine arts. In this she could have had many possible teachers. In the United States, for example, author and landscape architect Andrew Jackson Downing (1815–1852) wrote of the importance of character in *A Treatise on the Theory and Practice of Landscape Gardening Adapted to North America; with a View to the Improvement of Country Residences* of 1841.[5] In describing the range of possible and appropriate features that a landscape architect might project onto an American landscape, he spoke of "national character," "graceful and agreeable character," "artificial character," "military character," "sylvan character," and even "highly tasteful character."[6] Downing, who lived in Newburgh, New York, published extensively during the 1830s, and one might expect Minerva to have been familiar with his work.

The depth of her understanding was more subtly revealed, however, in her use of the analogy "our houses, like our faces." This phrase suggests the theory of facial expression articulated in a collection of drawings, *Caractères des passions sur les desseins* (1695–1720) by Charles Le Brun (1619–1690) court painter to Louis XIV. Amounting to a near alphabet of expressions, the traces and outlines of our facial features reveal our inner passions, dispositions, and character, according to Le Brun. Rapture, esteem, veneration, joy, sorrow, and fear were among the fifty drawings of expression included in the *Caractères des passions*. Painters were tasked with acquiring this knowledge to the benefit of their art. By the eighteenth

---

4 Parker, 362.
5 Andrew Jackson Downing, *A Treatise on the Theory and Practice of Landscape Gardening Adapted to North America; with a View to the Improvement of Country Residences* (New York and London: Wiley and Putnam, 1844), accessed via Hathi Trust Digital Library. I am indebted to Gabrielle Ruddick for having introduced me to Downing's interest in "character."
6 Downing, *Treatise on the Theory and Practice of Landscape Gardening*, 17, 25, 34, 49, 60, 74, and 77..

century, the French term *caractère* had been applied to architectural works and to their ability to communicate identifiable characteristics associated with human qualities. Hence, for architects no less than painters, artistic skill was predicated on notions of style and on the visual language of character. This was the disciplinary knowledge Minerva understood when she shared the principles of an art of representation with her suffragist sisters in her essay "Architecture as an Art."

She did so once more in an essay published in 1893, "An Uncultivated Field." Appearing in *Housekeeper's Weekly, a Journal of Home Help, Information, and Entertainment*, Minerva's essay spoke to the kind of expertise required of women when building their own homes. Her article was nothing less than a call to action, *"I appeal to you, my sister women, to…attend to your own homes."*[7] Indeed, tending to the design and construction of one's home required clients well versed in the art of architecture.

> As there are all kinds of clients, so there are all kinds of houses. They have seemed to me like people—the houses that are all front and show—like, shallow and superficial people; the selfish houses, with cramped front doors; the secretive houses, with small, ill-lighted windows; the giddy houses, with much flimsy ornament and many colors; the plain houses, like Quaker women in their quiet garb; the dignified houses, like well-rounded characters; the dainty house, like our society women; the jolly houses; the sad; dissipated, and extravagant—all have their counterparts in the human families who occupy them.[8]

Now, more than a century later, this statement might strike today's reader as out of keeping with modern cultural and political norms. Yet, its main tenet and that of Minerva's longer article, was that a great deal of effort

---

7   Minerva Parker Nichols, "An Uncultivated Field," *Housekeeper's Weekly*, June 10, 1893, 3–4.
8   Nichols, 3–4.

should be invested in the representation of one's home and that women had agency in this area. Being familiar with architecture's expressive potential was not only a form of individuation, but of empowerment. As Minerva reminded her readers:

> The chief charm of any house is its individuality. There are many things which houses or people possess in common; but the thing which charms us is the thing peculiar to a certain house or a certain person.

At a time when her suffragist sisters sought emancipation, Minerva promoted her architectural ability to deliver homes to them designed to their character and in support of their personal individuation.

Building in Text

At the end of the nineteenth century, vigorous debate on art and on the value of architecture in the built environment was common—in print, in schools, and professional practice. Minerva was never far from a good debate. Indeed, when eleven members of the crème de la crème of Philadelphia's architectural establishment were featured on Sunday, November 19, 1893, in a full-page article called "Art in Architecture," Minerva was among them. More precisely, a drawn portrait of her was at the center of a composition that featured the likes of Frank Furness, Frank Miles Day, Wilson Eyre, Walter Cope, and John Stewardson. At the close of the Chicago World's Fair, each architect was asked to pronounce themselves on the "Influence of the Columbian Exposition on American Building." Furness applauded Daniel Burnham's organizational prowess, whereas Stewardson was confident the White City had made an important impression on "the masses of technically uneducated people."[9] Minerva, whose piece was titled "An Architectural Object Lesson," alluded, not surprisingly, to "mistakes, misunderstandings and false notes," which surrounded her loss of the commission for the Fair's Queen Isabella Association Pavilion.[10] Notwithstanding, however, what must have been a professional setback, Minerva acquiesced with grace to calling the architectural event a success. She adopted the literary analogy of buildings as books, when comparing the 1893 World's Columbian Exposition in Chicago to the 1876 Centennial Exposition in Philadelphia, concluding that Burnham's plan had excelled in the features of its urban planning, its "lagoons, boats, bridges and pavilions."[11] In what concerned the buildings, according to Minerva:

> The architects of the World's Fair are to be congratulated on their harmony of design and for the general absence of that unrestrained originality which mars so many of our buildings ... we can only congratulate ourselves on the exhibition of a real devotion to art displayed. I have no regret that the buildings are temporary structures. They were the text-books of a great national architectural object lesson, and like the text-books of the college graduate, are only of value in so far as they have cultivated a higher standard of scholarship.[12]

Simultaneously critical and laudatory, the statement was masterfully written. On the one hand, the Columbian Exposition was deemed successful, having been the profession's point of reference for decades in what concerned the "harmony of design." It offered architects a veritable textbook on the art of architecture, its "higher standard of scholarship"

---

9   "Art in Architecture," *Times* (Philadelphia), November 19, 1893
10 "Art in Architecture." See also Margaret (Molly) Lester, "'Lady Architect': The Work and Writings of Minerva Parker Nichols in Late Nineteenth-Century Philadelphia," *Pennsylvania Magazine of History and Biography* 143, no. 1, 2019: 52–53.
11 "Art in Architecture."
12 "Art in Architecture."

contributing to its acclaim. On the other hand, as a temporary site with temporary structures, the Chicago fair offered little to those interested in the art of building. One wonders, in fact, if Minerva was not somewhat disappointed in the excessive ornamental exuberance of the fair's neoclassical building fronts. Her 1889 text published in the *Woman's Journal* and mentioned above reminded her readers that if "architecture is the highest form of art" this is not because it was "a decorative art … a plaything in the hands of the idle."[13] Rather, if architecture was the mistress of the arts it was because she embodied art by way of her construction. A "grotesque face" carved "on some doorway or bracket" executed by the "rude hand" of the stone-cutter or temple frescoes by "Raphael, Correggio, Michael Angelo, and Titian,"[14] were works of architectural art because they were materially contingent with building. Architects created art when they handled stone, wood, and brick. She noted: "As Americans, we are the guardians of the most matchless granite and marble, forests and mines, which, yielding like clay in the hands of the sculptor, come forth bearing the impression of our thoughts."[15]

To be clear, architects were not sculptors; their education was distinctly other. Whereas sculptors learnt how to produce statues destined for art galleries, "stone-cutters and carvers" were tasked with the "stationary and no[n] moveable art."[16] Building craftspeople labored in support of the "long line of busy travelers" who "as a familiar landmark on their journey" … "look up at" their artwork when they encounter it on a building.[17]

Minerva repeatedly disclosed in text her knowledge of the art of building. She did so in her careful but necessary parsing of the difference between sculpture and architecturally embedded sculpture, and when referring to the skill architects needed for making in-situ adjustments to

---

13 Parker, "Architecture as an Art," 362. See also Lester, "'Lady Architect'": 38.
14 Parker, "Architecture as an Art," 362.
15 Parker, 362.
16 Parker, 362.
17 Parker, 362.

both building proportions and architectural figures. According to Minerva, lack of this expertise—never easy to acquire—could not be concealed by added "originality," novelty, or fashion, and could only be learnt by attending "thoroughly equipped schools of architecture." Indeed, architectural knowledge was distinct and materially different in several ways from that of painters and sculptors. As she noted in "Architecture as an Art":

> The collection of plaster casts of architectural ornament, which is being collected for the New York Metropolitan Art Gallery, the sketch clubs, competitions, manual training-schools, and industrial art schools, [that] are much needed steps in the right direction; [yet] … the question of utility and construction enters so largely into the work, aside from its art and decoration, that a special training is indispensable to the architectural student.[18]

Four years earlier, only a year into her practice and while still a student at the Pennsylvania Museum and School of Industrial Art, Minerva had called upon both architects and clients to master matters of "utility and construction." Possibly familiar with the writings of ancient architect Marcus Vitruvius Pollio (ca. 90–20 BCE), who had theorized that all architects require the knowledge of *venustas*, *utilitas*, and *firmitas* (beauty, utility, and strength), she reminded her readers that "it is impossible to furnish or decorate an ill-planned house, and poorly proportioned rooms cannot be disguised by costly hangings and elaborate furniture."[19]

No matter how well ornamented, a poorly proportioned room would never be architecturally pleasing. This basic tenet of architectural theory was important to Minerva, who referred to it once more in June 1893, when she published in *Housekeeper's Weekly* an essay on the design and construction

---

18   Parker, 362.
19   Parker, 362. Minerva returned to the Vitruvian triad when, in her January 1891 article in the *Home-Maker*, she noted: "In judging the merit of any architectural work, its first virtue is utility, going hand in hand with stability. A building must not only be strong but have the appearance of repose." Parker, "Practical Dwellings."

of well-proportioned homes. Of great concern to her was the tendency among some clients to build homes that were far bigger than needed, a financially reckless and architecturally useless propensity, in her view.

> Don't try to get more house for the same amount of money than anyone else ever did; for the builder must either make you a present of his labor, or deceive you in the value in quality of the work and material.[20]

This age-old principle familiar to many an architect signaled Minerva's awareness of the art of distribution, the knowledge by which architects orchestrated the careful composition, proportion, and program of rooms: a skill she recommended all her clients possess, even if it required the ability to read plans.

> Women often seem so helpless when they come to design their own houses that the mere thought of a specification to be read or inspection of the plans, is enough to deprive the poor architect of their society for days. I assure you, French novels will seem dull compared with the delight of threading your way through the translation of plans, when you have once mastered the mechanical part of the drawing.[21]

Surely, only an architect would elevate the pleasure of reading a floor plan above that of reading a French novel. Time and again, Minerva articulated correspondences between drawings and words, between designs and texts. In "An Uncultivated Field," her 1893 essay in *Housekeeper's Weekly*, discussed above, she invited her "sisters" to be in command of architecture, to master its drawings, and to seek out its texts.[22]

---

[20] Nichols, "An Uncultivated Field," 3–4.
[21] Nichols, 3–4.

THE AGENCY OF WOMEN IN BUILDINGS AND TEXTS

This is the field which I would open to you, and you will be surprised at the new world it leads to. You will take a new interest in all the details, before unseen. The styles of architecture being to arrange themselves in groups, as do favorite authors or artists. It is a new and interesting book, that can be read every time you go on the street. Every country road has chapters of the tale.

Retiring the Pen

Minerva was no stranger to the printed word. Throughout her early career in Philadelphia from 1888 to 1896, her building projects were announced, featured, and described in local newspapers including the *Philadelphia Inquirer*, the *Philadelphia Times*, and the *Philadelphia Record*; in industry trade journals such as *Journal of Building, Scientific American Architects and Builders Edition; Builder Decorator and Wood-Worker; Carpentry and Building; California Architect and Building News*; and the *Philadelphia Real Estate Record and Builders Guide*; in women's journals including *Woman's Progress*; the *Home-Maker; Housekeeper's Weekly*; and the *Woman's Journal*. In *Housekeeper's Weekly*, for example, Minerva reminds us of the strength and perseverance that it takes to practice architecture:

> A word in closing for those of my sisters who think of architecture as a profession. Like the new land in the far West, there are many claims not taken. It requires courage, some capital, much labor in travelling, as the road is long.[23]

---

22 Nichols, 3–4.
23 Nichols, 3–4.

By 1896, we intuit in her words increasing tension between the demands of being an architect and those of being a woman, having well understood the difference during her move to Brooklyn from Philadelphia. Indeed, Minerva possessed a great deal of courage when in 1896, she openly criticized comments from "Louise Bethune, of Buffalo, who ... worked in this profession for a number of years," and who at the time was the only woman member "of the New York Chapter of the Architectural Association."[24] She "took exception" to the claim by Bethune (1856–1913):

> that there is no need whatever for a woman architect. No one wants her, no one yearns for her ... When the woman enters the profession, she will be kindly met and will be welcome, but not as a woman, only as an architect.[25]

Differently than Bethune, Minerva's career had focused on the spaces and places of women, for women, and by women: the home, the school, and women's clubs had all been central to her idea and exercise of architecture. Alongside her desire to build lay her ambition to elevate building in the minds of women:

> Is it not a reproach to the good sense of part of the human family that a woman will devote more time and thought to the making of a frock to be worn for one short season than to the planning of her home?[26]

Never fearful of upsetting her reader or client, Minerva reminded both that homes were as significant to a woman's sense of representation and identification as any dress or garment she chose to wear. An ardent author and

---

24 Minerva Parker Nichols, "Women as Architects," *Third Biennial, General Federation of Women's Clubs* (Louisville, KY: Flexner Brothers, 1896), 267.
25 Nichols, 267.
26 Nichols, 267.

commentator, she encouraged her "sisters" to follow in her footsteps and it was to them she directed her thoughts, words, deliberations, and ambitions. Unlike Bethune, Minerva was not ready to relinquish her identity as a woman. In fact, it was not in spite of being a woman that she practiced architecture, but because she was one.

> If every woman who thought of building a new home would make it a serious occupation of her life during the time of its planning and construction, and if every woman who enters the profession would determine that she would lay hold of the difficulties of design, construction, and ornamentation until she was master of her art, there would be great need of her.[27]

Sadly, this statement penned at the of age of thirty-four, was published in Nichols's final article. In 1896 her article "Women as Architects" celebrated the academic and professional progress made in architecture by women. She fêted their distinct "advantage over men, as in all the details of designing, women bring taste, tact and judgment."[28] She highlighted the fact that women were "practicing in almost every state in the Union." But, in an odd foreshadowing of her own inner tensions as a woman Minerva noted:

> It is well known that few men attain honorable recognition in the profession of architecture until early middle life. Ten or fifteen years of hard work bring with them the reward of labor well directed, and … recognized as such.[29]

---

27 Nichols, 267.
28 Nichols, 268.
29 Nichols, 268.
30 Lester, "Lady Architect," 39.

WRITINGS

She published this statement but a decade after having first apprenticed in 1886 in Philadelphia with Edwin W. Thorne.[30] According to her own claims, by 1896 she would have been well placed to "attain honorable recognition in the profession." And indeed she was, for as noted by Molly Lester, in the first eight years of Minerva's practice she had built forty projects, a remarkable record for any architect, let alone a woman sole practitioner at the close of the nineteenth century. She had also, however, married in 1891, miscarried twins seven months later, and moved in 1896 with her husband to Brooklyn New York. With fewer professional contacts and clients, caring for one child with a second on the way, her words in "Women as Architects," were prescient:

> In conclusion, I must add one word on the vexed question of the professional life of married women. Ideally, one feels that marriage and the care of children should not displace professional life. That a woman is entitled to the development of her talents and abilities after as before marriage no one dare deny. For my part, I believe that nothing can take the place in life of a real and intelligent interest in some occupation or profession, the active practice of which must at times give place to the demands and responsibilities of child life, if the mother wishes to assume the responsibility. Every child that is invited into this world deserves and has the right to demand at the hands of her or his mother her first and best care and thought.[31]

By 1901, when she participated in the evening discussion at the Architectural League of New York on "Architecture as an Occupation for Women," it was reported that for Minerva, the "draughting-room [was] now secondary to the nursery," now that she had "been called to a higher sphere of action, that

---

31   Nichols, "Women as Architects," 269–270.
32   "Women in Architecture," *Woman's Journal*, January 5, 1901, 2.

of motherhood."[32] The days when she would write and publish new copy for her readers of the monthly the *Home-Maker* were mostly in the past.

More than a hundred years later, it is difficult to reconcile the denouement of her professional career with the vibrancy of its early beginnings. In June 1891, but six months prior to her marriage, her professional office was featured in the *Home-Maker* with a rendering of Minerva hard at work over her drafting table. The room included her tools, projects, and rolled up drawings. The accompanying narrative lauded her ingenuity and bravery:

> She has great industry, a fine sense of personal responsibility, a strong determination to fulfill just expectations at any personal sacrifice, a broad, just view of all interests concerned in her contracts, a reverence for honesty and truth, a modest but firm appreciation of her own power, and a love for and fidelity to the highest and best aims in her profession. She has fought her way to the front through difficulties and stands to-day on her merits, at the head of her profession: and although still a young woman, under thirty, she illustrates anew the fundamental law, that success in any direction is not a matter of sex, but of character and endowment. [33]

Unfortunately, plus ça change ...

---

33 "A Woman Architect," *Home-Maker* 6, no. 3 (June 1891).

WRITINGS

Architecture as an Art (1889)

The Woman's Journal

Editors Woman's Journal: I wish to interest you a little in art that so nearly affects every one that we cannot afford to be ignorant of its influence or possibilities. Our houses, like our faces, may not be beautiful, but they shall, at least, have the firm and rugged lines that denote character.

Looking over the splendid examples of the past, we find in each recognized style the influence of the times and people. The sombre (sic), symbolic Egyptian; the purity and simplicity of Greece; the glory of Rome. The Norman and early English built homes like forts. The delicate lines of Gothic, with its slender spires and pointed arches, speak eloquently of the elevation of the Christian Church. We have built best, at all times, in all countries, and all people, to the gods whom we worship.

The architectural triumphs of the present century are so closely connected with the money markets and exchanges, that we must have a very material form of worship in our temples.

Architecture is the highest form of art, but we lack sadly in developing its possibilities. We have grown to look upon decorative art as a plaything in the hands of the idle. The sculptor disdains the stone-cutter and the carver, but it is the stationary and the not movable art to which belongs the first place. A great sculptor with infinite labor produces a statue; it is given a place in some draped and darkened room, or, at best, in some art gallery. A stone-cutter, with a rude hand, carves a grotesque face on some doorway or bracket, and the long lines of busy travellers (sic) look up to it, as a familiar landmark on their journey. The great painters, Raphael, Correggio, Michael Angelo, and Titian, did some of their best work on the frescos of temples. In the nineteenth century a stencil plate will supply the art required for a large proportion of fresco decoration.

There was a time in ancient Florence when a new carving, a metal grille, or a decorated window, was a general topic of interest. Each individual built for the fame of Florence. Rome at its best was a city of unrivalled beauty, more because each building was a complement to its neighbor than on account of the separate value of each. As Americans, we are the guardians of the most matchless granite and marble, forests and mines, which, yielding like clay in the hands of the sculptor, come forth bearing the impression of our thoughts.

With time, and the establishment of architectural schools, America can rival the world in architectural beauty. What we need most is study, schools, and training. One sees everywhere originality, thought, and beautiful features, but the harmony that alone comes from careful training is sadly missing.

THE AGENCY OF WOMEN IN BUILDINGS AND TEXTS

Wealth and philanthropy are always opening new channels for advancement and education, and I hope in the near future we may have thoroughly equipped schools of architecture. The collection of plaster casts of architectural ornament which is being collected for the New York Metropolitan Art Gallery, the sketch clubs, competitions, manual training-schools, and industrial art schools, are much-needed steps in the right direction; but the question of utility and construction enters so largely into the work, aside from its art or decoration, that a special training is indispensable to the architectural student.

Every woman's home is her dominion, and should yield, under her direction and planning, the largest possible amount of comfort and pleasure to her subjects. It is impossible to furnish or decorate an ill-planned house, and poorly-proportioned rooms cannot be disguised by costly hangings and elaborate furniture.

The old colonial houses, with their defects, were better than the fantastic designs we meet in our every-day walk. The stately dames and lords of the seventeenth century would have felt cramped and ill at ease in the pocket-edition castles now being published.

Architecture is not a thing that alone concerns the owner and the builder. The man or woman who erects a crude or fantastic building has wronged his neighbor and left a monument to his own folly. When we build patiently, when every one (sic), from the owner to the hod-carrier, is no longer in a fever of excitement to see the last brick in the highest chimney, we shall have better work. Now it is like Jack and the magic bean-stalk. Yesterday we passed an open lot, a few tin cans straggling weeds, a sportive goat, and the small boy. To-morrow a building whose cornice looks disdainfully down on its neighbors, a monster mushroom of bricks and mortar, a menace to life and health.

Minerva Parker
Philadelphia, Penn.

An Uncultivated Field (1893)

Housekeeper's Weekly

As weeds grow in a rich field, plowed in deep brown furrows and left uncultivated, so our architecture, sown on the soil of rich natural products and national prosperity, has been left uncultivated so long that it has grown to weeds. And I appeal to you, my sister women, to at least clear out your own door-yards and attend to your own homes. It is a duty (not a pleasure) you owe yourselves and your families to rectify some of the evils which have crept into home-making.

I shall try to show you some of the weeds, that you may not cultivate them in your garden; show you some planted by the builders, and not a few by yourselves, and try to indicate something of the method by which the field may be redeemed and made productive.

The old proverb, "Fools build houses for wise men to live in," has long been the stock argument against all advice to build your own homes. It is a labor-saving argument for the man of the household, and a source of constant profit to the builder and speculator, who are both, like the clown, "willing to play the part of fool," if you are willing to pay them well for the trouble and loss of respect. And they have made steps up and steps down, for no earthly reason, unless it were to make stumbling-blocks and extra labor—put doors where you will never want them, and left them out where you would naturally think doors would be most needed; placed windows where they look out on the garden or the pig-sty (sic), if there be one, and erected solid walls on southern exposures. They make bath-rooms in which you can have no heat, the place of all others where you most require it. If there is a pantry, it is in some dark corner where you are in danger of putting the flat-irons in the best china.

This proverb really meant, "Fools build houses, and it takes [italic in original] wise men to live in them" and be comfortable, and escape bodily harm from the numerous pitfalls.

The chief charm of any house is its individuality. There are many things which houses or people possess in common; but the thing which charms us is the thing peculiar to a certain house or a certain person.

Women often seem so helpless when they come to design their own houses that the mere thought of a specification to be read or an inspection of the plans, is enough to deprive the poor architect of their society for days. I assure you, French novels will seem dull compared with the delight of threading your way through the translation of plans, when you have once mastered the mechanical part of the drawing.

Architectural clients are of many kinds. There is the entirely satisfactory client, who knows what she wants, and knows when she has it; who knows just the style in which she wishes her house to be built, and of what material. She has taken into account that a house of wood is all right in the country, and is absurd in the city; that a dressed stone house in the country looks like a milkmaid in a ball dress. And there is the other client, who gives general directions, and allows the architect to develop the plan. These two sit high in the favor of the architect.

But there is the woman who wants a large house, and wants it to be a very cheap house, finished with all the late improvements; and if in an unguarded moment you draw the house which she desires, she becomes more and more delighted with her plan as it grows. Then comes a week of anxiety while waiting for the bids. At last they arrive, and are about one-half more than the client can or will pay. The architect and builder come in for much blame; and you begin the operation of cutting down.

No patient ever flinched under the surgeon's knife as a client flinches under the amputation of cherished anticipations. She feels robbed. You suggest pine in place of the hardwood finish. She submits graciously. Cheaper hardware is added. The floors are changed from oak to pine. You speak of the open fire-places, with tiles and mantels, but she tells you that she had forgotten that she must have an *extra* one! The reduction in the floor and hardware are absorbed in adding it. You are not getting on very well in the reduction, but cannot protest here, for fireplaces are poor places in which to insert the knife of economy. (There was a time not long ago when the splendid old fireplaces were walled up, as if they were the very doors by which evil spirits entered, who so vexed our ancestors in the days of witchcraft.)

We suggest the plumbing, but the client will not listen to that. We mention the fact that the house is large. *Large!* We are assured that it will require skill to pack the family in the house as it now is; and the furniture, which is large (I have noticed that people who have limited space always buy large furniture), must be sacrificed to allow them to get in at all. I think of the ornamental gable, only to find that it can not be spared.

But my client thinks of the kitchen; one window less will do. And the house might be two feet narrower, and need not have a cellar, but be built on piers, for all the world like the frost-bitten storks one sees on screens.

The cellar, once entered, seems a happy field for operations. The circulation is lo at that point, and the nerves are not active; so the cement floor is dispensed with, sacrificed on the altar of a bay or stained-glass window.

May we not hope, as a better understanding grows up between architect and client, that we will both come back to the simple dignity of our Colonial ancestors, borrowing their honest construction and beauty of design, then adding all the modern improvements in the way of lighting, heating and plumbing?

Than a word for the builder—for whom I have a profound respect, provided he does not try to be both architect and builder—a position which is not to the advantage of the house owner. You might as well expect a school boy to chastise himself when he plays truant, as to expect most builders to correct their own mistakes.

Don't try to get more house for the same amount of money than any one else ever did; for the builder must either make you a present of his labor, or deceive you in the value and quality of the work and material. Really good results only come from mutual respect on the part of both owner and builder. You should secure a contractor in whom you have a confidence, and then trust to his experience as far as matters of construction go, but keep full possession of the original design, which is your field of action. Do not allow him to deviate from that plan, unless by your suggestion. With the best intentions, builders often suggest change, simply because they have always done a certain thing, and do not look with favor on a new arrangement.

The money spent in securing the architect's services as superintendent is not ill-spent; but should you prefer to undertake the task yourself, be sure that you are as well posted as you would think it necessary to be in undertaking to be your own surgeon, lawyer, or optician. There are some rare souls who can do these things without previous knowledge; but I would warn you not to be too positive in your directions, or to insist on their literal fulfilment. You would be surprised often to see the result if the builder followed your instructions, literally. I cannot but respect the self-control of builders in receiving such instructions without the slightest suggestion to the amateur of their utter absurdity. If he tells you it cannot be done, you think him blunt; if he is politic, he does as he thinks best, and you are none the wiser; if he is dishonest, he detects your experience and plays upon it. If you had explained *what* you wanted, and not the *way* you wanted it executed, he would probably have served you better.

And there are the clients who want a bay like Mrs. A's, a porch like Mrs. B's, a roof like Mrs. C's, inside finish like Mrs. E's, the stair like some old photograph, and a doorway like the one found in some old print. By this time the fiend of the departed "crazy patchwork" has arrived to vex the architect, who tries in vain to harmonize these varied features in one design.

And there is the client who patiently spends days selecting carpets and wall paper, but cannot be induced to examine plans or read specifications; and the client who makes her own sketch,— often a good one, for which the architect gives her well-merited credit. Alas! she is so delighted with her labor that she assumes all the credit and glory of the building when finished, and will assure you that "the house was designed by herself—in fact, she was her own architect." She reluctantly admits that they did employ an architect, but you are given to understand that it was a useless precaution on her part; in fact, the architect was secured to take the blame if there was a failure—to do the mechanical work, and save the client the trouble of dealing with workmen.

As there all kinds of clients, so there are all kinds of houses. They have seemed to me like people— the houses that are all front and show—like shallow and superficial people; the selfish houses, with cramped front doors; the secretive houses, with small, ill-lighted windows; the giddy houses, with much flimsy ornament and many colors; the plain houses, like Quaker women in their quiet garb; the dignified houses, like well-rounded characters; the dainty house, like our society women; the jolly houses; the sad, dissipated, and extravagant—all have their counterparts in the human families who occupy them.

And the house that is very proper in front will grow uninteresting on the sides, with a small frame rear building, having a flat tin roof and short chimney. They remind me, not of people, but of the days when I was the mother of a large family of paper dolls. Standing in front, surveying them as they were propped up with invisible blocks of wood, I was delighted; moving to the side, I felt some disappointment. The glimmer of the front, combined with the scant apparel of the rear, was not gratifying to my maternal pride. When seen from the rear the entire sham was revealed, the straps on the shoulders alone suggesting the glory of the front. Now on the houses you see the cornice carried around the front and sides and neatly tucked around the shoulders of the rear, for all the world like the paper doll dresses! If our houses are to be so unsightly from the rear we must erect neat little signs, like the motto, "Keep off the grass," saying, "This house to be inspected from this point only. Any person found looking at it from the rear will be liable to the law." Or, far better, we might give up this senseless practice. Rich people, who need practice no economy, make the front of their house of cut stone and the rear of plain brick, simply because it has been a long standing practice,—a kind of shallow deceit which deceives no one.

THE AGENCY OF WOMEN IN BUILDINGS AND TEXTS

This is the field which I would open to you, and you will be surprised at the new world it leads to. You will take a new interest in all the details, before unseen. The styles of architecture being to arrange themselves in groups, as do favorite authors or artists. It is a new and interesting book, that can be read every time you go on the street. Every country road has chapters of the tale. Traveling takes on a new charm; and you come to known and understand the people by the houses in which they live.

And a word in closing for those of my sisters who think of architecture as a profession. Like the new land in the far West, there are many claims not taken. It requires courage, some capital, much labor in traveling, as the road is long, and a real love talent for the work. These, with a thorough training in some recognized school of architecture, are both your tools and capital. With this equipment you need fear no competition or jealousy, for the love of art and justice is so strong in the members of the architectural profession that you have but to prove ability to be admitted as a worthy member.

WRITINGS

Women as Architects (1896)

Third Biennial, General Federation of Women's Clubs

The last century has witnessed a remarkable change in the position of women in the professional world. Previous to 1871, women did not appear in the census as practicing physicians, and the names of women appear as architects in our census for the first time twenty years later, in 1891. Though it is well known that a few women were practicing previously to that time, this is the first official recognition of them in the profession.

At the time the circular was issued by the Women's Board of the Columbian Exposition, inviting competitive drawings for the Woman's Building at Chicago, it was, I understand, seriously doubted whether a sufficient number of women might be found prepared to enter such a competition. Twenty-one sets of drawings were submitted, a number of women who were practicing architects at the time not entering the competition, either through lack of time or because they disapproved the conditions of the competition, the remuneration for services being much less than that given the designers of any of the other buildings. The significant fact was that in 1891 twenty or thirty women were both willing and competent to undertake work of such a serious character, and that the first and second prizes justly went to the graduates of the Massachusetts School of Technology in Boston. The other plans may have been as good in composition or general plan, but doubtless lacked the finish of detail and execution which can come only from thorough training under the most competent masters. It is useless to enter the profession of architecture without a thorough training grafted upon a real love for the expression of art in building. Architecture must be accepted as one of the professions where the chief reward is in the consciousness of work well done, and not in anticipation of large financial returns. It is simply an art, and one of the oldest and most honorable.

Miss Hayden, who designed the Woman's Building in Chicago, is at present, I understand, in the office of a decorator in Boston. Miss Howe, who received second prize, has recently opened her office in Boston for the practice of architecture.

At the present time, seven women are studying architecture in the School of Technology in Boston, four of whom receive their degrees this year. Three of the four wish to enter active practice in offices at once.

Miss Hand and Miss Gannon, of the New York School of Design, are practicing with distinguished success. I recently heard a member of a large land company speak of their work with unstinted praise. Miss Elsie Murcur, of Pittsburg, designed the Woman's Building recently erected in Atlanta for the Cotton States Exposition, and the women of the South may be justly proud of the beautiful building which they contributed to the exposition. Every public recognition of woman's work makes it easier for other women to achieve success and to do better things in their chosen occupations. Perhaps no woman has won a more deserved success in architecture than Louise Bethune, of Buffalo, who has worked in this profession for a number of years, one of the few women, if not the only one, who are members of the New York Chapter of the Architectural Association. She said some time ago, in speaking on the subject of women in architecture, that she would change it to "Woman and Architecture," and that "when women entered the professional field to become physicians, they filled a long-felt want. There is no need whatever for a woman architect. No one wants her, no one yearns for her. There is no one line in architecture to which she is better adapted than a man. The woman architect is always conservative. She has exactly the same work to do that a man has. When the woman enters the profession, she will be kindly met and will be welcome, but not as a woman, only as an architect."

I must take exception to one point only, and that is: "There is no need whatever of a woman architect." There is great need that every woman should be educated in architecture. She must know, if she be a tenant, the possibilities and adaptabilities of a house, and if she be a prospective house owner, she must impress upon her future home the result of her own intelligent idea of what that place should be, having it put in practical shape by a skillful architect. Is it not a reproach to the good sense of part of the human family that a woman will devote more time and thought to the making of a new frock to be worn for one short season, than to the planning of her home?

If every woman who thought of building a new home would make it the serious occupation of her life during the time of its planning and construction, if every woman who enters the profession would determine that she would lay hold of the difficulties of design, construction and ornamentation until she was master of her art, there would be great need of her. I hear constantly of some young woman, who contemplates entering the profession as draughts woman or designer, unwilling to assume the superintendence of construction during the erection of her own designs. If women ever hold a respected position as architects, they must assume all of the duties and responsibilities; they must bring to it trained hands and eyes; they must enter the field determined not only to be architects, but to be the best of architects. The public is so disposed to look upon our work with kind and sympathetic eyes that we must judge our work by the standard of the highest architectural achievements, and be satisfied with nothing short of complete success.

A large proportion of all the buildings erected are intended for human habitations, and here it appears eminently fitting that women trained in the practice of architecture should execute their work with some advantage over men, as in all the details of designing, women bring taste, tact and judgment.

If home is woman's sphere, it must be admitted that she should build the home which she is to tend with such care. Women now hold a splendid position in painting and sculpture, and in the near future they will, doubtless, take an honorable position as architects. Women are now practicing in almost every state in the Union. It is well known that few men attain honorable recognition in the profession of architecture until early middle life. Ten or fifteen years of hard work bring with them the reward of labor well directed, and being recognized as such.

Miss Helen Treret, of New Orleans, is, I understand, a practicing architect. As the daughter of a well-known architect, she has some decided advantages. The great difficulty encountered by architectural students is the inability to obtain a position in the office of a skillful architect, and this she has had overcome for her.

M. de Monclos, of Paris, who won the third prize in the recent competition for the New Art Gallery to be erected in Fairmount Park, Philadelphia, makes no secret of the fact, I believe, that he was materially aided in the details of his plan by his wife, who takes a great interest in his work. She was before her marriage Miss Katherine C. Bartol, of Philadelphia.

Of the schools of architecture and general art schools, few, if any, exclude women. The art galleries and libraries are all open to them, facilities for the study of architecture being best in New York and Boston. In New York they have the benefit of the splendid collection of architectural casts in the Metropolitan Museum, and in Boston of the unsurpassed scientific and thorough training of the Massachusetts School of Technology.

A recently compiled table, giving the number of college women practicing the professions, gives the amazingly small number of ninety-one artists, including different branches, one only of these being possessed of a college diploma. The fact is greatly to the discredit of the professions and not to the discredit of the college. The same, I am sure, cannot be said a generation hence, when the women who are at present in our colleges have taken their places in their chosen occupations.

There is a large field for women as designers of furniture, stained glass and interior decorations, and as draughtswomen.

The question of remuneration might fittingly be discussed here. Financial success will depend on a question of skill and not of sex; but any who dream of long bank balances or luxurious returns for a limited expenditure of labor, I would advise to shun the architectural path. The returns are sufficient to sustain life and to afford some comforts, but are not sufficiently luxurious to dull the keen artistic sense of that artistic life which grows best in the attics of Paris and Rome, and thrives here on unsuccessful competition and in the shadow of unpaid bills. For the benefit of clients, I would like to say that all architects base their charges on a regular percentage of the cost of the building, and that "if the servant is worth hiring, he is worthy of his hire."

Little will ever be accomplished in the way of improving our architecture until there is a general interest in architecture, until every man and woman knows as much about designing as they know about music, until they are as familiar with ancient architecture as they are with ancient military history, until an exhibition of architectural drawings creates as much interest as a poster show, until an architectural medley is judged by the same standards as a musical medley, until higher education includes as much knowledge of the architecture of the Greeks and Romans as it now requires familarity (sic) with their languages.

I have had so much delight in my work in spite of its failures and disappointments, have met from my brother architects such a frank and generous recognition of my attempts to do acceptable work, such kindness from clients that the way has been anything but a thorny one.

In conclusion I must add one word on the vexed question of the professional life of married women. Ideally, one feels that marriage and the care of children should not displace a professional life. That a woman is entitled to the development of her talents and abilities after as before marriage no one dare deny. For my own part, I believe that nothing can take the place in life of a real and intelligent interest in some occupation or profession, the active practice of which must at times give place to the demands and responsibilities of child life, if the mother wishes to assume the responsibility. Every child that is invited into this world deserves and has the right to demand at the hands of her or his mother her first and best care and thought. The rearing of houses is, as it appears to me, a less noble occupation than the developing of a human life. One may still maintain all of the intellectual interest and enough of the practice of a profession to lift life out of the commonplace rut of inactivity. The professions are no longer confined to law, art,

THE AGENCY OF WOMEN IN BUILDINGS AND TEXTS

medicine and the pulpit. Every earnest woman has a profession or a ministry. So much work must be done to convert the crude material of mind and matter into beauty of form and spirit, that we are all co-laborers and not competitors.

    To the women of the Federation and of the individual clubs, I wish God-speed in the work of upbuilding a new acropolis, a temple whose white and gleaming walls shall adorn every city, from whose outer porch shall be heard only the voice of wisdom and of truth.

ACKNOWLEDGMENTS

Heather Isbell Schumacher
and William Whitaker

ACKNOWLEDGMENTS

Minerva Parker Nichols: The Search for a Forgotten Architect is the product of seven years' effort by a dedicated team of scholars, artists, and designers, as well as generous donors, without whom this project would not have been possible. We express our sincere thanks to all who contributed to the realization of this book and the exhibition it accompanies, most especially our curatorial collaborators Molly Lester and Elizabeth Felicella. Carrie Baker, Minerva's great-granddaughter, provided her unwavering support from the start, along with an insightful contemporary perspective on women's history.

For their vital and major support of our project, we acknowledge the Pew Center for Arts and Heritage. The Center's staff, particularly Marni Burke de Guzman, Angela Nace, Alfi Nurdin, Kelly Shindler, and Megan Wendell, energized our project in countless ways. We owe a specific debt of gratitude to Bill Adair, former Director of Exhibitions and Public Interpretation at the Center, for inviting us to participate in an "Archives Working Group," which profoundly impacted our thinking and led us to our collaboration with Elizabeth Felicella.

Crucial to the success of our exhibition and this book is the enthusiastic support and participation of the homeowners and stewards of Minerva's buildings as well as our institutional colleagues who graciously

ACKNOWLEDGMENTS

opened their doors—literally and figuratively—to our efforts. We thank: Kathleen Abplanalp; Linda and Tom Bickell; Christiaan Bouhuys; Sister Maria DiBello; Ellen and Alex Dyakiw; Christopher Grosso; Elizabeth Hoffman; Kailey Holden; Mark Jacobs; Deborah Kost; Andrew Leather; Kristin Lett and David Seator; Rebecca and Matt Lisowski; Judy Lustig and TJ Scully; Judi MacKarey and David Madison; Laura Marder and Ronald Erhman; Ami and Bruce Musser; Shawn Nau; Nichole Pugliese and Matthew Gingras; Allison Scanlon; Heidi Sentivan and Mary Woodling; Christine and Adam Shaw; Priscilla Simioni; Rachel and Daniel Solomon; David Swajeski and Donna Swajeski; Sister Mary Trainer; Janessa Wilde; and Rebecca Wickes. We are particularly grateful to Aaron Wunsch, who has been supportive of this work since Molly Lester's thesis work in 2011–12, and to Minerva's extended family, who shared insights and invaluable collection materials which energized our research. Jeffrey Cohen, Joseph Elliott, Sophie Hochhäusl, Adrienne Pruitt, and Shilpa Mehta each, in their own way, provided sage advice as our curatorial approach developed.

We mined many archival sources in our efforts to document Minerva's life and work, and are grateful for the thoughtful assistance of the following individuals: in California, Chris Ervin, Santa Barbara Historical Museum; Nanci Elliott, Santa Barbara Women's Club; Jace Turner, City of Santa Barbara; Dorothy Lazard, Oakland History Center; in Connecticut, Julie Hughes and Nick Foster of the Wilton Historical Society; in Delaware, Edward Richi, Delaware Historical Society; in the District of Columbia, Catherine Lavoie, Mary MacPortland, Scott Keyes, Jarob Ortiz, and Marcella Stranieri, and their colleagues at the Historical American Building Survey, National Park Service; in New Jersey, Ricky Gerhardt, Longport Historical Society; Mary Hussey, Office of the Monmouth County Clerk, Archives Division; in Illinois, Leslie Martin, Chicago History Museum, Abakanowicz Research Center; in Massachusetts, Diana Carey, Schlesinger Library, Harvard University; Robert H. Malme,

ACKNOWLEDGMENTS

Hingham Historical Society; and Esme Rabin, Buckingham Browne & Nichols School; in Pennsylvania, Susannah Carroll, The Franklin Institute; Erin Hess, Reconstructionist Rabbinical College in Wyncote; Margaret Huang, the Philadelphia Museum of Art; Bruce Laverty, Athenaeum of Philadelphia; Maria Lynn, Adams County Historical Society in Gettysburg; Greg Prichard, Radnor Historical Society in Wayne; Laura Stroffolino, Print and Picture Collection, Free Library of Philadelphia; Melody Totten, Connelly Library, Moore College of Art and Design; and Sarah Weatherwax, The Library Company of Philadelphia; in Virginia, Kellee Blake, National Archives-Mid Atlantic Region; Jasmine Collins, Eastern Shore Public Library; Dennis Custis, Eastern Shore of Virginia Historical Society; Ellen Johnson, Eastern Shore Railroad Museum; and Sherry W. Mayes, Circuit Court of Accomack County; in New York, Allyson Malinenko, Center for Brooklyn History of the Brooklyn Public Library; in Texas, William Grace, Tyrrell Historical Library of Beaumont; and in Washington, Ruba Sadi, of the University of Washington Libraries Special Collections.

Michael Grant led our marketing and publicity in collaboration with Rachel Judlowe, while Christopher Cataldo, Jennifer Sorrentino, Nadine Beauharnois, Tiara Campbell, Jessica Dejesus, Ronald Powell, and Jenny Thuman kept track of the finances. In addition, we thank: Fritz Steiner, John Caperton, Mark Harper, Sandi Mosgo, Allison Olsen, Shae Spahl, and Karl Wellman. Our student researchers and interns—Parima Kotanut, Calvin Nguyen, Elizabeth Sexton, and Peehu Sinha—offered brilliant assistance with the many details. We are grateful to Harvey Kroiz, Larry Korman, and Peter Shedd Reed for their long-term support of the work of the Architectural Archives.

We are especially thankful to Marianna Thomas who skillfully guided a team of Temple University preservation students through the process of documenting five sites designed by Minerva in measured drawings. Gabe Albion, Oksana Kaleeva, Igor Kiselev, Changfeng Luo, and Jhon

ACKNOWLEDGMENTS

Velazco all contributed to this important effort. Kiselev, a key organizer of the students' work, passed away unexpectedly as this project neared completion. His kind spirit and mentorship will be treasured by all who knew him.

This publication benefited from the enthusiastic support and guidance of Despina Stratigakos and Franca Trubiano, each of whom have contributed important essays to this publication. John Bartelstone "pinch hit" for our colleague Elizabeth Felicella to complete an essential last round of photography, while Evan Laudenslager of Black and White on White, Gerard Franciosa of My Own Color Lab, and Sebastiaan Hanekroot of Colour & Books, oversaw the intricacies of darkroom printing and optimization for digital files for publication. LTI Lightside handled film processing and Fotocare was an invaluable source of supplies and guidance throughout the project. Lauren Mitchell has been endlessly helpful in the photography process from beginning to end, and her willingness to dive into the project wherever she was needed. George Stoltz provided special support to Felicella's project, as well as valuable feedback on her essay. We are thrilled to work with book designer Olivia de Salve Villedieu, who deftly negotiated the challenges and opportunities in this project. Johanna Halford-MacLeod brought careful editorial attention to our texts and our storytelling and Sarahh Scher provided valuable indexing and proofreading expertise. Our thanks also go to Nick Geller and Katherine Boller of Yale University Press, our enthusiastic partner in distributing this publication.

Lastly, we are especially grateful for the lively, first-hand accounts of Minerva provided by her grandson Patrick Baker, as well as for the care, skill and wit of John Taylor, who has been involved in exhibition installations at this university for over 50 years—including this project. Taylor put a perfect capstone on our project as the final touches were being made on the installation by recounting that he had learned to dance in the "living room" of Minerva's New Century Club in Philadelphia.

INDEX

INDEX

Note: Page numbers in italics indicate images. All buildings are by Minerva Parker Nichols unless otherwise indicated.

Abel, Elizabeth, 58–59
American Architect, 30
American Architect and Building News, 46, 48, 51, 58
Archambault (Frank L.) house, 36, 184, *185,* 212
"An Architectural Object Lesson" (Parker Nichols), 52, 307
Architecture and Building
    "An Architectural Object Lesson" (Parker Nichols), 52, 307
    "Architecture as an Art" (Parker Nichols), 303–304, 305, 308–309, 316–317
    "Art in Architecture" (Parker Nichols), 52, *53,* 306–308
Ashmead (Isaac) house, *35,* 36, 48, 75n60, *87,* 179, *179*
Avery, Rachel Foster, 58
    Rachel Foster Avery house, Mill-Rae, 42, *104–111,* 223, *223–225,* 225
The Baddest Day, and Other Favorite Stories (Nichols family), 18, 72
Baker, Adelaide Nichols (Minerva's daughter), 56, 57, 59, 78n152
    John and Adelaide Baker house, *69,* 70, 72, *165–169,* 289, *289–290,* 296
    John and Adelaide Baker house, Guard Hill, 70, *71,* 291, *291–293,* 294, 296
    and Minerva's legacy, 16, 17, 18
    Return to Arcady, 65, *66,* 67, 68, 283, 288
Baker (Sylvester J. Jr.) house, 236
Barber (Margaret M.) house, *40,* 41, 260, *260*
Baugh (Mrs.) house, 222
Beale (J. Frank) house, 199, *199*
Beecher, Catherine, 38–39, 43, 76n74
Beerman (George) house, 214
Bennett, Henry R., 42, 50, 193
Bewley, Sarah E.W., 188
    Sarah E.W. Bewley house, 42, 189, *189*
Blanchard, Louise (Blanchard Bethune), 38, 46, 58, 75n62
Board of Lady Managers (World's Columbian Exposition), 46, 48, 226–227
Brooke, Emma Williams, 76n82, 187
Brooke, Lewis T., 42, 76n82, 177, 178, 233
    Lewis T. Brooke house, 186–187, *187*
    See also Overbrook Land and Improvement Company
Brooklyn Bureau of Charities, 59, 62, 64, *66,* 68, 72, 278, 286
    Northern District Building, 62, 280
Browne and Nichols School for Boys, *60,* 61–62, 72, *273,* 273–276

See also Nichols, Edgar (Minerva's brother-in-law)
buildings with location unknown
    George Beerman house, 214
    F. B. Crooke house, 214
    house for the *Home-Maker,* 251, *251*
    prototype for a nursery school, 278, *279*
    sketch for a cottage, 211
    unidentified house (1896), 271, *272*
    unidentified house (ca. 1930s), 294, *295*
California buildings (built/undetermined)
    Maria Nye Johnson house, 57, 262
    Ida V. Stambach house, 250
Campbell Sisters (Jane and Mary A.), twin houses for, 248, *248–249,* 261
Caractères des passions [...] (Le Brun), 304–305
Carpentry and Building, 33–36, *34,* 51, 52, 177
Carter (James H.) row houses, 213
Cathedral of St. John the Divine, 67, 285
Centennial Exposition (Philadelphia), 15, 27, 307
Chadbourne, Elizabeth Stanton, 50, 193
Cheltenham Township, 27, 48, 49, 184, 222, 269
Christy, George W., 42, 200
    George W. Christy house, 182, *182–183*
    See also Elm Land and Improvement Company
Civil War, the, 22, 23, 28, 49, 179
Clements, Gabrielle de Veaux, 238, 261
Cohen, Jeffrey, 29–30
Colonial Revival
    in Minerva's house designs, 41, 223, 228, 248, 255, 264, 289, 296
    in Minerva's interiors, 261, 269
Connecticut buildings (built/undetermined), 70, 299
    homes for veterans, 22, 72, 299
    John and Adelaide Baker house, *69,* 70, 72, *165–169,* 289, *289–290,* 296
    John and Adelaide Baker house, Guard Hill, 70, *71,* 291, *291–293,* 294, 296
    Charles A. and Gertrude R. Lubrecht house, 70, *71,* 72, *170–175,* 296, *297–298*
    William and Minerva Parker Nichols house, 65, *66,* 67, 68, 70, *161–163,* 282–283, *282–283,* 294
    unidentified house (ca. 1930s), 294, *295*
Crooke (F. B.) house, 214

Davis (Edward J.) house, 195, *195*
Delaware buildings (built)
    First Unitarian Church of Wilmington, 254
    New Century Club of Wilmington, 43, *45,* 72, 83, *139–151,* 255, *255–259,* 258, 261
Doane, Amanda (Amanda Parker, Amanda Maxwell; Minerva's mother), 24, *25,* 67, 68, 70, 74n28, 222
    boardinghouse management, 26, 39, 48, 49, 56,

331

INDEX

65
    investments, 48, 49–50, 76n93, 179, 184, 193, 222
    marriage to John Parker, 22–23
    marriage to Samuel Maxwell, 26–27, 49, 72n19, 74n22
Doane, Lucretia (Minerva's grandmother), 23–24, 74n6
Doane, Sarah (Aunt Sudie; Minerva's aunt), 23, 24
Doane, Seth Brown (Minerva's grandfather), 23–24, 25, 74n31
Downing, Andrew Jackson
    A Treatise [...], 304
Eagle Iron Foundry, 252, *253*
Elm Land and Improvement Company, 182
    houses for, 200, *200*, 215
First Church of Deerfield, 68, 70, 287
First Unitarian Church of Gouverneur, 278
First Unitarian Church of Wilmington, 254
Franklin Institute Drawing School, 28, 29–30, 32, 52, 177, 247
Furness, Frank, 52, *53*, 54, 306
Furness, William Henry, 54, 57
Gallagher (Elizabeth E.) house, 42, 203, *204*
Gaskell (Esther R.) house, 42, 254
Grew, Mary, 57
Griffiths, Adelaide. *See* Parker, Adelaide
Griffiths, Nye Winifred (Minerva's niece), 29, 50, 70, 72
Guano, Emmanuel, macaroni factory for, 217
HABS. *See* Historic American Buildings Survey
Hackley School, projects for, 62, 277, *277*
Harper, Ida Husted, 62, *63*, 65
Hartel (Eliza C.) house and store, 201, *202*
Hayden, Sophia, 51, 56, 58, 61
    Woman's Building (World's Columbian Exhibition), 46–48, *47*, 59, 226–227, 247, 261, 322
Historic American Buildings Survey (HABS), 18, 81–83
    twin houses for Jane and Mary A. Campbell and, *135–137*
    Isaac Ashmead house and, *87*
    Rachel Foster Avery house, Mill-Rae and, *104–111*
    John and Adelaide Baker house, Guard Hill and, *165–169*
    Francis Jordan Jr. house and, *113–119*
    F. Millwood Justice house and, *89–93*
    Charles A. and Gertrude R. Lubrecht house and, *170–175*
    house for the Moore Brothers and, *153–159*
    Frank Wallace Munn house and, *120–125*
    John Rugan Neff house and, *84*
    New Century Club of Philadelphia and, *14*, 81
    New Century Club of Wilmington and, 83, *139–151*
    William J. Nicolls house and, *127–133*
    William P. Painter house and, *103*
    William and Minerva Parker Nichols house (Wilton, CT) and, *161–163*
    Mary Potts house and, *95–97*
    Edward Y. Taylor and Harriet Potts Taylor house and, *98–101*
    Joshua H. Witham house and, *85*
Home-Maker, 51, 57, 64, 302, 314–315
    house for, 251, *251*
    Frank Wallace Munn house and, 230, *231*, 244
    William J. Nicolls house and, 244, *244*
Housekeeper's Weekly
    "An Uncultivated Field" (Parker Nichols), 51, 305–306, 309–311, 318–321
Howe, Lois Lilley, 59, 61, 78n148
Huff (William A.) Cottage, *177*, 178
Johnson, Maria Nye, 50, 215
    Maria Nye Johnson house, 57, 262
Johnson (C. F.) house, 42, 215
Jones, Lewis, 233
    Lewis Jones house, 234, *234–235*
    See also Overbrook Land and Improvement Company
Jordan (Francis Jr.) house, 55, *113–119*, 228, *228–229*
Justice, F. Millwood, 54
    F. Millwood Justice house, *89–93*, 190, *190–192*
Keim (John O.) house, 269, *269–270*
Kennedy (John M.) house, 201, 213

Le Brun, Charles
    Caractères des passions [...], 304–305
Lester, Molly, 12, 19, 313–314
Lippincott, Horace G. and Caroline, 27, 29, 39
Lubrecht (Charles A. and Gertrude R.) house, 70, 71, 72, *170–175*, 296, *297–298*
macaroni factory for Emmanuel Guano and Antonio Raggio, 217
Maine buildings (built)
    William I. Nichols summer house, 62, 68, 281, *281*
Massachusetts buildings (built)
    Browne and Nichols School for Boys, *60*, 61–62, 72, 273, *273–276*
    First Church of Deerfield, 68, 70, 287
    William and Minerva Parker Nichols house, 68, 70, 288
Massachusetts Institute of Technology (MIT), 46, 59, 61
    See also Hayden, Sophia
Maxwell, Amanda M. *See* Doane, Amanda
Maxwell, Samuel (Minerva's stepfather), 26–27, 49, 74n19, 74n22
Maxwell, Samuel Raymond (Minerva's half brother), 27, 29, 49, 70
Maxwell (Amanda M.) house, 48, 184

INDEX

McCammon (Emma de Crano) house, 246
Megargee (Irwin N.) house, Pen-y-Bryn, 267, *268*
misogyny and sexism, 46, 48, 52, 54
    pay discrepancies, 46, 55–56, 78n148, 247
Model Dwellings Association, 58, 68, 72
Moore Brothers, house for, 263, *263*
Munn, Frank Wallace, 42, 54
Munn (Frank Wallace) house, 21, 55, *120–125*, 200, 230, *230–232*, 234
Narberth, PA buildings (built)
    Edward J. Davis house, 195, *195*
    Elm Land and Improvement Company houses, 200, *200*
    F. Millwood Justice house, *89–93*, 190, *190–192*
    George W. Christy house, 182–183, *182–183*, 200
    John M. Kennedy house, 201
    Sarah E.W. Bewley house, 189, *189*
    Sylvester J. Baker Jr. house, 236
    William R. Wright house, 188, *188*, 200
National Register of Historic Places, 225, 258
Neff (John Rugan) house, 33, *35*, 36, *84*, 177
New Century Club of Philadelphia, 58, 255, 299
    building, *14*, 15, 16–18, 42, 43, *44*, 55, 72, 237–239, *237–242*, 261
    building commission, 15, 57, 236
    building demolition, 16–17, 18
    Historic American Buildings Survey (HABS) and, *14*, 17, 81
    Minerva's participation in, 56, 72
    See also New Century Guild of Working Women
New Century Club of Philadelphia member connections, 57, 208, 218, 236, 248
    Rachel Foster Avery, 58, 225
    Emma Williams Brooke, 76n82, 187
    Emily Sartain, 54, 56
New Century Club of Wilmington, 43, *45*, 72, 83, *139–151*, 255, *255–259*, 258, 261
New Century Guild of Working Women, 42, 43, 58–59, 237
    Guild house, 266
    See also New Century Club of Philadelphia
New Jersey buildings (built)
    house for the Moore Brothers, 263, *263*
    Elizabeth Newport house, 211
    Sarah A. Stewart house, 218, *219*
Newport (Elizabeth) house, 211
New York buildings (built/undetermined)
    Brooklyn Bureau of Charities, Northern District Building, 62, 280
    Cathedral of St. John the Divine, 67, 285
    First Unitarian Church of Gouverneur, 278
    Hackley School projects, 62, 277, *277*
    John W. T. Nichols house, The Kettles, 284, *284*
    housing studies for Alfred T. White, 286
New York League of Unitarian Women, 64, 65
New York Real Estate Record and Builders' Guide, 62

New York Times, 54, 72
Nichols, Caroline (Minerva's daughter), 61, 67
Nichols, Edgar (Minerva's brother-in-law), 54, 61, 273
    See also Browne and Nichols School for Boys
Nichols, John Doane (Minerva's son), 61, 78n152, 282
Nichols, Minerva Parker. *See* Parker Nichols, Minerva
Nichols, William ("Bill"; Minerva's son), 61, 66, 78n152
Nichols, William Ichabod (Minerva's husband), 54–55, 57, 58, 59, *60*
    declining health and death, 65, 67, 68, 79n182
Nichols (John W. T.) house, The Kettles, 284, *284*
Nichols (William and Minerva Parker) house (Hingham, MA), 68, 70, 288
Nichols (William and Minerva Parker) house (Wilton, CT), 65, *66*, 67, 68, 70, *161–163*, 282–283, *282–283*, 294
Nichols (William I.) summer house, 62, 68, 281, *281*
Nicolls (William J.) house, *127–133*, 244, *244–245*, 263
nursery school prototype, 278, *279*
Oak Lane Land Company, 48, 179, 184
Onyx, Herbert P., 55, 59
Overbrook Farms, 233, 247
Overbrook Land and Improvement Company, 196, 228, 234
    projects for, 233
Painter (William P.) house, *103*, 184, 212, *212*
Palmer, Bertha, 46, 77n128
Parker, Adelaide (Griffiths, Minerva's sister), *25*, 29, 48, 49, 50, 70, 76n93
Parker, Amanda. *See* Doane, Amanda
Parker (Minerva) house, 222
Parker Nichols, Minerva, *60*
    in Brooklyn, 59–68
    early life, 22–26, *25*
    education, 24, 26, 27–33, *31*, 38
    family relationships, 48–50, 52–55, 56–57, 314
        (*see also* Baker, Adelaide; Doane, Amanda; Nichols, William Ichabod)
    in Massachusetts, 68, 70, 287, 288
    as reformer, 22, 57–58, 62, 64–65, 72
    widowhood, 68–73, *69*, *73*
    in Wilton, CT, 65–67, *66*, 68
    The Baddest Day, and Other Favorite Stories, 18, 72
Parker Nichols, Minerva, commercial buildings (built), 50, 193
    Browne and Nichols School for Boys, *60*, 61–62, 273, *273–276*
    Eagle Iron Foundry, 252, *253*
    Hackley School projects, 62, 277, *277*
    macaroni factory for Emmanuel Guano and

333

INDEX

Antonio Raggio, 217
Riverside Buildings, 67
Parker Nichols, Minerva, journalistic coverage, *21*, 37, 41–42, 210, 223, 296
   Philadelphia Inquirer profile, 70, 72
   Philadelphia Real Estate Record and Builders' Guide profile, 42, 76n81
   San Francisco Chronicle profile, 62, *63*, 65
Parker Nichols, Minerva, personal designs
   William and Minerva Parker Nichols house (Hingham, MA), 68, 70, 288
   William and Minerva Parker Nichols house (Wilton, CT), 65, *66*, 67, 68, 70, *161–163*, 282–283, *282–283*, 294
   office, 262
   Minerva Parker house, 222
Parker Nichols, Minerva, professional life, *10*
   apprenticeship, 32–33, 36–37, 59, 177–179, *178*, 313 (*see also* Archambault (Frank L.) house; Ashmead (Isaac) house)
   Carpentry and Building competition, 33–36, *34*, 177
   as collaborator, 58–59, 184, 205, 210
   early work, 33–37 (*see also* individual buildings)
   homes for veterans, 22, 72, 299
   independent practice, *10*, 37–48, 50, 54–56, 57, 196, 233, 262 (*see also* individual buildings)
   as teacher, 55–56
   See also New Century Club of Philadelphia
Parker Nichols, Minerva, writings, 46, 47, 51–52, 58, 302–315
   on architecture as expression, 302–306
   on the value of architecture, 306–311
   and withdrawal from full-time practice, 311–314
   "An Architectural Object Lesson," 52, 307
   "Architecture as an Art," 303–304, 305, 308–309, 316–317
   "Art in Architecture," 52, *53*, 306–308
   "An Uncultivated Field," 51, 305–306, 309–311, 318–321
   "Women as Architects," 311–313, 314, 322–325
   See also *Home-Maker*
Parksley Land and Improvement Company, 49–50, 193–194, *194*, 215
Pate (Edward C.) house, 215, *216*
Patterson (James A.) house, 196–197, *197–198*, 228, 233
   See also Overbrook Land and Improvement Company
Pennock (Abraham L.) house, 243
Pennsylvania buildings (built)
   Frank L. Archambault house, 36, 184, *185*, 212
   Isaac Ashmead house, *35*, 36, 48, *87*, 179, *179*
   J. Frank Beale house, 199, *199*
   Lewis T. Brooke house, 186–187, *187*
   Elizabeth E. Gallagher house, 42, 203, *204*
   Eliza C. Hartel house and store, 201, *202*
   Irwin N. Megargee house, Pen-y-Bryn, 267, *268*
   Francis Jordan Jr. house, 55, *113–119*, 228, *228–229*
   John O. Keim house, 269, *269–270*
   John Rugan Neff house, 33, *35*, 36, *84*, 177
   William J. Nicolls house, *127–133*, 244, *244–245*, 263
   William P. Painter house, *103*, 184, 212, *212*
   buildings for the Pennsylvania Central Railroad, 210
   houses for the Rutledge Mutual Land Improvement Association, 177–178, *177–178*
   Max M. Suppes house, 27, 37, 180, *180–181*
   See also Narberth, PA buildings (built); Philadelphia buildings (built)
Pennsylvania Central Railroad, 210
Pennsylvania Central Railroad, buildings for, 210
Philadelphia buildings (built)
   Rachel Foster Avery house, Mill-Rae, 42, *104–111*, 223, *223–225*, 225
   Margaret M. Barber house, *40*, 41, 260, *260*
   twin houses for the Campbell Sisters, 248, *248–249*, 261
   Eagle Iron Foundry, 252, *253*
   Frank Wallace Munn house, *21*, 55, *120–125*, 200, 230, *230–232*, 234
   Lewis Jones house, 234, *234–235*
   macaroni factory for Emmanuel Guano and Antonio Raggio, 217
   office for the architect, 262
   James A. Patterson house, 196–197, *197–198*, 228, 233
   Mary Potts house, 39, *40*, 208, *208–209*, 210, 261
   John O. Sheatz house, 264, *265*
   Edward Y. Taylor and Harriet Potts Taylor house, *98–101*, 205, *206–207*, 208, 210
   See also New Century Club of Philadelphia
Philadelphia Normal Art School, 27–28, 55, 59
Philadelphia Real Estate Record and Builders' Guide, 37, 48, 50, 75n63, 243, 255, 263
   Minerva's letter to, 33, 51
   profile of Minerva, 42, 76n81
Philadelphia Record, 210, 237–238
Philadelphia School of Design for Women, 28–29, 55–56, 59, 74n31, 77n128, 222, 261
Philadelphia Times, 223
   "Art in Architecture" (Parker Nichols), 52, *53*, 306–308
   "Pioneer Woman Architect Still Active at Age of 75" (*Philadelphia Times*), 70, 72
Plant (John B.) Cottage, 178, *178*
Potts, Mary, 252
Potts (Mary) house, 39, *40*, 208, *208–209*, 210, 261
Presbyterian Church at Oak Lane, 220, *221*

INDEX

Queen Anne style, 201, 208, 261
Queen Isabella Association Pavilion, 15–16, 43, 45–46, *47,* 56, 226–227, *226–227,* 307
    Board of Lady Managers and, 46, 77n128, 226–227 (*see also* Woman's Building, World's Columbian Exposition (Hayden))
Quindlen, Anna, 15, 16, 17
Raggio, Antonio, macaroni factory for, 217
Reading Railroad, 179, 244, 252, 269
Return to Arcady (Baker), 65, *66,* 67, 68, 283, 288
Riis, Jacob
    How the Other Half Lives, 68
Riverside Buildings, 67, 68, 286
Rutledge Mutual Land Improvement Association, 177
    houses for, 177–178, *177–178*
San Francisco Chronicle, 62, *63,* 65
Sartain, Emily, 54, 56, 222, 261
Sellers, Horace Wells, 208, 239
Sheatz (John O.) house, 264, *265*
sketch for a cottage, 211
Spring Garden Unitarian Church, 54, 57, 59, 225, 236, 237
Stambach (Ida V.) house, 250
Stephens, Alice Barber, 55, 261
Stewart, Sarah A., 261
    Sarah A. Stewart house, 218, *219*
Sudie (Aunt). *See* Doane, Sarah (Aunt Sudie)
suffrage movement, 22, 57–58, 243, 248, 250
    Minerva's writings and, 302, 303, 305, 306
    Rachel Foster Avery and, 223, 225
    women's clubs and, 43, 226
Suppes (Max M.) house, 27, 37, 180, *180–181*
Taylor (Edward Y. and Harriet Potts) house, *98–101,* 205, *206–207,* 208, 210
Texas buildings (undetermined)
    C. F. Johnson house, 42, 215
Thorne, Edwin W., 30, 32, 55, 75n50
    Isaac Ashmead house, *35,* 36, 48, *87,* 179, *179*
    Minerva's apprenticeship with, 32–33, 36–37, 59, 177–179, 313
    Minerva's collaboration with, 184, 205, 210
A Treatise [...] (Downing), 304
unbuilt buildings
    Mrs. Baugh house, 222
    Esther R. Gaskell house, 42, 254
    house for the *Home-Maker,* 251
    Amanda M. Maxwell house, 48, 184
    Emma de Crano McCammon house, 246
    New Century Guild of Working Women Guild house, 266
    Minerva Parker house, 222
    Parksley Land and Improvement Company projects, 49–50, 193–194, *194,* 215
    Abraham L. Pennock house, 243
    Presbyterian Church at Oak Lane, 220, *221*
    projects for the Overbrook Land and Improvement Company, 233
    projects for the Parksley Land and Improvement Company, 50, 193–194, *194,* 215
    row houses for James H. Carter, 213
    houses for Wendell and Smith, 247
    See also Queen Isabella Association Pavilion; Spring Garden Unitarian Church
"An Uncultivated Field" (Parker Nichols), 51, 305–306, 309–311, 318–321
unidentified house (1896), 271, *272*
unidentified house (ca. 1930s), 294, *295*
Unitarianism, 26, 68, 205, 208, 278, 281, 286
    First Church of Deerfield, 68, 70, 287
    First Unitarian Church of Gouverneur, 278
    Hackley School and, 62, 277, *277*
    New York League of Unitarian Women, 64, 65
    Spring Garden Unitarian Church, 54, 57, 59, 225, 236, 237
veterans, homes for, 22, 72, 299
Virginia buildings (built)
    Edward C. Pate house, 215, *216*

Wendell and Smith, 233
    houses for, 247
White, Alfred T., 67–68, 280
    housing studies for, 286
Wilmington, DE. *See* Delaware buildings (built)
Wilson, William C., 50, 193
Woman's Building, World's Columbian Exposition (Hayden), 46–48, *47,* 59, 226–227, 247, 261, 322
Woman's Journal
    "Architecture as an Art" (Parker Nichols), 303–304, 305, 308–309, 316–317
Woman's Progress, 21, 248
women's clubs, 42–43, 56
    See also New Century Club of Philadelphia; New Century Club of Wilmington; Queen Isabella Association Pavilion
Wood, Kathleen Sinclair, 18, 33
World's Columbian Exposition, 43, 52, *53,* 261, 306, 307–308
    Queen Isabella Association Pavilion, 15–16, 43, *47,* 56, 226–227, *226–227,* 307
    Woman's Building (Hayden), 46–48, *47,* 59, 61, 226–227, 247, 261, 322
    Women's Reception Rooms, Pennsylvania Exhibition, 261
Wright, William R., 189
    William R. Wright house, 188, *188,* 200

Yaneva, Albena
    Crafting History, 19

This catalogue is published on the occasion of the exhibition *Minerva Parker Nichols: The Search for a Forgotten Architect,* curated by Elizabeth Felicella, Heather Isbell Schumacher, Molly Lester, and William Whitaker.

Harvey and Irwin Kroiz Gallery, The Architectural Archives, University of Pennsylvania, Philadelphia, PA
March 21–July 22, 2023

Minerva Parker Nichols: The Search for a Forgotten Architect has been supported by The Pew Center for Arts & Heritage. The views expressed are those of the author(s) and do not necessarily reflect the views of The Pew Center for Arts & Heritage or The Pew Charitable Trusts.

Significant additional support for this publication has been provided by The Shedd Endowment for the Architectural Archives and Susan Hedrick.

Distributed by
Yale University Press
302 Temple Street
P.O. Box 209040
New Haven, CT
06520-9040
yalebooks.com/art

Copyright 2023 by The Trustees of the University of Pennsylvania. All rights reserved. No part of this publication, including illustrations, may be reproduced in any form (beyond that copying permitted by Sections 107 and 108 of the U.S. Copyright Law and except by reviewers for the public press) without written permission from the publishers.

ISBN 978-0-300-27517-9

Library of Congress Control Number: 2023917897

Editors: Heather Isbell Schumacher, Elizabeth Felicella, Molly Lester, and William Whitaker
Copyeditor: Johanna Halford-MacLeod
New photography: Elizabeth Felicella and John Bartelstone
Design: Olivia de Salve Villedieu
Lithography: Colour&Books
Printing: Wilco Art Books
Typeface: BB Modern, ABC Social

Printed in The Netherlands

Frontispiece: New Century Club of Wilmington. Auditorium detail [HABS-DE-352-16]

Photo Credits

The Architectural Archives, University of Pennsylvania, Philadelphia, PA. Carrie Baker Collection: 25, 40 (fig. 9), 60 (figs. 15-16), 66 (fig. 21), 69 (fig. 22), 79 (fig. 25), 198, 207, 229, 240-241, 248, 279, 289, 290, 293. Elizabeth Halsted Collection: 60 (figs. 17-18), 295. General Collection: 191, 204, 206, 209, 224, 256, 258. Mark Jacobs Collection: 292, 293. Willman Spawn Collection: 249. Buckingham, Browne and Nichols School Archives, Cambridge, MA: 273, 275; *Builder and Decorator: An Illustrated Monthly* (May 1888), courtesy of Bryn Mawr College, Canaday Library, Bryn Mawr, PA: 35 (fig. 8); *Carpentry and Building* (October 1886), courtesy of The Architectural Archives, University of Pennsylvania, Philadelphia, PA: 34; Cranaleith Spiritual Center, Philadelphia, PA: 223 (bottom left); Delaware Historical Society, Wilmington, DE: 257; Eastern Shore of Virginia Heritage Center, Parksley, VA. Parksley Land and Improvement Company Records: 194; Free Library of Philadelphia, Print and Picture Collection, photo by Frank H. Taylor: 44; *Harper's Weekly* 35, no. 1792 (April 25, 1891): 47; Harvard Art Museums / Fogg Museum, Transfer from the Carpenter Center for the Visual Arts, Social Museum Collection: 66 (fig. 20); Harvard University, Radcliffe Institute, Schlesinger Library, Adelaide Nichols Baker Papers, Cambridge, MA: 31, 221, 226, 227, 228, 255, 259, 269, 270, 272, 274, 276; Historical Society of Pennsylvania, Jane Campbell Scrapbook Collection, Philadelphia, PA: 238, 239, 242; Historic American Buildings Survey, Library of Congress, Prints and Photographs Division, Washington, DC. Photos by John Bartelstone: 113, 117, 119, 189; Photos by Elizabeth Felicella: frontispiece, 35 (fig. 7), 45 (fig. 12), 71 (figs. 23-24), 84, 85, 87, 89, 91-93, 95, 97-99, 101, 103-105, 107, 109, 111, 115, 120, 121, 123-125, 127, 129-131, 133, 135, 137, 139-141, 143, 145, 147, 149, 151, 153-155, 157, 159, 161, 163, 165-167, 169-171, 173, 175, 179, 188, 190, 192, 195, 199, 200, 208, 212, 219, 223 (top right), 225, 230, 232, 234, 235, 245, 263, 265, 268, 282, 283, 297, 298; Photos by George A. Eisenman: 14, 237 (top right); *Home Maker* (January 1891, April 1891, June 1891, September 1891, December 1891), courtesy of University of Washington Libraries, Special Collections Division, Seattle, WA: 10. 231, 242, 251; Johnstown Area Historical Association, Johnstown, PA: 180; King's Vies: Philadelphia (New York: Moses King, 1900), courtesy of The Athenaeum of Philadelphia: 253; Media Historic Archives Commission, Media, PA: 185, 202; *Memories of Four Score Years: Suppes, Waters, Unger, Wagoner, Jones, 1889-1968.* Privately published booklet, 1968, courtesy Historical Society of Pennsylvania, Philadelphia, PA: 181; Town of Parksley, Virginia: 216; Philadelphia City Archives, Philadelphia, PA: 197, 237 (bottom left); *Philadelphia Times* (November 19, 1893): 53; Radnor Historical Society, Radnor, PA: 187; Reconstructionist Rabbinical College Archives, Wyncote, PA: 40 (fig. 10), 260; Rutledge [promotional brochure], ca. 1897, courtesy of Mary Woodling, Rutledge, PA; *San Francisco Chronicle* (April 14, 1901): 63; *Scientific American Architects and Builders Edition*, Vol. 10, No. 6 (Dec 1890), courtesy of The Athenaeum of Philadelphia: 183, 183; Peter D. Taylor Collection: 284; William Whitaker: 277, 281; *Women's Progress* (May 1893), courtesy of Historical Society of Pennsylvania, Philadelphia, PA: 21